Thomas Schirrmacher

The Persecution of Christians Concerns Us All

The WEA Global Issues Series

Editors:

Bishop Efraim Tendero, Philippines
Secretary General, World Evangelical Alliance

Thomas Schirrmacher
Director, International Institute for Religious Liberty and Speaker for Human Rights of the World Evangelical Alliance

Volumes:

1. Thomas K. Johnson – Human Rights
2. Christine Schirrmacher – The Islamic View of Major Christian Teachings
3. Thomas Schirrmacher – May a Christian Go to Court?
4. Christine Schirrmacher – Islam and Society
5. Thomas Schirrmacher – The Persecution of Christians Concerns Us All
6. Christine Schirrmacher – Islam – An Introduction
7. Thomas K. Johnson – What Difference does the Trinity Make
8. Thomas Schirrmacher – Racism
9. Christof Sauer (ed.) – Bad Urach Statement
10. Christine Schirrmacher – The Sharia: Law and Order in Islam
11. Ken Gnanakan – Responsible Stewardship of God's Creation
12. Thomas Schirrmacher – Human Trafficking
13. Thomas Schirrmacher – Ethics of Leadership
14. Thomas Schirrmacher – Fundamentalism
15. Thomas Schirrmacher – Human Rights – Promise and Reality
16. Christine Schirrmacher – Political Islam – When Faith Turns Out to Be Politics
17. Thomas Schirrmacher, Thomas K. Johnson – Creation Care and Loving our Neighbors: Studies in Environmental Ethics
18. Thomas K. Johnson (Ed.) – Global Declarations on Freedom of Religion or Belief and Human Rights

"The WEA Global Issues Series is designed to provide thoughtful, practical, and biblical insights from an Evangelical Christian perspective into some of the greatest challenges we face in the world. I trust you will find this volume enriching and helpful in your life and Kingdom service."

Bishop Efraim Tendero, Secretary General, World Evangelical Alliance

Thomas Schirrmacher

The Persecution of Christians Concerns Us All

Towards a Theology of Martyrdom

70 Biblical-Theological Theses written for the
German Evangelical Alliance and its
Religious Liberty Commission

Reprint of the 2001 edition with a new appendix.

The WEA Global Issues Series
Volume 5

WIPF & STOCK · Eugene, Oregon

Wipf and Stock Publishers
199 W 8th Ave, Suite 3
Eugene, OR 97401

The Persecution of Christians Concerns Us All
Towards a Theology of Martyrdom
By Schirrmacher, Thomas
Copyright©2001 Verlag für Kultur und Wissenschaft
ISBN 13: 978-1-5326-0885-8
Publication date 4/19/2018
Previously published by Verlag für Kultur und Wissenschaft, 2001

Contents

Preface by the Very Rev. Johan Candelin 9

Preface by Julia Doxat-Purser 10

Preface by Rev. Rudolf Westerheide 11

Note on the third edition 13

A. **The Present Situation** 15
  1. The reason for this contribution 15
  2. A Theology of Martyrdom 17
  3. Wide Sections of Christians Are Being Persecuted 21
  4. The Theology of the Early Church Was Forged by Martyrdom 23
  5. The Question of the Persecution of Christians is Not Limited to the Early Church 24
  6. The Multi-faceted Reasons for Persecutions 27
  7. What is a Martyr? 27

B. **An Important Biblical Theme** 28
  8. Scriptures are taken out of context and trivialized 28
  9. Large Portions of Scripture Deal with Persecution 30
  10. Assistance in Revelations 32
  11. Historical Criticism and its Problems with the Martyr Texts in the New Testament 34
  12. The First Human Being to Die was a Martyr. 35
  13. The Old Testament Prophets Were Persecuted 36
  14. God's People persecutes God's People 40
  15. Christians also persecute both fellow Christians and others 41
  16. Persecution is an Ecumenical Topic 45
  17. The First Christian Martyr 46

C. **To Speak of Jesus is to Speak of Martyrdom** 46
  18. Jesus is the Prototype of the Martyr 46
  19. To Die for Friends is the Highest Form of Love 47

20. All Persecution is Actually Directed Towards Jesus 48
21. Continuation of the Suffering of Christ 48
22. Jesus as Role Model – The Martyrs as Role Models 49
23. A Theology of the Cross ('theologia crucis') 50

D. The Church under Persecution.. 52
24. No Church without martyrdom 52
25. Hatred towards God 53
26. The World's Hatred of God Originates in Satan's Hatred 54
27. The Holy Spirit – Consolation in Persecution 56
28. Joy in Persecution 58
29. Trusting God Alone 58

E. Behavior under Persecution... 59
30. Never aspire to persecution 59
31. It is Legitimate to Flee Persecution 61
32. Not All Suffering is for Christ's Sake 63
33. Assistance for the Weak 64
34. Praying for the Persecutor 66
35. Persecutors Become Converts 67

F. Missions and Martyrdom 68
36. The Fruit of Martyrdom 68
37. Fruit is not Automatic 70
38. Martyrdom Accompanies World Missions 72
39. The Martyr as 'Witness'; the 'Testimony' of the Martyrs 73
40. The Victory and Defeat of the Prophets Belong Together 79
41. A Christian's Weakness is his strength 79
42. The Manifestation of the Children of God 80
43. The Outcry for Justice 81
44. Why are the Godless So Prosperous? 82

G. Contra a Religion of Prosperity 84
45. Christianity is not a Religion of Prosperity (Romans 5:1-5) ... 84
46. The Theology of Wealth-and-Health-Gospel is Questionable 85
47. Denial and Suffering 85
48. Fight the Good Fight of Faith 86
49. Martyrdom is the Protest Against the Assault on the Soul. 86

Contents

- 50. The Spectacle before the Invisible World 87
- 51. The Vision of the Heavenly Places 87
- 52. Scripture Does Not Restrict Persecution to the 'Last Days' 90

H. The State and Persecution 91
- 53. There are Many Kinds of Persecution 91
- 54. Martyr Terminology must not be Abused Politically 93
- 55. Against the Perfection of Power 93
- 56. Loyal Citizens 95
- 57. Praying for a Peaceful Life 97
- 58. Resisting the State 98
- 59. The Persecution of Christians Can Develop into Genocide 101
- 60. The Persecution of Christians can be Part of Immense Mass Murders 102
- 61. Persecution of Christians under National Socialism 103

I. Practical Compassion 105
- 62. When One Member suffers 105
- 63. The Body's Intervention for its Martyrs Exposes Its Own Condition .. 107
- 64. Communion is the Ideal Place to Remember Suffering Believers 107
- 65. the Martyrs in Worship 108
- 66. Education on Persecution 110
- 67. We Need Confessors 111
- 68. Perseverance is Essential 112
- 69. Church Structure and Persecution 112
- 70. We Need Concrete Ideas 113

Appendix 1: Human Rights and Christian Faith 115
- Man as Creation and Image of God 115
- The Christian Roots of Human Rights 116
- Enlightenment or Forgiveness and Repentance? 117
- Human Rights Precede the State 118
- The Meaning of Romans 13 119
- On the Separation of Church and State 120
- God Knows no Partiality 121

Appendix 2: Faith is a Human Right 125

Appendix 3: A response to the high counts of Christian martyrs per year (2011) 131

Appendix 4: Religious Freedom and the Persecution of Christians.. 137
    Four negative Developments.. 142
    Four positive Developments 145

Selected Bibliography on Persecution of Christians............................ 151

Web-adresses 175

About the Author... 177

Preface by the Very Rev. Johan Candelin

Director of the Religious Liberty Commission of the World Evangelical Alliance

There is a story told about Professor Albert Einstein. He prepared questions for some students when his secretary said: "But, professor, these are the same questions you gave last time". "I know", said Einstein, "but I have changed the answers!". We live in a time where the answers are new to old questions. The world is not the same it was some years ago. At the same time some questions and answers do never change. We need to know which one changes and which one do not. We need to do this in the complicated world we live in where the tension between foreign policy, globalisation and religion poses new questions about religion, especially Islams relation to Christianity. We need to protect the freedom for Muslims in the west but also protect the freedom for Christians in the Muslim world. They often feel forgotten by us.

In this situation I can highly recommend Dr Thomas Schirrmachers new book. It gives a clear and logical insight in many of the questions even people who consider themself non-religious people now ask. It can best be read with an open Bible and some open daily newspaper. It will give a supprisingly new insight into what it means to live in " a time like this".

Preface by Julia Doxat-Purser
Socio-Political Representative & Religious Liberty Coordinator for the European Evangelical Alliance

Christians have brothers and sisters from almost every culture. Belonging to a family brings responsibilities. The Bible makes it abundantly clear that the Church is to be united, to act as one Body, to care for each part. Looking after one another and standing in solidarity when suffering comes is a key part of God's provision for his children.

Suffering comes in many forms but the one that Scripture tells all Christians to expect is persecution for one's faith. As Thomas Schirrmacher's theological study will demonstrate, the Bible has a tremendous amount to teach us about persecution. Without a Biblical understanding, we are unlikely fully to grasp the nature of the spiritual battle, nor what it means to be sheep among wolves and, at the same time, both a wise serpent and innocent dove.

As religious liberty coordinator for the European Evangelical Alliance, it is a privilege to work alongside Christians across Europe. Some know the realities of persecution through firsthand experience. Others, like me, are fortunate enough to have only indirect knowledge. But we can learn from one another. And together, we can make a difference to the Suffering Church, as we pray, give practical help and speak for the voiceless in the public sphere. For the time being, most European Christians are enjoying a breathing space when it comes to major oppression. That does not mean, however, that we should not be wise and vigilant when it comes to responding to more subtle pressures that could so easily end up blocking the Church from witnessing as it must. As citizens of countries where we are free to dialogue with political leaders, we have a particular responsibility to be advocates for persecuted Christians who live under different kinds of political regimes.

The wonders of internet technology enable me to work with Thomas Schirrmacher on religious liberty issues both within a European context and under the umbrella of the World Evangelical Fellowship's Religious Liberty Commission. Electronic communication enables the global Church to share information, give advice and speak with a united voice on behalf of persecuted Christians. But, if we are to know how to pray, speak and act, we must rely on Scripture. I am delighted, therefore, that this book puts the Bible's teaching on persecution centre stage.

Preface by Rev. Rudolf Westerheide
German and European Evangelical Alliance

Only a few years ago, reports about persecuted Christians seemed unreal to us. We were shocked by the descriptions of the unimaginable cruelty being practiced in prisons and concentration camps – somewhere far away in Siberia, perhaps – but the whole thing was only as relevant as a somewhat exotic description of a foreign world. Reports of martyrs and of their steadfastness under dreadful torture moved us – particularly because it reminded us of our own indifference.

Following the fall of the Iron Curtain, the situation has changed in two ways. On the one hand, most of the former East Block now enjoys religious liberty. Praise God! On the other hand, new travel possibilities give us the opportunity to meet believers who have survived the concentration camps. At international meetings of the Evangelical Alliance, prosperous young Christians from Germany sit next to older Romanian believers who have endured years of imprisonment for their faith. The suffering of the persecuted takes on a face and becomes a living reality, and the very healthy realization that these men and women who have proven themselves in the fire are still vulnerable to human weakness and vanity.

At the same time, we must face the fact that the threat of religious and national intolerance towards Christians has become part of European reality. In the sunny vacation land of Greece, the missionary commitment of Evangelical believers brings them into serious confrontation with the authorities and may lead to career problems and imprisonment. The experiences of our Turkish fellow-believers reminds us that Islamic repression has already reached Europe.

This new situation, combined with the horror stories from other parts of the world, unavoidably forces us to confront the subject of the persecution of Christians. We realize that those who suffer for their faith are not Someone Else, but the Body of Christ. We are involved, when young Christian women are sold into slavery in the Sudan – we cannot evade the responsibility of bearing their burdens in prayer and petitioning the Lord to care for them in a special way. At the same time, we must recognize the reality of repression and persecution as an intrinsic element of our Christian existence, and acknowledge that our own complete religious liberty is an exception to the rule.

A commission of the German Evangelical Alliance has dedicated itself to this task in preparation for the Day of Prayer for the Persecuted Church. It soon became clear that the disclosure of the facts was not enough; that we require a new Biblical-theological and ecclesiastical review of the subject. Professor Dr. Thomas Schirrmacher, President of the Martin-Bucer-Seminary in Bonn, presents us with the following study. The persecution of Christians belongs essentially and historically to the most fundamental themes of the Evangelical Alliance. With the presentation of this document, we wish most urgently that Evangelical believers give the subject new depth and attention.

Prefaces 13

Note on the third edition

This third edition of 2018 contains the text of the 2001 and 2008 editions in new layout, which have been translated from the original German edition of 1998.

Literature and other informations reflect the situation two decades ago. Some of the persons writing the forewords have different positions meanwhile.

The introduction (proposition 1) from 2001 has been shortened, the discussion of the yearly numbers of marytrs there has been replaced by a new appendix 3 of 2011.

Beside appendix 3, appendix 4 is also new, a lecture given 2013 at the party headquarter of Mrs Merkel's party, the Christian Democratic Union.

A. The Present Situation

1. The reason for this contribution

Hebrews 10:32-35: "Remember those earlier days after you had received the light, when you stood your ground in a great contest in the face of suffering. Sometimes you were publicly exposed to insult and persecution; at other times you stood side by side with those who were so treated. You sympathized with those in prison and joyfully accepted the confiscation of your property, because you knew that you yourselves had better and lasting possessions. So do not throw away your confidence; it will be richly rewarded."

The author of the Letter to the Hebrew seeks to embolden his readers in times of suffering so that they are reminded of how God helped them in earlier times of suffering (verse 32).

What is truly interesting in this text, however, is that the Letter to the Hebrews designates all readers as such, as those who have "endured in the great contest in the face of suffering," independent of whether this occurred through suffering or through vicarious association with suffering! The author of the Letter to the Hebrews puts *the sufferers (A) and those demonstrating compassion (B)* on the same footing. And then, in verses 33-34, the author emphasizes this close connection under the cross using an ABBA outline:

In verse 33, the readers are first of all addressed as those who in part have "themselves" endured much suffering (A), but "at other times" also suffered because they, in some cases, "stood side by side with those who suffered" (B). There are, then, *direct sufferers* (A), and sufferers who are in that position because they *suffer alongside others* (B)!

In verse 34 the order is reversed: To start with, it is mentioned that the readers have suffered with those in prison (B). Then it is mentioned that they themselves lost possessions (A).

That is precisely the objective of IDOP (International Day of Prayer for the Persecuted Church), which has been installed by the World Evangelical Fellowhip in 1996 as an option to show solidarity with the persecuted. Christians who suffer and Christians who stand side by side with those suffer seek to build a community of suffering. Prayer occurs simultaneously in countries where there is Christian persecution and where there is no persecution of Christians. If we do this, then we "do not throw away our confidence", and this confidence "will be richly rewarded" (verse 35).

A Christian never lives without Christian persecution! Either he is persecuted or he suffers with the fate of those who are persecuted. And whoever suffers, suffers at the same time with others who, perhaps, suffer even more!

The possibility that someone simply ignores the suffering of another individual or church and then enjoys the fact that things are going well for him, without this turning into thankful involvement for the sake of others, is something which does not even come to mind to the writer of the Letter to the Hebrews! For Christians to suffer and for other Christians to not suffer side by side? Unthinkable! Christians who turn to the other side while others suffer? Inconceivable! And yet this is precisely what applies to the large majority of Christians!

The part of the Church which is free of persecution, cannot ignore the large numbers of Christians under severe persecution and even threat of death, but must act, for "when one member suffers, all suffer," (1 Cor. 12:26). We must pray, give, confess and encourage the media and the politicians to deal with the subject. In doing so, we merely obey the Biblical commandment, "Remember them that are in bonds, as bound with them; and them which suffer adversity, as being yourselves also in the body." (Heb 13:3).

The Church arose out of persecution in New Testament times, and developed its earliest theology under the pressure of persecution and oppression. The following pages seek to demonstrate that martyrdom is not an embarrassing side effect of Christianity, but an intrinsic element of Old Testament, New Testament, Jewish and Early Church faith. At the same time, we will see that committed efforts to aid persecuted Christians cannot be left up to a few enthusiasts, but, according the New Testament, is a central duty of the Christian Church.

The following theses deal only with Christian martyrdom, which is only one aspect of the more comprehensive subject of religious liberty and human rights.[1] This limitation is justified to a certain extent, for persecution

---

[1] See: my article on religious freedom in the German journal of Amnesty International: "Glauben ist ein Menschenrecht" (Titel). ai-Journal 8/2000: 6-9; as well as Thomas Schirrmacher. "Christlicher Glaube und Menschenrechte". Querschnitte 12 (1999) 3 (Mrz): 1-6; Thomas Schirrmacher. "Christlicher Glaube und Men-

A. The Present Situation

on religious grounds befalls mostly Christians; no other faith is so strongly persecuted than the Christian Church[2] – which has not always been the case.

2. A Theology of Martyrdom

Proposition: To a large extent, we lack a theology of martyrdom.[3] Academic theology[4] has dealt with the subject of martyrdom only in the

---

schenrechte" (Russisch). POISK: Ezemedel'naja Vsesojuznaja Gazeta [Publication of the Russian Academy of Sciences]. Nr. 48 (446) 22.-28. November 1997. p. 13., Thomas Schirrmacher. "Christlicher Glaube und Menschenrechte" (Russian). Utschitjelskaja Gazeta (Russian magazine for teachers). No. 2 (9667) 3.1.1998. p. 21 + No. 3 (9668) 20.1.1998. p. 21 + No. 4 (9669) 3.2.1998. p. 22.

[2] Nina Shea. In The Lion's Den, *op. cit.*, p. 4.

[3] The most important contributions known to me are:
Lutheran: Otto Michel. Prophet und Märtyrer. Beiträge zur Förderung christlicher Theologie 37 (1932), Vol. 2. Bertelsmann: Gütersloh, 1932; Dietrich Bonhoeffer. Nachfolge. Chr. Kaiser: München, 1950³; 1987¹⁶; [1937]; repr. Dietrich Bonhoeffer Werke, Vol. 4. Gütersloher Verlagshaus: Gütersloh, 1989¹; 1994²; Medardo Ernesto Gómez. Fire against Fire: Christian Ministry Face-to-Face with Persecution. Augsburg Publ.: Minneapolis (MN), 1990 [Original: Fuego contra fuego. Ediciones Liberación: o. O. (El Salvador), 1990]; Robert Kolb. For all the Saints. Changing Perceptions of Martyrdom and Sainthood in the Lutheran Reformation. Mercer University Press: Macon (GA), 1987;
Reformed: A.lfred de Quervain. Die Heiligung. Ethik Erster Teil. Evangelischer Verlag: Zollikon, 1946² [1942¹]. pp. 151-221 (Ch. III. "Das Kreuz im christlichen Leben");
Evangelical: Peter Beyerhaus. Die Bedeutung des Martyriums für den Aufbau des Leibes Christi (Eph. 1,22-23). Orthodoxe Rundschau 16 (1984): 4-24 (Special Issue); revised as: Die Bedeutung des Martyriums für den Aufbau des Leibes Christi. Diakrisis 25 (1999) 3: 131-141; Peter Beyerhaus. Martyrdom - Gate to the Kingdom of Heaven". p. 163-179. God's Kingdom and the Utopian Error. Tyndale: Wheaton (IL), 1992; Christof Sauer. Mission und Martyrium: Studien zu Karl Hartenstein und zur Lausanner Bewegung. edition afem - missions scripts 5. Verlag für Kultur und Wissenschaft Schirrmacher: Bonn, 1994; Josef Tson. Suffering, Martyrdom, and Rewards in Heaven. University Press of America: Lanham/New York, 1998 [Diss. Heverlee (B), 1996]; Paul A. Marshall. Their Blood Cries out: The Untold Story of Persecution against Christians in the Modern World. Word: Dallas, 1997; Herbert Schlossberg. A Frangrance of Oppression: The Church and Its Persecutors. Crossway Books: Wheaton (IL), 1991. p. 115-134 (Biblical-theological section);
Catholic: Karl Rahner. Zur Theologie des Todes. Quaestiones disputatae 2. Herder: Freiburg, 1958, particularly. "Exkurs über das Martyrium". p. 73-106 [*Ibid.*, . 1965⁵]; Oda Hagemeyer. "Theologie des Martyriums". Benediktische Monatsschrift 60 (1984) 309-315; Theofried Baumeister. Die Anfänge der Theologie des

Martyriums. Münsterische Beiträge zur Theologie 45. Aschendorff: Münster, 1980; Ivo Lesbaupin. Blessed are the Persecuted: The Early Church Under Siege. Orbis Books: Maryknoll (NY), 1987 [Original Portugiesisch]; Spire (Hodder & Stoughton): Sevenoaks (GB), 1988; Georg Stoll. "Gefahr für Leib und Leben". Stadt Gottes: Familienzeitschrift der Steyler Missionare 122 (1999) 9 (Sept): 8-10; *Miscellaneous*: Jan Pit (Ed.). Jeden Tag geborgen: 366 Andachten verfolgter Christen. Hänssler: Neuhausen, 1998; William Carl Weinreich. Spirit and Martyrdom. University Press of America: Washington D.C., 1981 [Diss. Basel, 1977]; Harry W. Tajra. The Martyrdom of St. Paul: Historical and Judicial: Context, Traditions, and Legends. Wissenschaftliche Untersuchungen zum Neuen Testament 67. Mohr Siebeck: Tübingen, 1994; John S. Pobee. Persecution and Martyrdom in the Theology of Paul. Journal for the Study of the New Testament Supplement Series 6. JSOT Press: Sheffield, 1985; Scott Cunningham. Through Many Tribulations: The Theology of Persecution in Luke-Acts. Journal for the Study of the New Testament Supplement Series 142. Sheffield Academic Press: Sheffield (GB), 1997; Daniel Boyarin. Dying for God: Martyrdom and the Making of Christianity and Judaism. Stanford University Press: Stanford (CA), 1999; Norman H. Hjelm (Ed.). Out of the Ashes: Burned Churches and the Community of Faith. NelsonWord: Nashville (TN), 1997; Nina Shea. In The Lion's Den: Persecuted Christians and What the Western Church Can Do About It. Broadman & Holman: Nashville (TN), 1997; Ready for the End Battle. Open Doors: Johannesburg (South africa), n. d. (ca. 1980), repr. Jan Pit. Persecution: It Will Never Happen Here? Open Doors: Orange (CA), 1981; John Rutherford. "Persecution". Sp. 23-24 in: James Orr (Ed.). The International Standard Bible Encyclopedia. 5 Vols., Vol. 4. Wm. B. Eerdmans: Grand Rapids (MI), 1957 [1939]; Merill Tenney. "Persecution". p. 403 in: Everett F. Harrison. Baker Dictionary of Theology. Baker Book House: Grand Rapids (MI), 1975;

Asian: Bong Rin Ro. "Need for a Theology of Suffering". Asia Theological News 14 (1988) 3: 2-3; Bong Rin Ro (Ed.). Christian Suffering in Asia. Evangelical Fellowship of Asia: Taichung (Taiwan), 1989, particularly.: Ken R. Gnanakan. "A Biblical Perspective on Suffering" S. 23-30 und Jonathan Chao. "Witness in Suffering". p 43-54; "Christian Suffering and Persecution". Asian Perspectives, Heft 9. (The Declaration of the 4th ATA Theological Consultation in Hong Kong). Asia Theological Association (ATA): Taichung (Taiwan), 1984; "A Theology of Suffering". Themenheft Asia Theological News 14 (1988) 3; particularly . "A Letter to the Churches in Asia". Asia Theological News 14 (1988) 3: 4-5 und John Richard. "Preparing for Suffering". p. 8-9;

Africa: Festo Kivengere (1921-1988). The Spirit is Moving. Africa Christian Press: Nairobi (Kenia) & Lagos: London, 1976; Festo Kivengere. I Love Idi Amin: The Story or Triumph under Fire in the Midst of Suffering and Persecution in Uganda. Marshall, Morgan and Scott: London, 1977; Revell: Old Tappan (NJ), 1977; Festo Kivengere. Ich liebe Idi Amin: Uganda heute, Triumph der Liebe mitten in Leiden und Verfolgung. Hänssler: Neuhausen, 1978^1; 1979^3; Festo Kivengere. Revolutionary Love. African Evangelistic Enterprise: Nairobi (Kenia), 1981; Tokunboh Adeyemo. "Persecution: A Permanent Feature of the Church". Evangelical Ministries/Ministères Evangélique (Association of Evangelicals of Africa and

A. The Present Situation 19

context of early church history (the first three centuries AD), if at all.[5] Evangelical theology generally ignores the issue, leaving it up to specialized mission boards and their publications. A series of Evangelical conferences in the 70's and 80's,[6] however, and the success of the International

---

Madagascar) Mar-Aug 1985: 3-9; Tokunboh Adeyemo. De gemeente zal altijd vervolgd worden. n. d.; Tortured for Christ. Themenheft Evangelical Ministries/Ministères Evangélique (Association of Evangelicals of Africa and Madagascar) Mar-Aug 1985, particularly . Herman Boonstra. "La Persecution: Formule de Dieu pour la Croissance". p. 11-13; Philip Makau Kavuo. "Unchain My Brethren". p. 14-15; Emmanuel S. A. Ayee. "Persecution: A Bible Study Guide". S. 1925; Brother Andrew (Ed.). Destined to Suffer? African Christians Face the Future. Open Doors: Orange (CA), 1979; particularly . Tokunboh Adeyemo. "Persecution: A Permanent Feature of the Church". p. 23-36 und Dan Kyanda. "The Attitude of the Prepared Christian". p. 97-104; Ready for the End Battle. Open Doors: Johannesburg (South africa), n. d. . (ca. 1980), repr. Jan Pit. Persecution: It Will Never Happen Here? Open Doors: Orange (CA), 1981; Daniel Kyanda. "Mission and Persecution". Arbeitspapier der gleichnamigen Arbeitsgruppe auf der World Consultation on Frontier Mission, Edinburgh 1980.unpublished paper; Idoti und David M. Davies. With God in Congo Forests During the Persecution Under Rebel Occupation as Told by an African Pastor. Worldwide Evangelization Crusade: Bulstrode, Gerrards Cross (GB), 1971;

Lexica: Wilhelm Schneemelcher. "Christenverfolgungen". Col. 257-260 in: Hermann Kunst, Siegfried Grundman (Ed.). Evangelisches Staatslexikon. Kreuz Verlag: Stuttgart, 1966¹; Wilhelm Schneemelcher. "Christenverfolgungen". Col. 324-327 in: Hermann Kunst (Ed.). Evangelisches Staatslexikon. Kreuz Verlag: Stuttgart, 1975² (See also the bibliography); Eduard Christen. "Martyrium III/2.". p. 212-220 in: Gerhard Krause, Gerhard Müller (Ed.). Theologische Realenzyklopädie. Vol. 22. Walter de Gruyter: Berlin, 1992; Rudolf Freudenberger u. a. "Christenverfolgungen". p. 23-62 in: Gerhard Krause, Gerhard Müller (Ed.). Theologische Realenzyklopädie. Vol. 8. Walter de Gruyter: Berlin, 1981.

4   In Germany, academic theology is dominated by the Roman Catholic and Lutheran State churches and their faculties at state universities. Evangelical seminaries are not recognized by German universities and the state churches.

5   The situation has worsened. The Evangelische Staatslexikon included an article on "Christenverfolgungen" in its first two editions (Wilhelm Schneemelcher. "Christenverfolgungen". Col. 257-260 in: Hermann Kunst, Siegfried Grundman [Ed.]. Evangelisches Staatslexikon. Kreuz Verlag: Stuttgart, 1966¹; repr. Col. 324-327 in: Hermann Kunst [Ed.]. Evangelisches Staatslexikon. Kreuz Verlag: Stuttgart, 1975²), but the latest edition (1987³) has eliminated the contribution without replacing with any other detailed discussion of the subject, although it plays a significant role in the question of the relationship between Church and State.

6   The most significant Evangelical conferences on Martyrdom have been:
1977: Ingrid Kastelan. "Verfolgung ist letztendlich Verheißung". idea 45/1977 (7.11.). p. I-II (No report);
Konferenz der AEM "Gemeinde in Bedrängnis" 2.-6, Nov. 1977 in Burbach-

Day of Prayer for Persecuted Christians, in which about 300,000 local churches participated, encourage expectations of change.

Eduard Christen has pointed out that the occupation with the persecution of Christians up until 311 AD has been fairly acceptable, but that there is almost no Biblical evaluation of the subject or on persecution from 311 AD to the present, and that we are far removed from a desperately needed systematic documentation of the subject or a 'Theology of Martyrdom.'[7] The lack of Biblical-theological studies and reflection on the subject is conspicuous, even in American Evangelicalism, which generally disseminates information about international persecution. I can only agree with Patrick

---

Holzhausen;

1978: Love Africa '78 Congress in Blantyre, Malawi, Mai 1978: Brother Andrew (Ed.). Destined to Suffer? African Christians Face the Future. Open Doors: Orange (CA), 1979;

1978: AEPM/EFMA/IFMA Konferenz Overland Park (Kansas) 25.-29, Sept. 1978: Edwin L. Frizen, Wade T. Coggins (Ed.). Christ and Caesar in Christian Missions. William Carey Library: Pasadena (CA), 1979;

1980: Daniel Kyanda. "Mission and Persecution". Report of the group of the same name in the World Consultation on Frontier Mission, Edinburgh 1980. unpublished;

1983: "The Yakunin Hearing July 22-26, 1983 Vancouver ..." (Christian Solidarity International). Program, but no report;

1984: 4. Theologische Konsultation der Asia Theological Association (ATA) in Hong Kong, 1984: Christian Suffering and Persecution. Asian Perspectives, Nr. 9. (The Declaration of the 4th ATA Theological Consultation in Hong Kong. Asia Theological Association (ATA): Taichung (Taiwan), 1984;

1984: Meeting of the Theologischen Kommission der World Evangelical Fellowship / Weltweiten Evangelischen Allianz in St. Chrischona / Basel, Result of the so-called. "Baseler Brief": "The Basel Letter" Col. 8-18 in: Christian Suffering and Persecution. Asian Perspectives, NR. 9. (The Declaration of the 4th ATA Theological Consultation in Hong Kong. Asia Theological Association (ATA): Taichung (Taiwan), 1984;

1988: AfeM-Jahrestagung 1988: Urgemeinde und Endzeitgemeinde - Missionarische Existenz in Zeugnis und Leiden: Vier Referate der Jahrestagung des Arbeitskreises für evangelikale Missiologie (AfeM). Idea Dokumentation 3/1988;

1988: Konferenz der Asiatischen Evangelischen Allianz / Evangelical Fellowship of Asia "Die Kirchen inmitten des Leides" Hong Kong 24.-27.2.1988: Bong Rin Ro (Ed.). Christian Suffering in Asia. Evangelical Fellowship of Asia: Taichung (Taiwan), 1989; "A Theology of Suffering". Themenheft Asia Theological News 14 (1988) 3, particularly . "A Letter to the Churches in Asia". pp. 4-5 and on the reason for the Conference, John Richard. "Preparing for Suffering". p. 8-9; See also the reports: "Prepare for Sufferings Says a Letter to Asia's Churches". Evangelical World May 1988: 1-2 and in idea 24/1988 (16.3.). p. 2-3

[7]   Eduard Christen. "Martyrium III/2.". *op. cit.*, p. 212.

Johnstone's plea for the development and propagation of a Martyrology, the doctrine of persecution.[8]

3. Wide Sections of Christians Are Being Persecuted

Proposition: A large percentage of Christians today, particularly Evangelical Christians, no longer live in prosperity and legal security, but under persecution. These believers understand both the Old and the New Testaments much more realistically than Western Christians.

"The martyrdom of Christ's Church has achieved a new pinnacle in this century"[9] and the Western Church with its great deficit in a theology of martyrdom needs to learn from its fellow believers in countries and situations under persecution, either through contact with individuals or with their literature.[10]

---

[8] Patrick Johnstone. "Preparing 3rd World Believers for Church Growth under Persecution". Worldwide Thrust (WEC USA) Nov/1978: 3-7, here p. 3.

[9] Peter Beyerhaus. Die Bedeutung des Martyriums für den Aufbau des Leibes Christi. Diakrisis 25 (1999) 3: 131-141, here p. 134; See also: Andrew Chandler (Ed.). The Terrible Alternative: Christian Martyrdom in the Twentieth Century. Cassell: London, New York, 1998; Ann Ball mit Paul Marx, Stephen Dunham. The Persecuted Church in the Late Twentieth Century. Maginificat Press: Avon (NJ), 1990 (Catholic point of view); on a part of the world seldom discussed in this respect: Martin Lange, Reinhold Iblacker (Ed.). Christenverfolgung in Südamerika: Zeugen der Hoffnung. Herder: Freiburg, 1980; in English; Martin Lange, Reinhold Iblacker (Ed.). Witnesses of Hope: The Persecution of Christians in Latin America. Orbis Books: Maryknoll (NY), 1981.

[10] *For example, Asian:* Petrus Oktavianus. "Die Narde ausschütten". p. 120-128 in: Otto Riecker (Ed.). Ruf aus Indonesien, Hänssler: Neuhausen, 1973³ [1971¹]; Chua Wee Hian, Frank Saphir Khair-Ullah, Subodh Sahu. "Evangelism in the Hard Places of the World". p. 464-473 in J. D. Douglas (Ed.). Let the Earth Hear His Voice: International Congress on World Evangelization Lausanne, Switzerland. World Wide Publ.: Minneapolis (MN), 1975; Bong Rin Ro (Ed.). Christian Suffering in Asia. Evangelical Fellowship of Asia: Taichung (Taiwan), 1989 (8 general contributions 15 reports), particularly; Ken R. Gnanakan. "A Biblical Perspective on Suffering" p. 23-30 and Jonathan Chao. "Witness in Suffering". p. 43-54; "Christian Suffering and Persecution". Asian Perspectives, Heft 9. (The Declaration of the 4th ATA Theological Consultation in Hong Kong. Asia Theological Association (ATA): Taichung (Taiwan), 1984; Met Q. Castillo. The Church in Thy House. Alliance-Publishers: Malina (Philippinen), 1982;
Africa : Preparing Believers for Suffering and Persecution: A Manual for Christian Workers. Hope: Bulawayo (Simbabwe), n. d. (ca. 1979). 15 S.; Ready for the End Battle. Open Doors: Johannesburg (South africa), n. d. (ca. 1980), repr. Jan Pit. Persecution: It Will Never Happen Here? Open Doors: Orange (CA), 1981; Broth-

Most of the German studies and texts on Martyrology were, naturally, written during the Third Reich. Among the most prominent are: the Protestants Otto Michel (1932), Hans Freiherr von Campenhausen (1936), Dietrich Bonnhoeffer (1937), Hellmuth Frey (1938), Hans-Weren Surkau (1938), Ethelbert Stauffer (1933 & 1941), Ernst Günther (1941), Alfred de Quervain (1942), Friedrich Graber (1943) and in France, André Grabar (1943), and the Catholic Albert Ehrhard (1932).[11]

---

er Andrew. Destined to Suffer? African Christians Face the Future. Open Doors: Orange (CA), 1979, particularly . Tokunboh Adeyemo. "Persecution: A Permanent Feature of the Church". p. 23-36 and Dan Kyanda. "The Attitude of the Prepared Christian". p. 97-104; Daniel Kyanda. "Mission and Persecution". Arbeitspapier der gleichnamigen Arbeitsgruppe auf der World Consultation on Frontier Mission, Edinburgh 1980. unpublished. Peter Hammond. Faith under Fire in Sudan. Frontline Fellowship: Newlands (South africa), 1996; Peter Hammond. In the Killing Fields of Mozambique. Frontline Fellowship: Newlands (South Africa), 1998; See also Brother Andrew. Battle for Africa. Revell: Old Tappan (NJ), 1977 and Patrick Johnstone. "Preparing 3rd World Believers for Church Growth under Persecution". Worldwide Thrust (WEC USA) Nov/1978: 3-7

Latin America: Medardo Ernesto Gómez. Fire against Fire: Christian Ministry Face-to-Face with Persecution. Augsburg Publ.: Minneapolis (MN), 1990 [Original: Fuego contra fuego. Ediciones Liberación: (El Salvador), 1990] (Lutheran); Ivo Lesbaupin. Blessed are the Persecuted: The Early Church Under Siege. Orbis Books: Maryknoll (NY), 1987 [Original Portuguese]; Spire (Hodder & Stoughton): Sevenoaks (GB), 1988 (Brasilian; Catholic);

Former Iron Curtain; Josef Tson. Suffering, Martyrdom, and Rewards in Heaven. University Press of America: Lanham/New York, 1998 [Diss. Heverlee (B), 1996]; Ivan Vasiljevitch Moisejev. Eine Märtyrergeschichte. Aktionskomitee für verfolgte Christen: Rheinbach, 1982^5; See also. Manfred Fermir. Christen in der Verfolgung. Anregungen: Arbeitshefte für den Religionsunterricht ... 3. R. Brockhaus, 1979; G. P. Wiens [= Georgii Petrovich Vins]. Zeugnis vor der Kommission für Sicherheit und Zusammenarbeit in Europa 7 Juni 1979. Missionswerk Friedensstimme: Köln, n. d. [1979]; Georgi Vins. Auf dem Pfad der Treue. Missionswerk Friedensbote: Gummersbach, 1999; Georgii Petrovich Vins. Let the Wars Roar: Evanglists in the Gulag. Baker Book House: Grand Rapids (MI), 1989; Georgii Petrovich Vins. Chronique de la persécution religieuse. Éditions des Catacombes: Courbevoie (F), 1975; Georgii Petrovich Vins. De Kerk leeft nog! De Situatie van de Hervormde Baptisten in Rusland. Ed. von Henk Wolzak. J. H. Kok: Kampen, 1981; Georgii Petrovich Vins. Konshaubi: A True Story of Persecuted Christians in the Soviet Union. Baker Book House: Grand Rapids (MI), 1988; Georgii Petrovich Vins. Three Generations of Suffering. Hodder & Stoughton: London, 1976; Georgii Petrovich Vins. Testament from Prison. ed. by Michael Bordeaux. D. C. Cook Publ.: Elgin (IL), 1975.

[11] See Bibliography.

A. The Present Situation

4. The Theology of the Early Church Was Forged by Martyrdom

Proposition: **The persecution suffered by Christians under the Roman Empire prior to 311 AD has had a lasting influence on the Church's theology.**[12] "Although it took relatively few victims in spite of its long duration, this persecution has molded the developing Church's theology and structure more than any other factor."[13] Because the New Testament Church arose under persecution and developed its theology in the first centuries of its existence under the pressure of persecution and oppression, it is worthwhile to restudy the literary heritage of the persecuted Church.[14] "There is an abundant post-apostolic and patristic literature about martyrdom, particularly the documents on the martyrs and their sufferings,[15] as well as official transcripts of their trials and authentic eye witness reports."[16] Ethelbert Stauffer has noted that Eusebius' History of the

---

[12] See: Theofried Baumeister. Die Anfänge der Theologie des Martyriums. *op. cit.*, p. 1; Theofried Baumeister. "Märtyrer und Verfolgte im frühen Christentum". *op. cit.*, p. 169 und Albert Ehrhard. Die Kirche der Märtyrer. a. *op. cit.*, p. 117-121 and the whole book. This is true in a positive sense, but also in a negative sense, as the text shows.

[13] Rudolf Freudenberger et. al. "Christenverfolgungen". *op. cit.* p. 23.

[14] As an introduction I would recommend the Epistle of the Churches of Vienne and Lyon (177 A. D.), in Eusebius of Caesarea. Kirchengeschichte. Wissenschaftliche Buchgesellschaft: Darmstadt, 1984 [Lizenz von Kösel: München, 1981²]. p. 233-245 [5th Vol. Ch. 1-2] and Lactantius. De mortibus persecutorum. ed. by J. L. Creed. Clarendon Press: Oxford, 1984. Particularly valuable are the descriptions of the conduct of the church fathers Laktantius, Cyprian, Augustinus und Eusebius under persecution.

[15] For a good classification of this literature, see: Herbert Musurillo (Ed.). The Acts of Christian Martyrs. Clarendon Press: Oxford, 1972. pp. lii-liii in "Introduction" pp. xi-lxxiii. See also the numerous collections, *Ibid.*, (Greek/Latin and English translation); Rudolf Knopf, Gustav Krüger (Ed.). Ausgewählte Märtyrerakten. Sammlung ausgewählter kirchen- und dogmengeschichtlicher Quellenschriften 3. J. C. B. Mohr: Tübingen, 1929; revised by Gerhard Ruhbach *Ibid.*, 1965 (Greek Originals); Andreas Schwerd. Lateinische Märtyrerakten. Humanitas christiana 1. Kösel: München, 1960; Gerhard Rauschen. Frühchristliche Apologeten und Märtyrerakten. 2 Vols. Bibliothek der Kirchenväter. Kösel: Kempten, n. d. (German); Hugo Rahner. Die Märtyrerakten des zweiten Jahrhunderts. Zeugen des Wortes 32. Herder: Freiburg, 1954. See the list of German translations of sources Hans Dieter Stöver. Christenverfolgung im römischen Reich. Econ: Düsseldorf, 1983; Bechtermünz: Eltville am Rhein, 1990 (Edition 1983. p. 290-294).

[16] I. Bria. "Martyrium". *op. cit.*, p. . 267. Daneben gehören natürlich im weiteren Sinne noch Passionsdarstellungen und Märtyrerlegenden dazu; See also. Gerhard

Church, the first of its kind, was written from the view point of Martyrology[17] (a model for the present!).

Even though we ought to be wary of encouraging a *longing* for martyrdom, and although some developments were dubious,[18] the Early Church correctly understood, that the theory and practice of martyrdom in the first centuries of its life were the direct continuation of the doctrines and experiences of the New Testament Church. Those churches who exist without considerations of martyrdom deviate more strongly from the New Testament than those persecuted groups of the first centuries who, suffering martyrdom and valuing it highly, and thereby reached the entire Roman Empire with the Gospel.

5. The Question of the Persecution of Christians is Not Limited to the Early Church

Proposition: Martyrdom and the persecution of believers concerns not only the Early Church, for it has constantly accompanied Christianity throughout its history.[19] "Persecution of Christians and martyrdom took place in every century."[20] This must come to the attention of students of Church History. Many theological publications deal with the subject as if persecution had ended in the early centuries of European history. Many historical summaries end at the reign of Constantine,[21] thus not only ignor-

---

Ruhbach. "Märtyrerakten". p. 1303 in: Helmut Burkhardt, Uwe Swarat (Ed.). Evangelisches Lexikon für Theologie und Gemeinde. Vol. 2. Brockhaus: Wuppertal, 1993.

[17] Ethelbert Stauffer. "Märtyrertheologie und Täuferbewegung". Zeitschrift für Kirchengeschichte 52 (1933): 545-598, here p. 548.

[18] See the contribution on the worship of the saints below, but caution is advisable. Theofried Baumeister. Die Anfänge der Theologie des Martyriums. *op. cit.*, pp. 252-257, has demonstrated that the Early Church, particularly the "Shepard of Hermas" has been falsely accused of teaching 'Rewards', a martyrology of merit.

[19] For a good summary, see: Jonah Spaulding. A Summary History of Persecution from the Crucifiction of Our Saviour to the Present Time. S. K. Gilman: Hallowell (ME), 1819.

[20] Gerhard Ruhbach. "Märtyrer". p. 1303 in: Helmut Burkhardt, Uwe Swarat (Editors.). Evangelisches Lexikon für Theologie und Gemeinde. Vol. 2. Brockhaus: Wuppertal, 1993.

[21] See, for example, Albert Ehrhard. Die Kirche der Märtyrer: Ihre Aufgaben und ihre Leistungen. J. Kösel & F. Pustet: München, 1932; H. Last. "Christenverfolgung II (judicial)". Col. 1208-1228 and J. Vogt. "Christenverfolgung I (historical)". Col. 1159-1208 in: Reallexikon für Antike und Christentum. Vol. 2. Hirsemann: Stuttgart, 1954. *Ibid.*, p. 1159 defines the persecution of Christians simply

A. The Present Situation

ing and making light of the massive persecutions of the Twentieth Century,[22] of which Chuck Colson writes: "more Christians have been martyred for their faith in this century alone than in the previous nineteen centuries combined."[23] Such accounts also ignore the fact that persecution has always played a role in Church History and Missiology,[24] for, "The history of the Church is also the history of her persecution."[25] To ignore the subject is to disregard the persecutions[26] carried out in all the religious wars and disputes, the results of the French Revolution,[27] the Christians in the

---

as the persecution by the Romans (and partly by the Jews in the Roman Empire)! This limitation of the issue to the first centuries occurs even in Geoffrey W. Bromiley. "Persecute". p. 771-774 in: Geoffrey W. Bromiley (Ed.). The International Standard Bible Encyclopedia. Vol. 3. Wm. B. Eerdmans: Grand Rapids (MI), 1986; John Rutherford. "Persecution". p. 23-24 in: James Orr (Ed.). The International Standard Bible Encyclopedia. 5 Vols. Vol. 4. Wm. B. Eerdmans: Grand Rapids (MI), 1957 [1939] oder I. Bria. "Martyrium". *op. cit.*, oder Michael Slusser. "Martyrium III/1.". p. 207-212 in: Gerhard Krause, Gerhard Müller (Ed.). Theologische Realenzyklopädie. Vol. 22. Walter de Gruyter: Berlin, 1992.

[22] See: James C. Hefley, Marti Hefley, James Hefley. By Their Blood: Christian Martyrs of the Twentieth Century. Baker Book House: Grand Rapids (MI), 1994 und Johannes Herzog. "Märtyrer". pp. 166-167 in: Friedrich Keppler (Ed.). Calwer Kirchenlexikon. Vol. 2. Calwer Verlagsg.: Stuttgart, 1941. p. 166-167.

[23] Chuck Colson. "Foreword". S. ix-xii in: Nina Shea. In The Lion's Den: A Shocking Account of Persecution and Martyrdom of Christians Today and How We Should Respond. Broadman & Holman: Nashville (TN), 1997. p. ix.

[24] Bernard Ruffin. The Days of Martyrs: A History of the Persecution of Christians from Apostolic Times to the Time of Constantine. Our Sunday Visitor: Huntington (IN), 1985; See also the contributions in Diana Wood (Ed.). Martyrs and Martyrologies. Papers Read at the 1992 Summer Meeting and the 1993 Winter Meeting ... Ecclesiastical History Society. B. Blackwell: Oxford, 1993 and W. J. Sheils (Ed.). Persecution and Toleration. Papers Read at the ... Ecclesiastical History Society. B. Blackwell: Oxford, 1984.

[25] Franz Kardinal Hengsbach. "Vorwort". pp. 5-6 in: Gebetstag für die verfolgte Kirche 1991. Arbeitshilfen 85. Sekretariat der Deutschen Bischofskonferenz: Bonn, 1991. p. 6.

[26] On various periods of European history, see: Brad Stephan Gregory. Salvation at Stake: Christian Martyrdom in Early Modern Europe. Harvard Historical Studies 134. Harvard University Press: Cambridge (MA), 1999; Lutz E. von Padberg. Die Christianisierung Europas im Mittelalter. Reclam: Stuttgart, 1998; Lacey Baldwin Smith. Fools, Martyrs, Traitors: The Story of Martyrdom in the Western World. A. A. Knopf: New York, 1997; Northwestern University Press: Evanston (IL), 1999^{Tb} (teilweise weltlich); Joseph N. Tylenda. Jesuit Saints and Martyrs. Loyola University Press: Chicago 1984^1; Loyola Press: Chicago, 1998^2; F. Graeme Smith. Triumph in Death: The Story of the Malagasy Martyrs. Evangelical Press: Welwyn (GB), 1987; 1994^{Tb}.

[27] Rudolf Freudenberger et. al. "Christenverfolgungen". *op. cit.*, pp. 45-48.

Islamic World,[28] as well as the mass executions of Christians in Asia; specifically in Japan (1587-1635), China (1617, 1665, 1723, 1724, 1736, 1811, 1857, 1900-1901) and Korea (. 1784, 1791, 1801, 1815, 1827, 1839, 1846, 1866, 1881, 1887), to name only a few examples. Even prior to the Twentieth Century, many states had prohibited and suppressed the Christian faith (for example, Japan, 1635-1854, Madagascar since 1835, and continually in Saudi Arabia).[29]

The often barbarously persecuted minority churches and Anabaptist movements have recognized that the entire history of the Church has been molded by persecution, as Stauffer has stated: that unfortunately, 'the Martyr Apocalypse did not arise in the established Churches, but in the 'heretical fellowships',[30] such as the Waldensians or the Protestants in the confrontation with the Roman Church, the Baptists with the Catholics and the

---

[28] *Ibid.*, pp. 35-38 . See also the example of Egypt in: Martyrs and Martyrdom in the Coptic Church. Saint Shenouda the Archimandrite Coptic Society: Los Angeles (CA), 1984; John Eibner (Ed.). Christians in Egypt: Church under Siege. Institute for Religious Minorities in the Islamic World: Zürich, Washington, 1993; on the present situation, see Herbert Schlossberg. A Frangrance of Oppression: The Church and Its Persecutors. Crossway Books: Wheaton (IL), 1991. pp. 25-50; Andrea Morigi, Vittori Emanuele Vernole, Priscilla di Thiene. Die Religionsfreiheit in den Ländern mit überwiegend islamischer Bevölkerung. Schriftenreihe von 'Kirche in Not/Ostpriesterhilfe'. KIN/OPH: München/Luzern/Wien, 1999 (primarily Catholic victims); Eberhard Troeger. "Verachtung, Bachteile - Unrecht, Tod? Christsein in islamischen Ländern". Confessio Augustana 1/2000: 29-33; "Facing the Fire: Christians Under Persecution". Crossroads (Middle East Christian Outreach) Nr. 70: March 1988: 2-9; Abram J. Wiebe. "Special Problems with Islamic Governments": p. 95-102 in: Edwin L. Frizen, Wade T. Coggins (Ed.). Christ and Caesar in Christian Missions. William Carey Library: Pasadena (CA), 1979 and Christine Schirrmacher. "Human Rights and the Persecution of Christians in Islam". Chalcedon Report No. 375 (Oct 1996): 13-15; Christine Schirrmacher. "Menschenrechte und Christenverfolgung in der islamischen Welt". Querschnitte 12 (1999) 4/5 (Apr/Mai): 1-8; Christine Schirrmacher. "Menschenrechte und Christenverfolgung in der islamischen Welt". S. 24-35 in: Max Klingberg (Hg.). Märtyrer heute. Schulte & Gerth: Asslar, 2000; Christine Schirrmacher. "Wenn Muslime Christen werden - Glaubensabfall und Todesstrafe im Islam". S. 36-49 in: Max Klingberg (Hg.). Märtyrer heute. Schulte & Gerth: Asslar, 2000; Lorenz Müller. Islam und Menschenrechte. Diss. Hamburg, 1996.

[29] Dates from "Christenverfolgungen". Col. 1115-1120 in: Josef Höfer, Karl Rahner (Ed.). Lexikon für Theologie und Kirche. Vol. 2. Herder: Freiburg: 1986 (repr from 1958). p. 1120 (predominantly Catholic martyrs.); See also. Rudolf Freudenberger et. al., . "Christenverfolgungen". *op. cit.*, pp. 38-44 on China, Japan, Korea and Vietnam.

[30] Ethelbert Stauffer. "Märtyrertheologie und Täuferbewegung". *op. cit.*, p. 553.

Protestants, or the Baptists and the Mennonites against the Orthodox Church in the former Iron Curtain countries. The Anabaptists realized what all should have known: "The true congregation has always been a congregation of martyrs. That is the basic concept of the Baptist theology of history."[31]

6. The Multi-faceted Reasons for Persecutions

Proposition: The reasons for the persecution of Christians are often multi-faceted and seldom purely religious.[32] **Political, cultural, national, economic and personal motives may also play a role.**

The Old Testament demonstrates this clearly. Queen Jezebel's hatred toward God and His prophets was mixed with a desire for power, as well as for personal gain (1 Kings 16-19). In St. John's Revelation, hatred for the Church is augmented by political and economic issues. Another example is the Ephesians craftsmen who instigate a riot, because they consider Paul's message a threat to their welfare (Acts 19:23.29). In Acts 16, Paul and Sills are imprisoned after exorcising a fortune telling demon out of a slave girl, because her owners are angry at the lost of their profit (Acts 16:16-24).

We lack the space to deal with the variety of motives and grounds behind all the waves of persecution in all their historical or geographical depth. We must, however, be aware that there has never been a persecution solely on religious grounds, that there is always a confusing blending of religious concerns with cultural and social problems.

7. What is a Martyr?

Proposition: A martyr is a Christian who suffers death of his own free will, as the penalty for the confession of his faith or the refusal to deny it or one of its dogmas, principles or practices.[33] "Martyrdom, as we use the term nowadays, means death for the sake of the Christian faith or Christian custom."[34] There is actually no difference between those 'per-

---

[31] *Ibid.*, p. 560.
[32] Gerhard Ruhbach. "Christenverfolgung/-en". *op. cit.*
[33] David B. Barrett. World Christian Encyclopedia. Nairobi etc.: Oxford University Press, 1982. p. 833.
[34] Karl Rahner. Zur Theologie des Todes. Quaestiones disputatae 2. Herder: Freiburg, 1958, particularly. "Exkurs über das Martyrium". pp. 73-106 [*Ibid.* 1965⁵]. p. 73.

secuted because of their faith' and those persecuted for their 'active support of justice';[35] the Book of Revelations demonstrates clearly that persecution due to practice or custom may be considered true persecution.[36] The Anti-Christian government (the Beast) oppresses the "saints: here are they that keep the commandments of God, and the faith of Jesus." (Rev. 14:12) and will thus fail. Revelations 12:17 describes those persecuted by the Dragon in the same way. The Christians are quite naturally first described as those who obey God's commandments, and only then as those who belong to Jesus Christ, which is the same thing. Both equally attract the hatred of the wicked.

B. An Important Biblical Theme

8. Scriptures are taken out of context and trivialized

Proposition: We have trivialized too many verses by taking them out of their context of persecution and suffering. We must learn anew to understand them against their own background.

A typical example is Jesus' admonition that Christians should be *Salt of the Earth*, a word which reminds us that the fate of our world should be important to us. Seldom, however, do we point out the obvious consequences of faith, which Jesus describes as the willingness to die! The Old Testament prophets were the salt of the earth, as we should now be: "Blessed are they which are persecuted for righteousness' sake: for theirs is the kingdom of heaven. Blessed are ye, when men shall revile you, and persecute you, and shall say all manner of evil against you falsely, for my sake. Rejoice, and be exceeding glad: for great is your reward in heaven: for so persecuted they the prophets which were before you. Ye are the salt of the earth: but if the salt have lost his savour, wherewith shall it be salted? it is thenceforth good for nothing, but to be cast out, and to be trodden under foot of men." (Matt. 5:10-13).

A further example is the admonition to look to Jesus, "... the author and finisher of our faith; who for the joy that was set before him endured the cross, despising the shame, and is set down at the right hand of the throne of God. For consider him that endured such contradiction of sinners against

---

[35] Gebetstag für die verfolgte Kirche 1993: China. *op. cit.*, p. 11.
[36] Otto Michel. Prophet und Märtyrer. Beiträge zur Förderung christlicher Theologie 37 (1932), Vol. 2. Bertelsmann: Gütersloh, 1932. p. 42.

B. An Important Biblical Theme

himself, lest ye be wearied and faint in your minds. Ye have not yet resisted unto blood, striving against sin. And ye have forgotten the exhortation which speaketh unto you as unto children, My son, despise not thou the chastening of the Lord, nor faint when thou art rebuked of him," (Heb. 12:2-5) which portrays the Lord's steadfastness in suffering and martyrdom as a model for us. Looking to Jesus, which enables us to endure, is not simply role playing or meditation, but a concrete recollection that Jesus suffered, because He knew what awaited Him afterwards, and imitation of His example. The writer of Hebrews had persecution in mind, as he wrote these words, for he has just mentioned the "cloud of witnesses" (12:1), which he has discussed in detail in Chapter 11.

When Jesus calls us to deny ourselves, and challenges us to take up our cross, he is not speaking in psychological terms[37] – self contempt or minority complexes – but simply means the willingness to suffer martyrdom. "Then said Jesus unto his disciples, If any man will come after me, let him deny himself, and take up his cross, and follow me. For whosoever will save his life shall lose it: and whosoever will lose his life for my sake shall find it." (Matt. 16:24-25). Note that this scripture is part of His first major Passion Discourse in 10:16-42. The terms 'Cross' and 'Persecution' are, for all practical purposes, identical.

---

[37] The association of love with God's commandments explains the admonition, "Thou shalt love thy neighbor as thyself." Some understand this sentence as a psychological idea, that one can only love others, when one loves oneself. Others understand self-love to be in total opposition to the self-denial which Jesus requires (Mt 16,24; Mk 8,34; Lk 9,23), and understand 'as thyself' to be a concession to human egotism. When we study the Laws of God, we see that both views are equally right and wrong. Since God commands us to take care of ourselves and to rejoice, Jesus' statement cannot demand a fundamental self-denial. When He tells us to earn our living or to enjoy our food, such activities cannot be wrong. His commandment to consider the interests of others before our own, cannot be annulled by psychlogical theories. The Bible does not pit the individual against society, or the individual's needs against those of others; it is neither individualistic nor socialistic, but protects the private sphere of the individual without freeing anyone from social responsibility. The Golden Rule in Matthew 7:12 combines self-love and the love for others inseparably: "Therefore all things whatsoever ye would that men should do to you, do ye even so to them: for this is the law and the prophets." Man's highest goal, eternal life and eternal fellowship with God is founded on tow principles; God takes first place in our lives, and man submits humbly to Him, and will praise Him eternally as Lord and Savior. On the other hand, this is the best thing a person can do for himself.

9. Large Portions of Scripture Deal with Persecution

Proposition: Large portions of Scripture can only be understood in the context of past or anticipated martyrdom.

Otto Michel, writing about the New Testament, says, "The language of martyrdom, the contemplation of martyrdom and the history of martyrdom are integral elements of the early Christian tradition, themes which recur continually. None of the early Christian literature is untouched by the subject; on the other hand, none of the early Christian literature can be completely understood without it."[38] Michel designates the Epistle to the Hebrews, 1 Peter[39] and the Revelation of St. John as 'Martyr Writings'[40] in the purest sense of the word, for their purpose is to prepare the congregations for martyrdom or to comfort them under it. The failure to recognize this often leads to a misunderstanding of the Epistle to the Hebrews.[41] "Read against the background of a theology of martyrdom, Hebrews loses its abstractness and becomes very true to life."[42] Especially Revelations, which we will discuss later on, often suffers under the failure of Western believers to recognize the issue of assistance for a suffering Church.[43]

Only three books of the New Testament do not mention persecution. Four were especially written, to encourage persecuted Christians and persecution was a major topic of Jesus, Paul, Peter and John.[44] Whole books were written for persecuted Christians, especially 1Timothy, 1Peter and

---

[38] See Otto Michel. Prophet und Märtyrer. Beiträge zur Förderung christlicher Theologie 37 (1932), Vol. 2. Bertelsmann: Gütersloh, 1932. p. 42.

[39] *Ibid.*, p. 40-42; See also Theofried Baumeister. Die Anfänge der Theologie des Martyriums. *op. cit.*, pp. 204-209 and William Carl Weinreich. Spirit and Martyrdom. University Press of America: Washington D.C., 1981 [Diss. Basel, 1977]. p. 63-69.

[40] Otto Michel, Prophet und Märtyrer, *op. cit.*, p. 36.

[41] *Ibid.*, pp. 37-40.

[42] *Ibid.*, p. 39; See also Theofried Baumeister. Die Anfänge der Theologie des Martyriums. *op. cit.*, pp. 200-204 and William Carl Weinreich. Spirit and Martyrdom. University Press of America: Washington D.C., 1981 [Diss. Basel, 1977]. pp. 69-71.

[43] *Ibid.*, p. 39; See also Theofried Baumeister. Die Anfänge der Theologie des Martyriums. a. a. O. pp. 211-228, particularly 219-227, and William Carl Weinreich. Spirit and Martyrdom. a. a. O. p. 73-78, and the list of verses below on derivatives of 'martyr'.

[44] Taken from Patrick Johnstone. "Preparing 3rd World Believers for Church Growth under Persecution". *op. cit.*, p. 4.

Revelations[45]. The book of Acts[46] contains only two chapters which do not mention persecution.[47] Paul's entire missionary practice and theology[48] is saturated with the subject of martyrdom, as we will see.[49] Paul could see himself only as a martyr.[50]

Biblical Examples of persecution:
Old Testament
• Abel murdered by Cain (Gen. 4:2-10; Mat 23,:5; Luke 11.51; Heb. 11:4; 12:24)[51]
• Isaac suffers from the Philistines' envy, leading to end of persecution (Gen. 26:12-33)
• Israel by Pharaoh and the Egyptians. Result: God liberates them from slavery.(Exodus 1-15)
• David by Saul – Result: David is protected shielded by God. (1Sam. 18-27; Ps 31,13; 59,1-4)
• 85 Priests of Nob killed by Saul and Doeg (1Sam. 22)
• Prophets killed by Queen Jezebel (1Kings 18:3-4)

---

[45] Taken from Preparing Believers for Suffering and Persecution: A Manual for Christian Workers. Hope: Bulawayo (Simbabwe), n. d. (ca. 1979). 15 pp. p. 6.

[46] On the theology of martyrdom in Acts, see: Scott Cunningham. Through Many Tribulations: The Theology of Persecution in Luke-Acts. Journal for the Study of the New Testament Supplement Series 142. Sheffield Academic Press: Sheffield (GB), 1997. Apg 186-294 + 295-342; William Carl Weinreich. Spirit and Martyrdom. *op. cit.*, pp. 31-43; Theofried Baumeister. Die Anfänge der Theologie des Martyriums. *op. cit.*, 119-137.

[47] Preparing Believers for Suffering and Persecution: A Manual for Christian Workers. Hope: Bulawayo (Simbabwe), n. d. . (ca. 1979). 15 pp., p. 6.

[48] On the theology of martyrdom in Paul's writings, see John S. Pobee. Persecution and Martyrdom in the Theology of Paul. Journal for the Study of the New Testament Supplement Series 6. JSOT Press: Sheffield, 1985; Harry W. Tajra. The Martyrdom of St. Paul: Historical and Judicial: Context, Traditions, and Legends. Wissenschaftliche Untersuchungen zum Neuen Testament 67. Mohr Siebeck: Tübingen, 1994. pp. 1-117 (pp. 118-197 on Paul's martyrdom from post-biblical sources); Harry W. Tajra. The Trial of Paul. Mohr Siebeck: Tübingen, 1989; William Carl Weinreich. Spirit and Martyrdom. *op. cit.*, pp. 43-63; Theofried Baumeister. Die Anfänge der Theologie des Martyriums. *op. cit.*, pp. 156-200

[49] See also: Theofried Baumeister. Die Anfänge der Theologie des Martyriums. *op. cit.*, pp. 161-164 (on Gal), pp. 164-169 (on 1 Cor.)

[50] See John S. Pobee. Persecution and Martyrdom in the Theology of Paul. *op. cit.*, pp. 93-106.

[51] See below.

- Elijah persecuted by Ahab and Jezebel, leading to salvation by flight. (1Kings 18:10-19:2)
- Prophet (Elijah's colleagues) killed by Queen Jezebel (1Kings 19:14+10)
- Elisha threatened with death by the king. (2 Kings 6,:1). Result – one of the king's officers is trampled to death. (2 Kings 7:17-20)
- The prophet Hanani imprisoned by King Asa (2Chr 16,7-10)
- The prophet Zecharia lynched at King Joash's command. (2Chr. 24:20-22)
- The prophet Uriah killed by King Jehoiakim (Jer. 26:20-23)
- Jeremiah imprisoned several times, lastly in a dam cistern, leading to repeated liberation (Jer. 26:7-19; 37:1-38:13; See also the previous deliverance and those following in Jer. 20:24; 39:18)
- Schadrach, Meschach and Abednego in the fiery oven, leading to miraculous deliverance by an angel (Dan. 3)
- Daniel in the lions' den, leading to miraculous deliverance by God (Dan 6)

New Testament
- Jesus as an infant, but saved by flight to Egypt (Matt. 2:13-23)
- John the Baptist imprisoned and beheaded by Herod (Matt.14:3-13)
- Stephan stoned under Saul's command (Acts 6:8-8,3)
- Several Christians tortured by Herod (Acts 12:1)
- James executed by Herod (Acts 12:2)
- Peter and John in prison, leading to liberation by an angel (Acts 4:1-31)
- Paul: See below
- John exiled to Patmos (Rev. 1:9)

10. Assistance in Revelations

Proposition: The Revelation of John contains a forcible message,[52] which continually gives Christians encouragement in new historical

---

[52] On the subject of Martyrdom in Revelations, see: Hans von Campenhausen. Die Idee des Martyriums in der Alten Kirche. Vandenhoeck & Ruprecht: Göttingen, 1936¹; 1964². pp. 42-46.; Hans von Campenhausen. "Das Martyrium in der Mission". pp. 71-85 in: Heinzgünter Frohnes, Uwe W. Knorr (Ed.). Die Alte Kirche. Kirchengeschichte als Missionsgeschichte 1. Chr. Kaiser: München, 1974. p. 74-76; Bo Reicke. "The Inauguration of Catholic Martyrdom According to St. John the Divine". Augustinum (Rom) 20 (1980): 275-283 and Ivo Lesbaupin. Blessed are the Persecuted: The Early Church Under Siege. Orbis Books: Maryknoll (NY), 1987 [originally in Portuguese]; Spire (Hodder & Stoughton): Sevenoaks (GB), 1988. p. 62-95. On these subjects and on the question of which wave of persecu-

B. An Important Biblical Theme

situations. However we interpret the details of the revelation, we should agree on one point: the Church expands neither by power, wealth or force, but through the authority of Jesus, by the Word of God, by the Holy Spirit and by prayer.

Even when God permits religious and state powers to combine forces against the Body of Christ, appearances deceive – the false Church and the perverted State will never exterminate the Body of Christ, but are only digging their own graves. In the end, God will lead them to turn on each other, so that the State destroys the Church's religious opponents, as in Revelations, in which the secular power of the Beast suddenly executes God's judgment on the Whore of Babylon.

Jesus promised, "... I will build my church; and the gates of hell shall not prevail against it" (Matt. 16:18). God's Kingdom grows unchecked against all opposition from religious, philosophical, economic and political powers of this world, a principle clearly seen in the Old Testament, especially in the book of Daniel[53]. Did Jesus not repeat this assertion in all of the parables about corn fields and vineyards, as well as in the Great Commission? Has He not assured us that the very gates of Hell would be unable to withstand His Church? History repeatedly confirms Jesus' promise. Where is the Roman Empire, where is Manichaeism? Where are all the widely-spread ancient religions, who all attacked Christianity, but are now only familar to historians? Where is the world revolution promised by Nazism or Communism?

Can we not learn from John's Revelation, that Islam and Chinese Communism will also fail, when God in His wisdom decrees it? Speaking of himself, Paul once said, "Wherein I suffer trouble, as an evil doer, even unto bonds; but the word of God is not bound" (2 Timothy 2: 9). Is his statement not equally true for the spread of the Gospel; individual believers can be bound and kept under control, but not the Word of God or the Church. "Martyrdom always becomes necessary as sign and testimony of faith, when the world tries to gag or fetter God's people. When they can

---

tion is being referred to, see: Thomas Schirrmacher. "Gründe für die Frühdatierung der Offenbarung vor 70 n. Chr." pp. 129-154 in: David Chilton. Die große Trübsal. Reformatorischer Verlag Beese: Hamburg, 1996; also in Anstöße Nr. 17. pp. 1-4 (Supplement to Neues vom Euroteam 1/1998).

[53] For details see proposition 55.

not longer witness with words or deeds of faith and love, they have nothing left but the testimony of suffering and the act of dying."[54]

11. Historical Criticism and its Problems with the Martyr Texts in the New Testament

Proposition: Historical Criticism's late dating of New Testament frustrates the formulation of a theology of martyrdom.

Historical Criticism dates Old Testament texts concerning martyrdom very late. The book of Daniel, for example, is supposed to have been written in the 2nd century BC in the time of persecution under the Syrian ruler, Antiochos IV. Epiphanes (175-164 B. C.). The Old Testament apocryphal books such as the Supplement to the Book of Daniel or 2nd and 4th Maccabees were composed at this time.[55] The Martyr Epistles of Paul,[56] such as the Pastoral Letters or – depending on the author – Colossians and Ephesians are considered late forgeries, as well as the Revelation of St. John, which was supposedly neither composed by the apostle nor written prior to the events it describes.[57] Were these theories accurate, then the Jews and the Early Church would have had only a collection of fabrications written by later anonymous believers to comfort them.

The consequences of such late dating concern Jesus most of all, but most researchers assume that He never expected to be martyred nor believed Himself to have any sort of redemptive function.[58] A prominent study on

---

[54] Friedrich Graber. Der Glaubensweg des Volkes Gottes: Eine Erklärung von Hebräer 11 als Beitrag zum Verständnis des Alten Testamentes. Zwingli Verlag: Zürich, 1943. p. 262.

[55] Theofried Baumeister. Die Anfänge der Theologie des Martyriums. *op. cit.*, pp. 13-24; Theofried Baumeister. Genese und Entfaltung der altkirchlichen Theologie des Martyriums. *op. cit.*, pp.; Ernst Haag. "Die drei Männer im Feuer nach Dan. 3:1-30". p. 20-50 und Ulrich Kellermann. "Das Danielbuch und die Märtyrertheologie der Auferstehung". p. 51-75 in: J. W. Van Henten (Ed.). Die Entstehung der jüdischen Martyrologie. Studia Post-Biblica 38. E. J. Brill: Leiden, 1989 (These texts do provide a good review of Daniel's theology of martyrdom).

[56] Z. B. Theofried Baumeister. Die Anfänge der Theologie des Martyriums. *op. cit.*, pp. 191-200

[57] See: Thomas Schirrmacher. "Gründe für die Frühdatierung der Offenbarung vor 70 n. Chr." pp. 129-154 in: David Chilton. Die große Trübsal. Reformatorischer Verlag Beese: Hamburg, 1996 and the literature noted for a refutation.

[58] See; Hans F. Bayer. Jesus' Predictions of Vindication and Resurrection. J. C. B. Mohr: Tübingen, 1986, for an excellent refutation, which demonstrates that proph-

martyrdom in the Early Church tells us, for example, "In spite of the discussion of the last few years, the question of whether Jesus ascribed any redemptive function to His death cannot be conclusively resolved."[59] "We find no clear indications of the significance which Jesus Himself ascribed to His death."[60]

Otto Michel has countered, that scholars tend to reject 'early' statements of Jesus which indicate that He considered His death necessary, and sets against this his statement "Death proves its rights"[61] or "A true prophet is perfected by death in Jerusalem (Luke 13:32-33)".[62] Michel points to language of martyrdom – such as 'the cup of suffering' (Mark 10:39; 14:36) or the 'baptism of death' (Mark 10:39; Luke 12:50) which permeates Christ's entire ministry.

12. The First Human Being to Die was a Martyr.

Proposition. New Testament definitions declare Abel, the first human being who ever died or was ever murdered, a martyr for his faith.[63]

Jesus considered Abel the first martyr of history (Matt. 23:35; Luke 11:51) and his murder the first in the long line of persecution of the prophets by those who taught the Law but obeyed it only in outward piety (Luke 11:50). The Church Father Aurelius Augustinus wrote, "From Abel to the end of this world, the pilgrim Church strides forward between the world's persecution and God's consolation."[64]

Cain's sacrifice was just as proper in its external form as Abel's, but Abel sacrificed "by faith" (Heb. 11:4), while Cain's sacrifice was invali-

---

ecies of the Crucifixion in the Gospels can be traced to Jesus and that they were the central message of His teaching.

[59] Theofried Baumeister. Die Anfänge der Theologie des Martyriums. *op. cit.*, p. 70.
[60] *Ibid.*, pp. 69-70. See also: Eduard Lohse. Märtyrer und Gottesknecht. Forschungen zur Religion und Literatur des Alten und Neuen Testamentes 64 (NF 46). Vandenhoeck & Ruprecht: Göttingen, 1955.
[61] Otto Michel. Prophet und Märtyrer, *op. cit.*, p. 25.
[62] *Ibid.*
[63] Tokunboh Adeyemo. "Persecution: A Permanent Feature of the Church". p. 23-36 in: Brother Andrew (Ed.). Destined to Suffer? African Christians Face the Future. Open Doors: Orange (CA), 1979. p. 24. Compare the Title of; George Fox. Cain against Abel: Representing New-England's Church-Hirarchy in Opposition to Her Christian Protestant Dissenters. no publisher.: London (?), 1675. 48 pp.
[64] Cited in: Zitiert nach Peter Beyerhaus. Die Bedeutung des Martyriums für den Aufbau des Leibes Christi. *op. cit.*, 131.

dated by his jealousy and his rebellion against God (Gen. 4:6-7). Enraged at God's acceptance of Abel's sacrifice and the rejection of his own, Cain then murdered his brother: "Thus the Old Testament begins with the testimony that sacrifices meant to satisfy God by their external contents are reprehensible, that only a reverent attitude makes the sacrifice acceptable."[65].

The writer of the Book of Hebrews is quite aware that the blood of Jesus "... speaketh better things than that of Abel." (Heb. 12:4), but draws a parallel between the two. In Hebrews 11:4, he relates the death of Abel to the testimony (martyrdom) that he understands to be the testimony of righteousness given by God. "By faith Abel offered unto God a more excellent sacrifice than Cain, by which he obtained witness that he was righteous, God testifying of his gifts: and by it he being dead yet speaketh."

Persecution, by the way, is frequently triggered by jealousy and envy. Paul once noted, "The one preach Christ of contention, not sincerely, supposing to add affliction to my bonds" (Phil. 1:16). In order to illustrate the ideal of martyrdom, Clemens of Rome[66] adds a long section on envy to his letter and, writing about Paul, Peter and other apostles, says, "Because of envy and jealousy, the greatest and most righteous pillars were persecuted and fought to the death."[67]

13. The Old Testament Prophets Were Persecuted

Proposition: Persecution is not just a New Testament issue,[68] but permeates the Old. God-fearing people were persecuted in the Old Testament at all times, as well.

---

[65] Gustav Friedrich Oehler. Theologie des Alten Testaments. J. F. Steinkopf: Stuttgart, 1891³. p. 81.
[66] The 1st Letter of Clemens 5,1 bis 6,2, abgedruckt in "Der Klemensbrief". p. 1-107 in: Joseph A. Fischer (Ed). Die Apostolischen Väter. Kösel: München, 1981⁸ p. 30-33 and Theofried Baumeister. Genese und Entfaltung der altkirchlichen Theologie des Martyriums. *op. cit.*, pp. 42-47 (Nr. 21); see Theofried Baumeister. Die Anfänge der Theologie des Martyriums. *op. cit.*, pp. 229-247 und Hermann Strathmann. "martys, martyreo, martyria, martyrion". p. 477-520 in: Gerhard Kittel (Ed.) Theologisches Wörterbuch zum Neuen Testament. 10 Vols. W. Kohlhammer: Stuttgart 1990 (repr of 1933-1979). Vol . IV [1942]. p. 489-492, hier p. 511.
[67] 1st Letter of Clemens 5,2, "Der Klemensbrief". S. 1-107 in: Joseph A. Fischer (Ed.). Die Apostolischen Väter. Kösel: München, 1981⁸ p. 31.
[68] See: Hellmuth Frey. Die Botschaft des Alten Testamentes. Calwer Verlag: Stuttgart, 1938.

B. An Important Biblical Theme

According to Jesus, Abel was the first martyr (Matt. 23:35; Luk. 11:51). The last martyr of the Old Covenant was John the Baptist (Mat 14:1-12; see also 11:11-13).

Struggle, conflict, persecution and martyrdom are characteristic of true prophets. David once noted, "Many are the afflictions of the righteous: but the LORD delivereth him out of them all" (Psalm 34:19). Since only few of the Old Testament prophets were spared persecution, they are prototypes of martyrdom (Heb. 11:35-38+12:1; Acts 7:51-53; Mat 5:12; 23:31; James 5:10; 1 Thess. 2:15). Stephen asks, "Which of the prophets have not your fathers persecuted?" (Acts 7:52). In 1 Thessalonians 2:14-15, persecution comes from "... the Jews, Who both killed the Lord Jesus, and their own prophets, and have persecuted us; and they please not God, and are contrary to all men". Jesus reminds His disciples, "Rejoice, and be exceeding glad: for great is your reward in heaven: for so persecuted they the prophets which were before you." (Matt. 5:12), and warns the Pharisees and Sadduccees that they testify against themselves, that "... that ye are the children of them which killed the prophets" (Matt 23:31).[69]

Stauffer describes the martyrdom of the Old Testament prophets as the "Prologue to the Passion of Christ,"[70] and the parable of the Unjust Winegrowers (Mark 12:1-12) a "martyrdom-theological summary of Salvation History",[71] in which the prophets are Jesus' "predecessors".[72]

Later Jewish theology between Malachi and John the Baptist, above all in the apocryphal books, pay much attention to the subject of martyrdom.[73]

---

[69] See, . Johannes Beutler. "martyreo", "martyria", "martys". Col. 958-973 in: Exegetisches Wörterbuch zum Neuen Testament. 2 Vols. Vol. 2. W. Kohlhammer: Stuttgart, 1992². p. 959.

[70] Ethelbert Stauffer. Theologie des Neuen Testamentes. Bertelsmann: Gütersloh: 1941¹. p. 81.

[71] *Ibid.*, p. 80.

[72] *Ibid.*, p. 81.

[73] Ethelbert Stauffer. Theologie des Neuen Testamentes. Bertelsmann: Gütersloh: 1941¹; 1947⁴; 1948⁵ has summarised the Septuaginta' (LXX) and Apokrypha's handling of the subject, in 1941¹ S. 314-317; see pp. 164-167; See also: Otto Michel. Prophet und Märtyrer. *op. cit.*, pp. 16-24; William H. C. Frend. Martyrdom and Persecution in the Early Church: A Study of a Conflict from the Maccabees to Donatus. Basil Blackwell: Oxford, 1965; Anchor Books: Garden City (NY), 1967; John S. Pobee. Persecution and Martyrdom in the Theology of Paul. *op. cit.*, pp. 13-46; Daniel Boyarin. Dying for God: Martyrdom and the Making of Christianity and Judaism. Stanford University Press: Stanford (CA), 1999; H. A. Fischel. "Martyr and Prophet: A Study in Jewish Literature". Jewish Quarterly Review 37 (1946/47): 265-280+363-386; William Carl Weinreich. Spirit and Mar-

Since the 1ˢᵗ century BC, the idea that true prophets must suffer persecution and even die, was an integral part of Jewish theology.[74] It would be false, however, to assume that this view had no basis in the Old Testament.[75] The prayer of repentance offered by the Levites at the time of Nehemiah includes Israel's confession, "Nevertheless they were disobedient, and rebelled against thee, and cast thy law behind their backs, and slew thy prophets which testified against them to turn them to thee, and they wrought great provocations." (Neh. 9:26). Adolf Schlatter has demonstrated that the later Christian theology of martyrdom was derived from Jewish

---

tyrdom. *op. cit.*, pp. 3-15; Theofried Baumeister. Die Anfänge der Theologie des Martyriums. *op. cit.*, pp. 23-65 (See pp. 57-58 on Flavius Josephus); Theofried Baumeister. Genese und Entfaltung der altkirchlichen Theologie des Martyriums. *op. cit.*, pp. 3-15; J. W. Van Henten (Ed.). Die Entstehung der jüdischen Martyrologie. Studia Post-Biblica 38. E. J. Brill: Leiden, 1989; Kalman J. Kaplan, Matthew B. Schwartz (Ed.). Jewish Approaches to Suicide, Martyrdom, and Euthanasia. Jason Aronson: Northvale (NJ), 1997; Eugen Weiner, Anita Weiner. The Martyr's Conviction: A Sociological Analysis. Scholars Press: Atlanta (GA), 1990; J. W. Van Henten. The Maccabean Martyrs As Saviours of the Jewish People: A Study of 2 and 4 Maccabees. Supplements to the Journal for the Study of Judaism 57. E. J. Brill: Leiden (NL), 1997; F. W. Gaß. "Das christliche Märtyrerthum in den ersten Jahrhunderten, und dessen Idee". Zeitschrift für die historische Theologie 29 (1859) 323-392 + 30 (1860) 315-381; H. A. Fischel. "Martyr and Prophet: A Study in Jewish Literature". Jewish Quarterly Review 37 (1946/47): 265-280+363-386; Hans-Werner Surkau. Martyrien in jüdischer und frühchristlicher Zeit. Vandenhoeck & Ruprecht: Göttingen, 1938. pp. 9-81; Wolfgang Nauck. "Freude im Leiden". Zeitschrift für neutestamentliche Wissenschaft 46 (1955): 68-80, particularly pp. 73-77; Norbert Brox. Zeuge und Märtyrer: Untersuchungen zur frühchristlichen Zeugnis-Terminologie. Studien zum Alten und Neuen Testament 5. Kösel: München, 1961. pp. 132-173 + 18-23 und Ephraim Kanarfogel. "Martyrium II: Judentum". pp. 202-207 in: Gerhard Krause, Gerhard Müller (Ed.). Theologische Realenzyklopädie. Vol. 22. Walter de Gruyter: Berlin, 1992; Hermann Strathmann. "martys, martyreo, martyria, martyrion". *op. cit.*, pp. 489-492.

[74] H. A. Fischel. "Martyr and Prophet: A Study in Jewish Literature". Jewish Quarterly Review 37 (1946/47): 265-280+363-386 und Hans-Joachim Schoeps. "Die jüdischen Prophetenmorde". pp. 126-143 in the same issue. In the Early Church period; J. C. B. Mohr: Tübingen, 1950. See also F. W. Gaß. "Das christliche Märtyrerthum in den ersten Jahrhunderten, und dessen Idee". Zeitschrift für die historische Theologie 29 (1859) 323-392 + 30 (1860) 315-381. On the tradition of "Murder of the Prophets," see; Lukas John S. Pobee. Persecution and Martyrdom in the Theology of Paul. *op. cit.*, pp.108-110.

[75] From a Protestant point of view.

B. An Important Biblical Theme 39

theology, which arose out of Judaism's conflict with the Hellenistic world.[76]

Hans von Campenhausen assumes that the idea of martyrdom was too closely bound with Jesus to have originated in Judaism,[77] but ignores the fact that Jesus' own view of prophet and martyr had its roots in the Old Testament.[78] The most impressive demonstration of the line extending from the New Testament apostles and disciples back through Jesus and the Old Testament prophets can be found in Otto Michel, who considers all these prophets as potential or actual martyrs.[79] He writes, "In God's war with His people, in the war between God's elect and the godless powers of this world, in the evangelization of the peoples called to God, the prophet arises as a witness to men ('Martys'). This is the foundation of the Old Testament theology of martyrdom, in which proclamation by word and deed are simultaneously testimony for God and His truth. In the legal proceedings between God and the world, the prophet stands with his testimony and his confession on God's side; his death is merely the last element of his testimony. The origin of martyrdom is the prophetic office."[80]

Daniel Boyarin represents a new view of the bond of origin between Judaism and Christianity, in which the various schools and views of both religions can hardly be separated.[81] He rejects both the idea that the theology of martyrdom originated in Judaism (the view of W. H. C. Frend) and the insistence that it arose in Christianity under Roman persecution (the

---

[76] Adolf Schlatter. Die Märtyrer in den Anfängen der Kirche. Beiträge zur Förderung christlicher Theologie 19 (1915), Vol. 3. Bertelsmann: Gütersloh, 1915.
[77] Hans von Campenhausen. Die Idee des Martyriums in der Alten Kirche. Vandenhoeck & Ruprecht: Göttingen, 1936^1; 1964^2. pp. 21-29+42-46.
[78] See: Theofried Baumeister. Die Anfänge der Theologie des Martyriums. *op. cit.*, p. 3 und Theofried Baumeister. Genese und Entfaltung der altkirchlichen Theologie des Martyriums. *op. cit.*, p. XI.
[79] Otto Michel. Prophet und Märtyrer. Beiträge zur Förderung christlicher Theologie 37 (1932), Vol. 2. Bertelsmann: Gütersloh, 1932; See also: Marc Lods. Confesseurs et Martyrs: Successeurs des prophètes dans l'église des trois premiers siècles. Cahiers Théologique 41. Delachaux & Niestle: Neuchatel, 1958; Adolf Schlatter. Die Märtyrer in den Anfängen der Kirche. *op. cit.*, on the history of this position, see; Theofried Baumeister. Die Anfänge der Theologie des Martyriums. *op. cit.*, pp. 6-13.
[80] Otto Michel. Prophet und Märtyrer. *op. cit.*, pp. 11-12; For Acts and Luke, see: Scott Cunningham. Through Many Tribulations: The Theology of Persecution in Luke-Acts. *op. cit.*, pp. 307-313.
[81] Daniel Boyarin. Dying for God: Martyrdom and the Making of Christianity and Judaism. Stanford University Press: Stanford (CA), 1999.

view of G. W. Bowersock[82]), but sees a constant give-and-take between the two.

14. God's People persecutes God's People

Proposition: Beginning with the Old Testament, the prophets and the true believers have been persecuted not only by the Jewish or heathen states, but by the organized people of God.

Israel itself persecuted the Old Testament prophets, Jesus and the apostles[83] (James was the first martyr among the apostles.[84] Acts 2:12. Jesus excepted only John from martyrdom. John 21:15-21[85]). The Lord constantly reminded His contemporaries of the fact whenever he compared the spiritual leaders of His day with those who had murdered the Old Testament prophets (Matt. 5:10-12; 10:23; 23:34; Luk. 11:49; 13:34; 21:12; John 5:16; See also Stephan's defense in Acts 7:52 and Peter in Acts 2:23). The Pharisees and the scribes 'testify' against themselves, that they "are the children of them which killed the prophets" (Matt 23:21).[86] Paul declares the Jews to be the source of persecution; "For ye, brethren, became followers of the churches of God which in Judaea are in Christ Jesus: for ye also have suffered like things of your own countrymen, even as they have of the Jews: Who both killed the Lord Jesus, and their own prophets, and have persecuted us; and they please not God, and are contrary to all men" (1 Thess. 2:14-15), and concludes "But as then he that was born after the flesh persecuted him that was born after the Spirit, even so it is now" (Gal. 4:29).

In the New Testament, Christians are persecuted not only by the Gentile state, but also by the oblivious Visible Church, which oppresses true believers in the name of God. Both the Gentile government and the Jewish leaders torture, mistreat and murder Jesus. Acts and the Pauline literature also relate persecution with the Jewish people of God,[87] which is clearly demonstrated in Revelations, where the religious institution which persecutes the Church is identified with the Whore of Babylon. Jesus' pithy

---

[82] See his summary on p. 93.
[83] See: Otto Michel. Prophet und Märtyrer. *op. cit.*
[84] On the martyrdom of James, see: Hans-Werner Surkau. Martyrien in jüdischer und frühchristlicher Zeit. *op. cit.*, pp. 119-126 based on biblical and extrabiblical sources.
[85] Ibid, p. 27.
[86] See; . Johannes Beutler. "martyreo", "martyria", "martys". *op. cit.*, p. 959.
[87] Scott Cunningham. Through Many Tribulations. *op. cit.*, 301-307.

B. An Important Biblical Theme 41

statement is, "yea, the time cometh, that whosoever killeth you will think that he doeth God service" (John 16:2).

15. Christians also persecute both fellow Christians and others

Proposition: "No theology of martyrdom can deny the often proven fact that Christians themselves have spread death and persecution 'in the name of the Christian faith.'"[88] We need only remember the forced conversions in the Middle Ages, the colonization of Latin America, the Crusades, the oppression of heretics, the Inquisition and the Jewish pogroms.[89] Ever since 4th century, the term 'martyr' has been expanded to include Christians killed by other 'orthodox' Christians.[90]

During the Reformation, martyrdom and martyr books took on an ugly confessionalistic character. Catholics,[91] Orthodox, Protestants, [92] Angli-

---

[88] Eduard Christen. "Martyrium III/2.". *op. cit.*, p. 218; see the whole article and Gerhard Ruhbach. "Christenverfolgung/-en". *op. cit.*, p. 370.
[89] See: Ephraim Kanarfogel. "Martyrium II: Judentum". *op. cit.*, p. 204-205.
[90] Michael Slusser. "Martyrium III/1.". *op. cit.* p. 210 und Hans von Campenhausen. Die Idee des Martyriums in der Alten Kirche. *op. cit.* 1936[1]; 1964[2]. pp. 164-172.
[91] See also the biographies of Catholic Martyrs; John Wagner. The Big Book of Martyrs. Paradox Press: New York, 1997 (Juvenile literature); Bernardo Olivera. How Far to Follow? The Martyrs of Atlas. St. Bebes: Petersham (MA), 1997; Joseph N. Tylenda. Jesuit Saints and Martyrs. Loyola University Press: Chicago 1984[1]; Loyola Press: Chicago, 1998[2]; Asa Hollister Craig. Christian Persecutions. Burlington (WI), 1899 (Anti Protestant); Giancarlo Politi Pime. "Märtyrer in China (I)". China heute 19 (2000) 1/2 (197/198): 27-35 (mostly priests); Helmut Moll (Ed.). Zeugen für Christus: Das deutsche Martyrologium des 20. Jahrhunderts. 2 Vols. in Commision of the German Bisops' Conference (Deutschen Bischofskonferenz). Schöningh: Paderborn, 1999 (700 biographies, including Protestants, but only when they died with Catholiks), See also Gernot Facius. "'In unserem Jahrhundert sind die Märtyrer zurückgekommen'". Die Welt vom 18.11.1999. p. 12 (In 1994, Pope John Paul II. ordered all 104 Bishops' Conferences, to present Martyr lists); On the Third Reich, see: Walter Adolph (Ed.). Im Schatten des Galgens: Zum Gedächtnis der Blutzeugen in der nationalsozialistischen Kirchenverfolgung. Morus Verlag: Berlin, 1953 and On the present: Martin Lange, Reinhold Iblacker (Ed.). Christenverfolgung in Südamerika: Zeugen der Hoffnung. Herder: Freiburg, 1980 [Engl. Translation:] Martin Lange, Reinhold Iblacker (Ed.). Witnesses of Hope: The Persecution of Christians in Latin America. Orbis Books: Maryknoll (NY), 1981.
[92] John Foxe. Book of Martyrs. W. Tegg: London, 1851 [1563]; newest Editions: John Foxe. Foxe's Book of Martyrs and How They Found Christ: in Their Own Words. Christian Classic Series 3. World Press Library: Springfield (MO), 1998

cans,[93] Lutherans,[94] Calvinists and Puritans[95] all produced collections of martyr histories,[96] but each included only martyrs from its own group, denying the ugly truth that all denominations had their own victims but also persecuted Christians of other persuasions[97]. The Roman Catholic Church, for example, had approximately 6,850,000 martyrs since the year 1000, but has executed some 4,534,000 non-Catholic Christians during the same period.[98] The Anabaptists,[99] the Quakers and other groups are no different.[100] This mutual oppression has continued into modern times. The

[1563]; John Foxe. Foxe's Book of Martyrs. Thomas Nelson Publ.: Nashville (TN), 2000 [1563] or recently: Otto Michaelis. Protestantisches Märtyrerbuch: Bilder und Urkunden der evangelischen Märtyrerkirche aus vier Jahrhunderten. J. F. Steinkopf: Stuttgart, 1917 with Protestant martyrs from all Europen countries (without Anabaptists).

[93] See; Helen C. White. Tudor Books of Saints and Martyrs. University of Wisconsin Press: Madison (WI), 1963.

[94] Märtyrbuch: Denckwürdige Reden vnnd Thaten vieler H. Märtyrer ... L. König: Basel, 1597; Ludwig Rabus. Der Heiligen ausserwoehlten Gottes Zeugen, Bekennern vnd Martyrern ... 8 Vols. Balthasar Beck: Straßburg, 1552 & Samuel Emmel: *Ibid.*, 1554-1558; Ludwig Rabus. Historien der Märtyrer ... 2 Vols. Josias Rihel: Straßburg, 1571 & 1572; on Rabus, see: Gerhard Dedeke. Die protestantischen Märtyrerbücher von Ludwig Rabus, Jean Crespin, und Adriaen van Haemstede und ihr gegenseitigen Verhältnisse. Diss.: Universität Halle-Wittenberg, 1924; Robert Kolb. For all the Saints. Changing Perceptions of Martyrdom and Sainthood in the Lutheran Reformation. Mercer University Press: Macon (GA), 1987. pp. 41-84+7 and the whole book on Lutheran Martyr books (See the lists pp. 165-174); for recent examples; C. J. Fick. Die Märtyrer der Evangelisch-Lutherischen Kirche. Vol. 1. Niedner: Saint Louis (USA), 1854 and Otto Michaelis. Protestantisches Märtyrerbuch. Steinkopf: Stuttgart, 1917; See alsoJames Michael Weiss. "Luther and His Colleagues on the Lives of the Saints". The Harvard Library Bulletin 33 (1983): 174-195.

[95] See. J. C. Ryle. Fünf Märtyrer: Treu bis in den Tod. CLV: Bielefeld, 1995 und George Fox. Cain against Abel: Representing New-England's Church-Hirarchy in Opposition to Her Christian Protestant Dissenters. no publ.: London (?), 1675. 48 pp. on the persecution of Dissenters by the Anglican State church.

[96] See the lists above for bibliography.

[97] An objective example is: James C. Hefley, Marti Hefley, James Hefley. By Their Blood: Christian Martyrs of the Twentieth Century. Baker Book House: Grand Rapids (MI), 1994.

[98] Bong Rin Ro (Ed.). Christian Suffering in Asia. Evangelical Fellowship of Asia: Taichung (Taiwan), 1989 and David B. Barrett. Our Globe and How to Reach it. New Hope: Birmingham (AL), 1990. p. 18.

[99] See. Ethelbert Stauffer. "Märtyrertheologie und Täuferbewegung". *op. cit.*, .On the Anabaptist Martyr books, see especially pp. 557ff.

[100] This begins very early. See; Thielemann J. (= Janszoon) Braght. Der blutige Schauplatz oder martyrer Spiegel der Tauffsgesinnten oder wehrlosen Christen.

B. An Important Biblical Theme

Orthodox Church in Russia, for example, persecuted members of other churches.[101] In this context, Paul A. Marshall has criticized the liberal churches for only taking interest in persecuted Christians of other theological persuasions.[102] The fact that Christians themselves are martyred in the name of the Christian God, as dreadful as it is, is not foreign to Scripture. The Bible gives us two reasons:

1. Both Testaments make it clear that in spite of external obedience to Jewish or Christian forms, the organized people of God can become God's enemy and can both persecute prophets and commit the terrible sin of killing others 'in God's name' but in its own cause (compare 2 Tim. 3:5: "having a form of godliness, but denying the power thereof"). Jesus said "They shall put you out of the synagogues: yea, the time cometh, that whosoever killeth you will think that he doeth God service" (John 16:2). If Satan can take on the form of an angel of light, how much more can his servants take on the form of ministers of righteousness (2 Cor. 11:13-14).

2. The holy books of no other religion depict their followers so negatively as the Bible does the Jews and the Christians. Scripture describes very graphically the doctrine that Jews and Christians are also sinners and capable of the most dreadful sins, and denounces not only the atrocities carried out by of the Gentiles, but also those of the supposed (or true) people of God.

This pitiless self-criticism is integral to Judaism and Christianity, in contrast to other religions. No other faith criticizes itself so severely as Old Testament Judaism or New Testament Christianity. Scripture exposes the

---

Drucks und Verlags der Brüderschafft: Ephrata (PA), 1748/49 (Anabaptists till 1660) = Thieleman J. (= Janszoon) Van Bragt. The Bloody Theater of Martyrs Mirror of the Defenseless Christians. Mennonite Publ. House: Scottdale (SAU), 1951[6.engl.]; Herald Press: Scottdale (USA), 1987[15], 1998[geb] [Dutch Original: Bloedig tooneel, ca. 1660]; Isaac Ienington. Concerning Persecution. Robert Wilson: London, 1661. 31 pp. (on the Quakers), but also in the present. See;. Dave Jackson, Neta Jackson. On Fire for Christ: Stories of Anabaptist Martyrs, Retold from Martyrs Mirror. Herald Press: Scottdale (USA), 1989. On the 20th century, see. Aron A. Toews. Mennonite Martyrs: People Who Suffered for Their Faith: 1920-1940. Kindred Press: Winnipeg (CAN) & Hillsboro (KS), 1990. (Mennonites in the Soviet Union).

[101] Paul A. Marshall. Their Blood Cries out.*op. cit.*,. S. 119-143 Ch. "Christen gegen Christen".

[102] *Ibid.*, pp. 162-178 and Marshall's statements in Nina Shea. In The Lion's Den. *op. cit.*, pp. 14-15. See also the support given by 'liberal churches' in the USA for the Worldwide Day of Prayer for Persecuted Christians and for the Declaration of the National Association of Evangelicals.

errors of the leaders very clearly, and God often employs outsiders to recall His people to obedience. The Jewish author, Hannes Stein, writes, "In contrast to the holy writings of Mohammed, the Hebrew Bible is not a book, but a library, a colorful patchwork of stories, woven by a whole people over a period of centuries. None of Israel's misdeeds is omitted, no royal crime concealed. Paul Badde writes, 'Practically every book of the Bible up to the New Testament can be seen as a contradiction, objection or critical commentary of earlier or contemporary history.' As the result of this honest self-portrayal, Judeo-Christian society values self-criticism as a virtue, a characteristic of strength, not an admission of weakness. In Islamic culture the situation is radically different: to criticize one's own history is an unthinkable blasphemy, a danger to the very basis of revelation and an insult to the Prophet! Thus, Muslim countries can allow neither freedom of speech nor debates in freely elected parliaments."[103]

The Bible never classifies faith or unbelief according to race or nation, but describes Gentiles and unbelieving Jews with the same terms. During the Exodus from Egypt, not only did Egyptians harass the Israelites, but unbelieving Egyptians and Israelites both opposed the believing Egyptians and Israelites.[104] For this reason, those of the Egyptians who heed Moses' warnings were permitted to join the Israelites (Exodus 12:38. See also Numbers 11:4; Lev. 24:10), while the unbelieving Israelites were destroyed after worshipping the Golden Calf (Exodus 32).

Christianity becomes a monstrousity when it denies the true power of faith (2 Tim. 3:5, "who have a form of piety, but deny its power") or substitutes human laws and commandments for divine revelation (Mark 7:1-3; Isaiah 28:13-14). The New Testament criticizes the Jews because, when they studied Scripture, they disregarded the essential element, Jesus (John 5:39) and failed to submit themselves to Him (Romans 10:2-3). They appealed to the Word of God, but did not live according to it (Romans 2).

In identifying the Roman Catholic Church with the Whore of Babylon, Martin Luther and other Protestant scholars understood the Biblical principle, that the true Church is persecuted by the false one, although, 450 years

---

[103] Hannes Stein. Moses und die Offenbarung der Demokratie. Rowohlt Berlin Verlag: Berlin, 1998. p. 47.

[104] See; Jonathan Magonet. "Die Einstellung des Buches Exodus gegenüber Ägypten". Concilium 24 (1988): 439-445, hier pp. 439+441. Exodus distinguishes between the hardened Pharao and those of his officers and people who listened to God (*Ibid.*, p. 442). Since some Egyptians brought in their herds after hearing of the coming judgment (Exodus 9:20), they must have believed Moses.

later on, we question the idea that the Catholic Church of the Reformation period has been the only historical fulfillment of that symbol.

16. Persecution is an Ecumenical Topic

Proposition: Persecution is an ecumenical issue,[105] but unfortunately engenders no deeper unity among Christians.

Brother Andrew, a Dutch pioneer in serving persecuted Christians, once saw himself forced to admit that, "Much of the suffering in the universal Church is instigated by the erroneous idea that the 'Body of Christ' is identical with 'my church' (congregation, denomination, dogma)."[106]

It is an unfortunate fact of ecclesiastical history that persecution can also engender conflict and division between Christians.[107] We have already seen that almost all the ruptures in the first centuries were due to persecution and the results of the Church's dealing with it. An appropriate, if terrifying, modern example occurred in Korea, when the Japanese rulers (1910-1945) required all Koreans to kowtow to Shinto shrines in order to honor the Japanese Emperor and the sun goddess. After long resistance, in 1937 and '38, most Christian groups surrendered to the increasingly intolerable coercion, but were strongly divided (particularly the Presbyterians) on the significance of the required ceremony; was it a religious rite or merely a cultural formality? Sixty years later, the issue remains unresolved and the breach is still evident, even though the original problem is gone for a long time already.[108]

---

[105] "The Yakunin Hearing July 22-26, 1983 Vancouver ..." (Christian Solidarity International). Programmheft.
[106] Bruder Andrew. "Wir brauchen eine neue Sicht der leidenden Kirche". Geöffnete Türen. Rundbrief Geöffnete Türen (Frutigen, Schweiz). Febr 1980. pp 1-3, here p. 3; similarly; Preparing Believers for Suffering and Persecution: A Manual for Christian Workers. Hope: Bulawayo (Simbabwe), n. d. (ca. 1979). 15 pp. p. 7+8.
[107] See; Albert Ehrhard. Die Kirche der Märtyrer. pp. 122-267. Erhard demonstrates that many early dogmatic controversies and conflicts arose out of sects and heretic movements in the Early Church, and often were involved with persecution.
[108] See;. "Der geistliche Kampf um Korea". Supplement to HMK-Kurier M 11403. Xeroxed. Hilfsaktion Märtyrer Kirche: Uhldingen, 1997. 4 pp. und Peter Pattison. Crisis Unaware: A Doctor Examines the Korean Church. OMF Books: Sevenoaks (GB), 1981.

17. The First Christian Martyr

Proposition: Not by chance, the book of Acts relates the martyrdom of the first martyr of the New Covenant, Stephan[109] (Acts 6:8-8:3[110]), in great detail.

This event is, not by chance, also the first appearance of Saul of Tarsus (Acts 7:58; 8:1+3; 9:1), who began as a persecutor of the Christians but later became a persecuted missionary himself and played such a decisive role in missionary history. Typically, 1. Stephan sees himself as the successor of the Old Testament prophets (Acts 7:51-52), and 2. his persecution comes not from the state, but from the misguided people of God, in the person of their leaders, the high priests and the leading theologians, the Pharisees (such as Saul. Acts 6:12; 8:1). As in Peter's sermon at Pentecost (Acts 2:14-36), Stephan accuses God's people of crucifying their Messiah.

C. To Speak of Jesus is to Speak of Martyrdom

18. Jesus is the Prototype of the Martyr

Proposition: Jesus is the archetype of the martyr. "Early Christianity defined the work of Christ in the categories of martyr theology, and interpreted the fate of the martyrs according to the fate of Christ."[111] A letter written to the churches in Vienne and Lyon in 177 AD calls Him, "Christ

---

[109] See; Hans-Werner Surkau. Martyrien in jüdischer und frühchristlicher Zeit. *op. cit.*, pp. 105-119; Hans von Campenhausen. Die Idee des Martyriums in der Alten Kirche. Vandenhoeck & Ruprecht: Göttingen, 1936[1]; 1964[2]. pp. 57-59; Theofried Baumeister. Die Anfänge der Theologie des Martyriums. *op. cit.*, pp. 123-132; William Carl Weinreich. Spirit and Martyrdom. *op. cit.*, pp. 36-43. Jacob Thiessen. Die Stephanusrede: Apg 7,2-53, Verlag für Theologie und Religionswissenschaft: Nürnberg, 1999. Thiessen examines and interprets Stephan's speech from Old Testament and Jewish perspective and offers quite a bit of detail, but deals insufficiently with other views or with the subject of martyrdom.

[110] According to William Carl Weinreich. Spirit and Martyrdom. *op. cit.*, p. 38, Luke pays so much attention to Stephan, not because he was the first martyr, but because of the consequences of his martyrdom (Acts 8:1), but even under this aspect, the issue of martyrdom is central to the text. Besides, Luke need not have been so explicit; he mentions the death of James in a singe sentence (Acts 12:2), and could have abbreviated Stephan's discourse, as he did others in Acts.

[111] Ethelbert Stauffer. "Märtyrertheologie und Täuferbewegung". *op. cit.* p. 547-548.

C. To Speak of Jesus is to Speak of Martyrdom

the faithful and true martyr."[112] The prediction of His martyrdom accompanies His whole earthly ministry from the very beginning (for example; Matt: 16:21; 17:22-23; 10:17-19; 26:2). The Passion takes up the longest part of the Gospels and relates Judas' betrayal, the false accusations, the illegal trial, torture and the excruciating execution at the hands of Israel's leaders and the Roman government in great detail.[113] Paul consistently presented Jesus as the archetype of the martyr and as an example for all Christians.[114] The Early Church's documents on martyrdom[115] thus considered Jesus to be the prototype of the martyr, Who could not be excelled by any other.[116]

19. To Die for Friends is the Highest Form of Love

Proposition: To give one's life for others is the highest form of love in this world.

Because Jesus teaches clearly: "This is my commandment, That ye love one another, as I have loved you. Greater love hath no man than this, that a man lay down his life for his friends." (John 15:12-13), a Christian's love is continually oriented towards Jesus' greatest sacrifice of all, His death on the Cross: "And walk in love, as Christ also hath loved us, and hath given himself for us an offering and a sacrifice to God for a sweet-smelling savour." (Eph 5:2). For this reason, the husband should be willing to die for his wife; a denial of any dictatorial ideas of 'headship'! "Husbands, love your wives, even as Christ also loved the church, and gave himself for it;" (Eph. 5:25). The Early Church did well to consider martyrdom for Jesus' sake the highest proof of one's love for God.

---

[112] In Theofried Baumeister. Genese und Entfaltung der altkirchlichen Theologie des Martyriums. *op. cit.*, p. 91; See also Eusebius von Caesarea. Kirchengeschichte. *op. cit.*, pp. 233-245 [Book 5, Ch. 2-3].

[113] See: Hans-Werner Surkau. Martyrien in jüdischer und frühchristlicher Zeit.*op. cit.*, pp. 82-104. Surkau presents the Passion as a martyr report.On the idea of martyrdom in the Gospels, see; Theofried Baumeister. Die Anfänge der Theologie des Martyriums. *op. cit.*, pp. 66-119+137-150; on Luke, see; Lukas Scott Cunningham. Through Many Tribulations: The Theology of Persecution in Luke-Acts. *op. cit.*, pp. 23-185 + 295-342.

[114] See; John S. Pobee. Persecution and Martyrdom in the Theology of Paul. *op. cit.* 74-92.

[115] See the details in further theses.

[116] Leonardo Boff. "Martyrdom: An Attempt at Systematic Reflection". pp. 12-17 in: Johannes Baptist Metz, Edward Schillebeeckx (Ed). Martyrdom Today.*op. cit.*

20. All Persecution is Actually Directed Towards Jesus

Proposition: Jesus is the actual object of all persecution. For this reason, Jesus asks Saul, "Saul, Saul, why persecutest thou me?" (Acts 9:4; 22:7; 26:14), and identifies Himself as, "... Jesus whom thou persecutest" (Acts 9:5); 22; 8; 26:15).

The true reason for Christians' suffering is Christ, Who justifies the contradiction, "The clearer the Church recognizes Christ and testifies of Him, the more certain it will encounter the contradiction, the confrontation and the hatred of the Antichrist."[117] Jesus Himself frequently reminded the disciples, that they would be persecuted for His sake (for example: Matt. 10:22= Luke 21:17. "And ye shall be hated of all men for my name's sake"; Matt. 16:25 "For whosoever will save his life shall lose it: and whosoever will lose his life for my sake shall find it."; Luke 21:12 "But before all these, they shall lay their hands on you, and persecute you, delivering you up to the synagogues, and into prisons, being brought before kings and rulers for my name's sake.")

21. Continuation of the Suffering of Christ

Proposition: The suffering of the Christian is distinctive because it continues Christ's sufferings.

The recollection of Golgotha is essential to an understanding of the Church's sufferings. Howard A. Snyder describes the Cross as the guarantee of the Church's suffering, not its escape from persecution.[118] Paul did not regard his own suffering as redemptive,[119] but still describes it as "Fellowship with the suffering of Christ."[120] In 2 Corinthians 1:5 ("For as the sufferings of Christ abound in us, so our consolation also aboundeth by Christ."), Paul relates suffering under persecution with the sufferings of Christ. He repeats the idea more explicitly[121] in Colossians 1:24: "I now

---

[117] Martin Luthers Sämtliche Schriften. Ed. by Joh. Georg Walch. Verlag der Lutherischen Buchhandlung H. Harms: Groß Oesingen, 1986 (repr. of 1910²). Vol. V, p. 106.
[118] Howard A. Snyder. The Community of the King. IVP: Downers grove (IL), 1977.
[119] Auch im Martyrium des Polykarp Herbert Musurillo (Ed.). The Acts of Christian Martyrs. Clarendon Press: Oxford, 1972, 'Martyrium des Polykarp' pp. 2-21. The descriptions of the martyrdom of Polycarp (ca. 155-157 A. D.), for example, distinguish between the redemptive sufferifings of Christ and the sufferings of the martyrs.
[120] Otto Michel. Prophet und Märtyrer. op. cit., pp. 31-33.
[121] Harry W. Tajra. The Martyrdom of St. op. cit., pp. 52-54.

C. To Speak of Jesus is to Speak of Martyrdom

rejoice in my sufferings for you, and fill up that which is behind of the afflictions of Christ in my flesh for his body's sake, which is the church." Again, in Galatians 6:17, he writes, "From henceforth let no man trouble me: for I bear in my body the marks of the Lord Jesus.", and in Philippians 3:10, he wishes to "... know him, and the power of his resurrection, and the fellowship of his sufferings, being made conformable unto his death". In 2 Corinthians 4:8-10, he adds, "We are troubled on every side, yet not distressed; we are perplexed, but not in despair; Persecuted, but not forsaken; cast down, but not destroyed; Always bearing about in the body the dying of the Lord Jesus, that the life also of Jesus might be made manifest in our body."[122] In his words about 'fire' and 'testing', Peter shared Paul's view, and writes, "But rejoice, inasmuch as ye are partakers of Christ's sufferings; that, when his glory shall be revealed, ye may be glad also with exceeding joy." (1 Pet. 4:13).

22. Jesus as Role Model – The Martyrs as Role Models

Proposition: Jesus' martyrdom makes Him our role model when we suffer persecution.

Jesus Himself suffered just as much as the martyrs of His Church, and more. "For in that he himself hath suffered being tempted, he is able to succour them that are tempted." (Heb. 2:18; Heb 4:15). Martin Luther wrote, "The Lord Christ had to suffer persecution at the hands of the devil and the world: we should not desire anything better."[123] Jesus reminds His disciples, "Remember the word that I said unto you, The servant is not greater than his lord. If they have persecuted me, they will also persecute you; if they have kept my saying, they will keep yours also" (John 15:20. For the context, read 18-21). When we read His words, "Behold, I send you forth as sheep in the midst of wolves: be ye therefore wise as serpents, and harmless as doves." (Matt. 10:16), we must remember that He is the Lamb of God[124] sent among the wolves to suffer and die peacefully for others.

---

[122] See: William Carl Weinreich. Spirit and Martyrdom. *op. cit.*, p. 51-52.
[123] Martin Luthers Sämtliche Schriften. *op. cit.*, Vol. III, p. 691.
[124] Ludwig Bertsch SJ. "Predigtgedanken". p. 11-15 in: Gebetstag für die verfolgte Kirche 1992. Arbeitshilfen 99. Sekretariat der Deutschen Bischofskonferenz: Bonn, 1992. p. 14.

His own example, which plays such an important role in the New Testament,[125] includes His suffering and His dealing with persecution. Paul knew that the reality of his own sufferings had taught Timothy to handle such situations: "But thou hast fully known my doctrine, manner of life, purpose, faith, longsuffering, charity, patience, Persecutions, afflictions, which came unto me at Antioch, at Iconium, at Lystra; what persecutions I endured: but out of them all the Lord delivered me. Yea, and all that will live godly in Christ Jesus shall suffer persecution" (2 Tim 3:10-12). The Thessalonians also became not only imitators of Paul, Silas and Timothy under persecution, but also role models for the believers in neighboring provinces. "And ye became followers of us, and of the Lord, having received the word in much affliction, with joy of the Holy Ghost: So that ye were ensamples to all that believe in Macedonia and Achaia" (1 Thess. 1:6-7). "For ye, brethren, became followers of the churches of God which in Judaea are in Christ Jesus: for ye also have suffered like things of your own countrymen, even as they have of the Jews: Who both killed the Lord Jesus, and their own prophets, and have persecuted us; and they please not God, and are contrary to all men" (1 Thess. 2:14-15).

23. A Theology of the Cross ('theologia crucis')

Proposition: Without the offence of the Cross there would be no persecution.

Ethelbert Stauffer, writing about the discussion of the persecution of Christ and the apostles, says "This 'theology of martyrdom' finds the center of its framework and its meaning in the fact of the Cross."[126] Paul thus writes,[127] "And I, brethren, if I yet preach circumcision, why do I yet suffer persecution? then is the offence of the cross ceased." (Gal 5:11) – without the Cross, there would be no persecution. He accuses his opponents of

---

[125] See: Thomas Schirrmacher. "Jesus as Master Educator and Trainer". Training for Crosscultural Ministries (World Evangelical Fellowship) 2/2000: 1-4, and the longer version in German "Jesus als Meisterpädagoge". Bibel und Gemeinde 95 (1995): 17-22 = Querschnitte 11 (1998) 11 (Nov): 1-4 = Anstöße 14. p. 1-4 - Beilage zu Neues vom Euroteam 1/1997 und "Paulus und seine Mitarbeiter: Vom Umgang 'neutestamentlicher Missionare' miteinander". S. 64-81 in: Klaus Brinkmann (Ed.). Missionare und ihr Dienst im Gastland. Referate der Jahrestagung 1997 des afem. edition afem - mission reports 5. Verlag für Kultur und Wissenschaft: Bonn, 1998 = Evangelikale Missiologie 15 (1999) 1: 13-22.

[126] Ethelbert Stauffer. "Märtyrertheologie und Täuferbewegung". op. cit., p. 546.

[127] On Paul's view of the Cross and martyrdom, see: John S. Pobee. Persecution and Martyrdom in the Theology of Paul. op. cit., pp 47-73.

C. To Speak of Jesus is to Speak of Martyrdom 51

being circumcised only to escape persecution: "As many as desire to make a fair shew in the flesh, they constrain you to be circumcised; only lest they should suffer persecution for the cross of Christ." (Gal. 6:12; see also verse 14).[128] The 'Word of the Cross' is 'foolishness' to unbelievers (1 Cor. 1:18), an impediment to the Jews and nonsense to the Gentiles (1 Cor. 1:23), but the center of salvation history. The heart of the apostolic message is thus "Jesus Christ, and him crucified" (1 Corinthians 2:2). "But we preach Christ crucified" (1 Corinthians 1:23). The message of the Cross is thus the glory of the gospel as well as its foolishness (1 Cor. 1:17-25; Gal. 6:11-14). Theology is either a theology of the Cross ('theolgia crucis') or no theology at all, as Martin Luther[129] and John Calvin[130] have insisted.

"The Theologia Crucis teaches: "The resurrected Lord is the Crucified Lord,"[131] but we must not twist Jesus' death on the Cross into a human victory. Alfred de Quervain formulates this fact, "Not because of His glorious and victorious struggle, not because of His goodness, is Christ the Lord, but because of his obedience and faith in judgment."[132] "This death lacks not only the cultural, human halo of Socrates' death; it also lacks all that we consider lovely, edifying or conscious of victory."[133] "The essence

---

[128] Otto Michel. Prophet und Märtyrer. *op. cit.*, p. 33-34.
[129] Walther von Loewenich. Luthers theologia crucis. Luther-Verlag: Bielefeld, 1982⁶. Von Lowevenich demonstrates that Luther's theology of the Cross not only determined his earlier work (pp. 14-15) but also his view of all of the concrete sufferings of the Christian (pp. 135-144). Robert. A Kelly. "The Suffering Church: A Study of Luthers Theologia Crucis". Concordia Theological Quarterly 50 (1986): 3-17, shows that the theology of the Cross is the reason that persecution is so central to Luther's work. Robert Kolb. For all the Saints. Changing Perceptions of Martyrdom and Sainthood in the Lutheran Reformation. *op. cit.*, however, points out how quickly post- Reformation Lutheran theologians forgot this priority. For a collection of Luther's comments on persecution, see; Otto Michaelis. Protestantisches Märtyrerbuch. *op. cit.*, pp. 217-245. Ethelbert Stauffer. "Märtyrertheologie und Täuferbewegung". *op. cit.*, pp. 550-553, assumes that Luther summarises, renews and evaluates the theology of martyrdom formulated in previous centuries. Luther expected martyrdom for himself. In 1523, when two Augustatine monks, Heinrich Voes and Johann von Essen were burnt at the stake in Brüssel, he discussed their martyrdom at length and stated clearly that their fate should have met him first *Ibid.*, p. 551.
[130] *Ibid.*, p. 218.
[131] Alfred de Quervain. Die Heiligung. Ethik Erster Teil. Evangelischer Verlag: Zollikon, 1946² [1942¹]. p. 151.
[132] *Ibid.*, p. 152.
[133] *Ibid.*, p. 151.

of Christ's crucifixion is not its (humanly speaking) ignominy and lackluster, but the fact that Christ died as a Sinner for sinners."[134]

D. Church under Persecution

24. No Church without martyrdom

Proposition: "Martyrdom is a part of the Church,[135] part of its very essence,[136] and suffering is the mark of missions and the Church between Christ's ascension and His return,[137] for "... we must through much tribulation enter into the kingdom of God" (Acts 14:22). Paul writes, "Yea, and all that will live godly in Christ Jesus shall suffer persecution"[138] (2Tim. 3:12). From the Old Testament, he derives the doctrine, "But as then he that was born after the flesh persecuted him that was born after the Spirit, even so it is now" (Gal. 4:29). Jesus Himself warned the disciples, "The servant is not greater than his lord. If they have persecuted me, they will also persecute you" (John 15:20). Before sending the disciples out to preach (Matt. 10:16-42), He spoke almost exclusively about the impending persecution which is closely bound to their fate in His 'Martyrapocalypse'[139] (Mark 13). Peter describes persecution not as an oddity contradictory to faith, but, on the contrary, something to be anticipated and even

---

[134] *Ibid.*, p. 151.
[135] Oda Hagemeyer. "Theologie des Martyriums". Benediktische Monatsschrift 60 (1984) 309-315, here p. 309.
[136] Peter Beyerhaus. Die Bedeutung des Martyriums für den Aufbau des Leibes Christi. *op. cit.*, p. 131; Karl Rahner. Zur Theologie des Todes. *op. cit.*, pp. 73-106 [*Ibid.*, 1965^5]. See p. 91: "Thus martyrdom is part of the Church's essence".
[137] Tokunboh Adeyemo. "Persecution: A Permanent Feature of the Church". Evangelical Ministries/Ministères Evangélique (Association of Evangelicals of Africa and Madagascar) Mar-Aug 1985: 3-9; Tokunboh Adeyemo. De gemeente zal altijd vervolgd worden. n. d.
[138] On derivitives of 'dioko', 'persecute" see:. O. Knoch. "dioko". col. 816-819 in: Horst Balz, Gerhard Schneider (Ed.). Exegetisches Wörterbuch zum Neuen Testament. 2 Vols, Vol. 1. W. Kohlhammer: Stuttgart, 1992^2; Günther Ebel, Reinier Schippers, Lothar Coenen. "Bedrängnis, Verfolgung". pp. 60-64 in: Lothar Coenen et.al,. (Ed.). Theologisches Begriffslexikon zum Neuen Testament. Vol. 1. R. Brockhaus: Wuppertal, 1967; Günther Ebel, Reinier Schippers. "Persecution, Tribulation, Affliction". pp. 805-809 in: Colin Brown (Ed.). The New International Dictionary of New Testament Theology. Regency/Zondervan: Grand Rapids (MI), 1976. Vol. 2.
[139] Otto Michel. Prophet und Märtyrer. *op. cit.*, p. 30.

D. Church under Persecution

valued: "Beloved, think it not strange concerning the fiery trial which is to try you, as though some strange thing happened unto you: But rejoice, inasmuch as ye are partakers of Christ's sufferings; that, when his glory shall be revealed, ye may be glad also with exceeding joy" (1 Pet. 4:12-13).

Martin Luther emphasized this point by saying, "Even if he only teaches the Word of Christ, every sincere Christian must have his persecutors."[140] The believer is to take up the 'struggle with sufferings' (Heb 10:32), the cross (Heb 12:2), the opposition of unbelievers (Heb. 12:3), persecution (Mark 10:30; Acts 8:1; 13:50; Romans 8:35; 2 Cor. 12:10; 2 Tim. 3:11; 2 Thess 1:4) – that is 'all', together with Paul (2 Tim 2:10), for his faith.

25. Hatred towards God

Proposition: "Persecution is the consequence of the world's hatred towards God and towards His revelation in Christ."[141] (Matt. 10:22; Mark 13:13; Joh 15:18ff; Rev. 12:13). "The persecution of Christians arises out of the inner contradiction between the world's way of life and Christ's message and His Church."[142] As Martin Luther put it, "When a man becomes a Christian and begins to confess his faith with his words and his life, the world becomes angry and begins to persecute, to torment …"[143]

Jesus, Who repeatedly demonstrated that belonging to Him and to His Father always provokes an instinctive reaction in a world which chooses to live without God, calls this reaction 'hatred'.[144] "If the world hate you, ye know that it hated me before it hated you. If ye were of the world, the world would love his own: but because ye are not of the world, but I have chosen you out of the world, therefore the world hateth you" (John 15:18-19). This reaction reflects the close relationship between the life of the believer and the life of Christ.

The world hates Jesus, because, "The world cannot hate you; but me it hateth, because I testify of it, that the works thereof are evil" (John 7:7). With David, the Lord could say, "They hated me without a cause" (John

---

[140] Martin Luthers Sämtliche Schriften. *op. cit.* Vol. IV, p. 263.
[141] Tokunboh Adeyemo. "Persecution: A Permanent Feature of the Church". S. 23-36 in: Brother Andrew (Ed.) Destined to Suffer? *op. cit.*, p. 23.
[142] Heinrich Öhler. "Christenverfolgungen". p. 333 in: Friedrich Keppler (Ed.). Calwer Kirchenlexikon. Vol. 1. Calwer Verlagsb.: Stuttgart, 1937.
[143] Martin Luthers Sämtliche Schriften. *op. cit.*, Vol. XII, p. 542.
[144] Werner Stoy. Mut für Morgen: Christen vor der Verfolgung. Brunnen Verlag: Gießen, 1980². pp. 104-105.

15:25; Psalm 13:19). Even one's own family joins the world in its rejection (Mat 10:21-22+35-37), for "And ye shall be hated of all men for my name's sake: but he that endureth to the end shall be saved" (Matth. 10:22). John, who wrote most of the words about the world's hatred of Christians, concludes, "Marvel not, my brethren, if the world hate you" (1 John 3:13).

26. The World's Hatred of God Originates in Satan's Hatred

Proposition: "The root of the world's hatred is the ancient hatred of Satan, the Prince of this world,"[145] **(John 12:31; 14:30; 16:11).** Revelations portrays Satan as the Dragon who has been persecuting the Church ever since the birth of Christ: "And when the dragon saw that he was cast unto the earth, he persecuted the woman which brought forth the man child" (Rev. 12:13). When John tells us, "Fear none of those things which thou shalt suffer: behold, the devil shall cast some of you into prison, that ye may be tried; and ye shall have tribulation ten days: be thou faithful unto death, and I will give thee a crown of life" (Rev. 2:10). See also 3:13), we recognize that, although the Devil engenders all persecution, he is subject to God's sovereign rule and will succumb to God's final victory.

The "Devil" is the 'murderer' and 'liar' (John 8:44), the 'unworthy' (Gr. 'beliar'; 2 Cor. 6:15), who creates 'lawlessness' (2 Cor. 6:15). He is the 'Prince of the power of the air, ' and the 'spirit that now worketh in the children of disobedience: determines the "the course of this world" (Eph. 2:2). The 'Prince of this world' (John 16:11; 12:31), he is the 'king' of the demons, 'the angel of the abyss; his Hebrew name is Abaddon, his Greek name Apollyon (Rev. 9:11; see verses 1-11), which both mean 'destroyer'. He is "the ruler of the darkness of this world" (Eph 6:12), the 'accuser' (Rev. 12:10), the 'great dragon, the old serpent, the devil and Satan.' (Rev 12:9), who disseminates 'demonic doctrines' (1 Tim. 4:1). Because he appears as "an angel of light", his servants often "are false apostles, deceitful workers, transforming themselves into the apostles of Christ" (2 Cor. 11:13-14).

Satan can only act when God permits it. Prior to Jesus' victory on the Cross, he had access to the divine throne room (Job 1:6-12; 2:1-7; Zech. 3:1-2), but judgement fell on him and his demons, when Christ died, and

---

[145] Peter Beyerhaus. Die Bedeutung des Martyriums für den Aufbau des Leibes Christi. *op. cit.*, p. 133.

D. Church under Persecution

he was thrown onto the earth. Jesus' appearance had already signaled the end of the devil's rulership over the demons (Rev. 20:1-3).[146] In Matthew 12:28, Jesus says, "But if I cast out devils by the Spirit of God, then the kingdom of God is come unto you." When the Seventy return exhilarated at the success of their mission, He rejoices with them: "I saw Satan fall like lightning from heaven. Behold, I give you the authority to trample on serpents and scorpions, and over all the power of the enemy, and nothing shall by any means hurt you. Nevertheless do not rejoice in this, that the spirits are subject to you, but rather rejoice because your names are written in heaven" (Luke 10; 17-20). Revelations 12:9 and 13 describe the fall of Satan and his demons with the following words, "And the great dragon was cast out, that old serpent, called the Devil, and Satan, which deceiveth the whole world: he was cast out into the earth, and his angels were cast out with him." He is the "... the star fallen from heaven unto the earth (Rev. 9:1), and the dragon, who threw a third of the stars of heaven to earth with his tail" (Rev. 12:4).

Ever since the commencement of the Kingdom of God, the Holy Spirit convicts "... of judgment, because the prince of this world is judged" (John 16:11). "And having spoiled principalities and powers, he (Jesus) made a shew of them openly, triumphing over them in it" (Col. 2:15). Satan and his forces cannot escape the eternal fire (Matt. 25:41; Rev. 20:10), as Scripture assures us, "And the angels which kept not their first estate, but left their own habitation, he hath reserved in everlasting chains under darkness unto the judgment of the great day" (Jude 6); "For if God spared not the angels that sinned, but cast them down to hell, and delivered them into chains of darkness, to be reserved unto judgment" (2 Pet. 2:4). This last text probably refers to Psalm 107:10-11, "Such as sit in darkness and in the shadow of death, being bound in affliction and iron; Because they rebelled against the words of God, and contemned the counsel of the most High."

The last three scriptures demonstrate Satan's problem – he had received an sphere of authority from God (Ultimately, all authority comes from God.), but demanded more – he wanted to be like God! I use the expression used in Genesis to describe the Fall of man (Gen. 3:5), in which Satan attempts to persuade Man to commit the same sacrilege, exchanging the theonomic authority given in God's covenant with one's own autonomous rulership – an illusory misery, as Adam soon discovered! Assuming that

---

[146] Most Post- and Ammillenial theologians believe the angel with the key to the abyss to be Jesus at His triumph over Satan on the Cross. Premillenialists, however, consider this an future event and a 'normal' angel.

Ezekiel 28:11-19 and Isaiah 14:12-18 are descriptions of Satan as well as of human rulers, provide us with an eloquent depiction of Hybris (arrogance towards God), which strives to overstep God-given limits and to become God.

Jesus can only promise "... I will build my church; and the gates of hell shall not prevail against it" (Matt 16:8), because he has already defeated Satan!

27. The Holy Spirit – Consolation in Persecution

Proposition: The Holy Spirit, 'the Comforter' (John 16:16+26) gives Christians the strength to endure persecution,[147] even to rejoice in the most difficult conditions. "If ye be reproached for the name of Christ, happy are ye; for the spirit of glory and of God resteth upon you: on their part he is evil spoken of, but on your part he is glorified" (1 Pet. 4:14).[148] The Spirit of Glory, which had rested on the Messiah (Isaiah 11:2) brings His glory to those who seem to have lost all glory, such as Stephan, whom Luke describes as "... being full of the Holy Ghost" (Acts 7:55) during his defense and his execution,[149] as he saw the Glory of God in Heaven.

The Holy Spirit is the "Spirit of Truth, whom the world cannot receive, because it seeth him not, neither knoweth him: but ye know him; for he dwelleth with you, and shall be in you" (John 14:17; See also 15:26 and 16:7). He is the difference between Christians and our rebellious world, and the only person Who can overcome the world (John 16:8). He testifies that Satan is already defeated (John 16:11).

In Luke 21:12-15, Jesus announces that He will give wisdom to the persecuted when they stand before their judges, wisdom that will become a testimony. Who will provide this wisdom if not the Holy Spirit? The paral-

---

[147] For the most thorough study, see: William Carl Weinreich. Spirit and Martyrdom. University Press of America: Washington D.C., 1981 [Diss. Basel, 1977]; See also: Karl Holl. "Die Vorstellung von Märtyrer und die Märtyrerakte in ihrer geschichtlichen Entwicklung" [1914]. pp. 68-102 in: Karl Holl. Gesammelte Aufsätze zur Kirchengeschichte. Vol. 2: Der Osten. J. C. B. Mohr, 1928; Marc Lods. Confesseurs et Martyrs: Successeurs des prophètes dans l'église des trois premiers siècles. Cahiers Théologique 41. Delachaux & Niestle: Neuchatel, 1958; and Eduard Christen. "Martyrium III/2.". *op. cit.*, pp. 214-215 und Werner Stoy. Mut für Morgen. *op. cit.*, pp. 46.

[148] On 1 Peter 4:14, see: William Carl Weinreich. Spirit and Martyrdom, *op. cit.*, pp. 64-65.

[149] *Ibid.* pp. 36-43. Acts 6:5 also describes Stephan as a man full of faith and the Spirit. (Acts 6:8).

D. Church under Persecution

lel text in Matthew 10:19-20 speaks of the 'Spirit of your Father', Who will testify before our judges. William Carl Weinrich notes that Jesus spoke seldom of the Holy Spirit's function, but when He did so, frequently described Him as helper and comforter in persecution (Matt. 10:17-20; Mark 13:9-11; Luke 21:12-19).[150] No wonder that Paul follows the Lord's example in his catalogue of his sufferings by attributing his endurance to the Holy Spirit (2 Cor. 6:6). In Philippians 1:19, he writes, "For I know that this shall turn to my salvation through your prayer, and the supply of the Spirit of Jesus Christ." He reminds the Thessalonians, that "ye became followers of us, and of the Lord, having received the word in much affliction, with joy of the Holy Ghost" (1 Thess 1:6-7).[151]

The Early Church was constantly aware that only the Spirit of God could provide the persecuted with wisdom and strength to endure. According to Tertullian,[152] the Spirit accompanies us into prison;[153] the 'Holy Spirit, the Instructor'[154] prepares the believers for their sufferings. A letter written in 177 A. D. from the churches of Lyon and Vienne mentions a leading Roman citizen in Gaul, who sprang to the assistance of the Christians and was himself condemned for his interference: "He, the comforter of the Christians, who had the Comforter, the Spirit of Zacharias, in himself, as the fullness of his love clearly shows ..."[155] The Ecclesiastical Directions of Hippolyt (early 3rd c. A. D.), advises the church not to lay hands on believers who they are to be ordained as deacons or presbyters, if they had been imprisoned or tortured, for they have already received the honor of presbyter through their testimony: they are to be considered Charismatics, since the Holy Spirit had given them their testimony in court.[156]

---

[150] Ibid, pp. 55-56.
[151] *Ibid.*, pp. 57-58.
[152] After he had become a Catholic.
[153] Tertullian, An die Märtyrer 1,3, in: Theofried Baumeister. Genese und Entfaltung der altkirchlichen Theologie des Martyriums. *op. cit.*, pp. 104-107.
[154] *Ibid.*, pp. 113.
[155] Letter of the Churches of Vienne and Lyon, in: Eusebius von Caesarea. Kirchengeschichte. *op. cit.*, p. 235 [5th. Book, Ch. 1, V.10].
[156] Theofried Baumeister. "Märtyrer und Verfolgte im frühen Christentum". Concilium 19 (1983) 3: 169-173, here p. 170; Text Theofried Baumeister. Genese und Entfaltung der altkirchlichen Theologie des Martyriums. *op. cit.*, p. 135 (Hippolyt, Apostolische Tradition, Absatz 9).

28. Joy in Persecution

Proposition: The presence of the Holy Spirit and the comfort of God enable the believer to rejoice even under persecution.[157]

"But rejoice, inasmuch as ye are partakers of Christ's sufferings; that, when his glory shall be revealed, ye may be glad also with exceeding joy" (1 Pet. 4:13; See also: 1 Pet. 1:6). Peter had learned this from his Master, who said, "Blessed are ye, when men shall revile you, and persecute you, and shall say all manner of evil against you falsely, for my sake" (Matt.5:11). Martin Luther, writing in a similar vein, says, "We have no reason to complain, when the world persecutes us and kills us, but rather to rejoice and to be glad."[158] This advice is quite practical – doesn't Luke tell us that Paul and Silas prayed and sang praises to God in prison (Acts 16:25)? Have you ever noticed that the Epistle to the Philippians, the New Testament letter which deals with persecution more than all the others, is also the most joyful letter? "Rejoice in the Lord alway: and again I say, Rejoice" (Phil. 4:4).[159]

29. Trusting God Alone

Proposition: In persecution, we learn not to rely on ourselves, but to trust God alone. Paul writes, "But we had the sentence of death in ourselves, that we should not trust in ourselves, but in God which raiseth the dead" (2 Cor. 1:9). This lesson is not only meant for those suffering persecution, but for the universal Church, unless she closes her eyes to the fate of the persecuted.

Because God will never abandon His persecuted children, Paul dedicates a whole chapter of 2 Corinthians (2 Cor. 1:3-11) to the comfort he had received from Christ and from the Father in his own sufferings. He continually emphasises the comfort and aid which God gives. "Notwithstanding the Lord stood with me, and strengthened me" (2 Tim. 4:17).

Two points are important here:

---

[157] Wolfgang Nauck. "Freude im Leiden". Zeitschrift für neutestamentliche Wissenschaft 46 (1955): 68-80; Werner Stoy. Mut für Morgen. *op. cit.*, pp. 74-76.
[158] Martin Luthers Sämtliche Schriften. *op. cit.*, Vol. IX, p. 758.
[159] On the subject of persecution in the Epistle to the Philippians, see: Theofried Baumeister. Die Anfänge der Theologie des Martyriums. *op. cit.*, pp. 176-182; Harry W. Tajra. The Martyrdom of St. Paul. *op. cit.*, pp. 58-72; William Carl Weinreich. Spirit and Martyrdom. *op. cit.*, pp. 55-56 n. d.

1. Nothing and no one can estrange Christ from the believer (Rom. 8:31-39), not even persecution (verse 35).[160]

2. God will never permit persecution to become unbearable, for He knows exactly how much the individual can endure. "There hath no temptation taken you but such as is common to man: but God is faithful, who will not suffer you to be tempted above that ye are able; but will with the temptation also make a way to escape, that ye may be able to bear it" (1 Cor. 10:13).[161]

E. Behavior under Persecution

30. Never aspire to persecution

Proposition: A Christian should not seek after persecution. In contrast to the occasional tendency of some Early Church believers, to seek after martyrdom for its rewards and blessings, we must remember that it is God's prerogative, not ours, to determine who is to suffer martyrdom. The believer has no right to pursue persecution.

The tendency to seek after martyrdom became prevalent by about 107-108 A. D, as Ignatius, Church Father and the Bishop of Antioch,[162] executed under the Emperor Trajan, admonished the Roman believers not to hinder his martyrdom, which they apparently could have done.[163] Other

---

[160] See Clemens of Alexandria's comments on this text in: Clemens of Alexandria, Teppiche IV, 14, 96, 1-2, in Theofried Baumeister. Genese und Entfaltung der altkirchlichen Theologie des Martyriums. *op. cit.*, pp. 133+135 (Nr. 49).

[161] Paul does not restrict this promise to situations of persecutions – it concerns all temptation, but is so general in nature, that we can apply it to persecution.

[162] Theofried Baumeister. Die Anfänge der Theologie des Martyriums. *op. cit.*, pp. 262-263+272-274 (on Ignatius, see pp. 260-289); Theofried Baumeister. Genese und Entfaltung der altkirchlichen Theologie des Martyriums. *op. cit.*, pp. 49-55; William Carl Weinreich. Spirit and Martyrdom. *op. cit.*, pp. 111-222; Hans von Campenhausen. Die Idee des Martyriums in der Alten Kirche. Vandenhoeck & Ruprecht: Göttingen, 1936¹; 1964². pp. 71-73; Werner Stoy. Mut für Morgen. *op. cit.* pp. 39-40 und I. Bria. "Martyrium". *op. cit.* p. 267; See also the positive representation in: Otto Michel. Prophet und Märtyrer. *op. cit.*, pp. 54-60, especially p. 57. The older opinion, that Ignatius had not distinguished his own martyrdom from that of Jesus or believed his death to be atonr for the sins of others, must be rejected: see; William Carl Weinreich. Spirit and Martyrdom. *op. cit.*, pp. 111-115.

[163] See his letter to the Romans: "Die Sieben Ignatius-Briefe". pp. 111-225 in: Joseph A. Fischer (Ed.). Die Apostolischen Väter. Kösel: München, 1981⁸. pp. 182-193,

Church Fathers, such as Cyprian[164] and the opponents of the Donatists, thought differently and endorsed the flight from martyrdom.[165] The earliest extant description of martyrdom,[166] "The Martyrdom of Polycarp" (ca. 155-157 A. D.) assumes that the Church Father died against the will his will, as it was in Jesus' case.[167] Clemens of Alexandria writes, "We rebuke those who throw their lives away,"[168] and adds explicitly, "We say of them that, having chosen to depart from this life in this way, they do not die as martyrs ..."[169]

In this respect, the issue is similar to slavery. Paul, who enjoined slaves to work hard and to prove their faith as slaves, could also write, "Let every man abide in the same calling wherein he was called. Art thou called being a servant? care not for it: but if thou mayest be made free, use it rather" (1 Cor. 7:20-21).

The Bible portrays man as a slave of sin, entangled in his rebellion against God. When he accepts divine judgment and the sacrificial death of

---

especially. 7,2 (p. 191): "and in love is eager for death", as well as 2,1-4,3 + 6,1-3; and 'An die Trallianer' 1,1 (p. 179).

[164] See the excerpts of Cyprian's letter to Fortunatus in: Theofried Baumeister. Genese und Entfaltung der altkirchlichen Theologie des Martyriums. *op. cit.*, pp 152-161 (Nr. 57); more complete in: Edelhard L. Hummel. The Concept of Martyrdom According to Siant Cyprian of Carthage. The Catholic University of America Studies in Christian Antiquity 9. The Catholic University of America: Washington, 1946.

[165] On the rejection of deliberate martyrdom, see: Bernhard Kriegbaum. Kirche der Traditionen oder Kirche der Märtyrer? Die Vorgeschichte des Donatismus. Innsbrucker theologische Studien 16. Tyrolia-Verlag: Innsbruck, 1986. pp. 77-81 n. d. and Donald W. Riddle. "From Apokalypse to Martyrology": Anglican Theological Review 9 (1926/27): 260-280, here, p. 271.

[166] Albert Ehrhard. Die Kirche der Märtyrer. *op. cit.* p. 37. We also have a letter of 156 A. D. from the church in Smyrna to the church in Philomelium in Greater Phrygia about the same event, which Eusebius used, see Eusebius von Caesarea. Kirchengeschichte. See Albert Ehrhard. Die Kirche der Märtyrer. *op. cit.*, p. 37, zugleich ist ein Brief aus dem Jahr 156 n. Chr. der Gemeinde in Smyrna an die Gemeinde von Philomelium in Großphrygien über dasselbe Ereignis, daß Eusebius übernommen hat: Eusebius von Caesarea. Kirchengeschichte. *op. cit.*, pp. 206-215 (4. Book, Ch. 14-15). See below for further literature.

[167] Martyrium des Polykarp 1,2 = S. 2-5 in: Herbert Musurillo (Ed.). The Acts of Christian Martyrs. Clarendon Press: Oxford, 1972, 'Martyrium des Polykarp' pp. 2-21;. William Carl Weinreich. Spirit and Martyrdom. *op. cit.*, pp.166-167.

[168] Klemens von Alexandrien, Teppiche IV, 4, 17, 1-4, in: Theofried Baumeister. Genese und Entfaltung der altkirchlichen Theologie des Martyriums. *op. cit.*, p. 131 (Nr. 47).

[169] *Ibid.* (Teppiche IV, 4, 17, 1).

E. Behavior under Persecution

Christ on the Cross, he is called by God to a new life. Forgiveness of sin liberates him to a new life, but this new life with God does not automatically improve all conditions immediately. Even when still a slave, he can serve God fully (which has nothing to do with approving slavery – Paul combats slavery and recommends Christians to release their slaves in 1 Cor. 7:21 and in the Epistle to Philemon[170]), but faith in Christ corrects our values. It is not labor which makes life worthwhile, but the Creator and Savior, who gives us our work. The power of Christianity lies in the demand of justice from others on the basis of God's justice, but, independent of external conditions, continues to thank and glorify God even when justice is denied. Inner liberty precedes external freedom.

In the same way, the Christian is to be steadfast under persecution, but to rejoice all the more when he can avoid it, or when it comes to an end – which is the justification for our commitment to combat the persecution of our brothers and sisters. We can take action to avoid, end or point out persecution. Besides, in His first address on persecution, Jesus said, "Behold, I send you forth as sheep in the midst of wolves: be ye therefore wise as serpents, and harmless as doves" (Matt. 10:16). Christians may not deny their Lord, but they certainly may look for clever ways to avoid persecution!

31. It is Legitimate to Flee Persecution

Proposition: Both the Old Testament and the New make it clear that a believer may flee immanent persecution.[171]

Jesus left Judaea for Galilee when John the Baptist was arrested (Matt. 4:12), and later remained there when the Jews wanted to kill Him (John 7:1). He hid when the Jews tried to stone Him (John 8:59; 10:39). God had also commanded His parents to flee to Egypt in order to protect Him from Herod (Matt. 2:13-18). The Christians in the first church fled Jerusalem (Acts 8:1) and Paul escaped from Damascus (Acts 9:25; 2 Cor. 11:32-33) and from Antioch (Acts 14:5-7).[172] In Revelations 12:6, the church flees from the Devil into the wilderness. Jesus even instructs the disciples to flee, "But when they persecute you in this city, flee ye into another: for verily I say unto you, Ye shall not have gone over the cities of Israel, till

---

[170] Herbert M. Carson. The Epistle of Paul to the Colossians and Philemon. The Tyndale New Testament Commentary. Wm. B. Eerdmans: Grand Rapids (MI), 1979 (repr. from 1960). especially pp. 21-24.
[171] Werner Stoy. Mut für Morgen. *op. cit.*, pp. 40-42.
[172] Acts 20:3 may also indicate that Paul was avoiding a difficult situation.

the Son of man be come" (Matt. 10:23), which Cyprian, Bishop of Carthage later cites.

The Old Testament also describes many similar situations.[173] Obadia hid 100 prophets from Queen Jesebel in two caves (1 Kings 18:4+13). 7000 other believers were also hidden in 1 Kings 19:1-18; Rom. 11:3-4). Elijah also fled from the same queen to Mount Horeb (1 Kings 19:1-18) and the Prophet Uria tried to flee from King Joiakim (Jer. 26:20).

In a few exceptional situations, believers did go to meet certain death. Jesus and Paul both returned to Jerusalem to be arrested (Acts 10:19-25), and, according to the earliest church traditions, Peter, who had left Rome, returned to be executed, after he had been called back by a vision.[174] These are, however, 1. key persons in salvation history and 2. key situations in salvation history, 3. commanded directly by God (for example, Acts 20:22-23).

A particular issue in the Early Church was the liberty of bishops and elders to flee,[175] a question which led to much controversy.[176] Jesus' warning against the 'hireling' who abandoned his flock to the wolves (John 10:11-13)[177] was understood to forbid such flight, but Jesus' instructions to flee (see above) to permit it. Cyprian referred to Matthew 10:23 when he fled from Rome, leading his church from his hiding place, which brought him intense criticism from the Roman congregation.[178] The most prominent bishop who remained and was executed, was Polycarp, whose example long carried weight in the argument against flight,[179] whereas Cyprian and

---

[173] William Carl Weinreich. Spirit and Martyrdom. *op. cit.*, p. 1.
[174] Carsten Peter Thiede. Simon Peter. The Paternoster Press: Exeter (GB), 1986. p. 185-194.
[175] See: Bernhard Kötting. "Darf ein Bischof in der Verfolgung die Flucht ergreifen?". pp. 220-228 in: Ernst Dassmann (Ed.). Vivarium: Feschrift Theodor Klauser zum 90. Geburtstag. Jahrbuch für Antike und Christentum, Ergänzungsband 11. Aschendorff: Münster, 1984, for the best summary.
[176] *Ibid.* p. 221-222.
[177] *Ibid.*, p. 221.
[178] *Ibid.*, pp. 223-224 and Adolf von Harnack. Die Mission und Ausbreitung des Christentums in den ersten drei Jahrhunderten. VMA-Verlag: Wiesbaden, n. d.(repr. from 1924⁴). p. 215; See also Cyprian's letter to Fortunatus; excerpts in Theofried Baumeister. Genese und Entfaltung der altkirchlichen Theologie des Martyriums. *op. cit.*, pp. 152-161 (Nr. 57); more completely in: Edelhard L. Hummel. The Concept of Martyrdom According to Siant Cyprian of Carthage. *op. cit.*
[179] Alvyn Pettersen. "'To Flee or not to Flee': An Assessment of Athanasius's De Fuga Sua". pp. 29-42 in: W. J. Sheils (Ed.). Persecution and Toleration. Papers Read at the ... Ecclesiastical History Society. B. Blackwell: Oxford, 1984. p. 29.

Athanasius were the most prominent bishops who did flee.[180] The Church finally adopted the position that a bishop might not flee out of fear or cowardice, but could do so if it served the interest of his church, the classical 'conflict of duty',[181] as justified by Cyprian, Athansius and Augustine,[182] who taught that the decision could only be made according to the Spirit's leading in the concrete situation.[183]

32. Not All Suffering is for Christ's Sake

Proposition: Not all suffering is for Christ's sake: when Christians commit crimes, they must be punished and suffer just like all others.

Jesus' promise, "Blessed are ye, when men shall revile you, and persecute you, and shall say all manner of evil against you" (Matt. 5:11) is restricted by the words "falsely, for my sake". Paul reminds us that the State is to punish us as it does other offenders (Romans 13:4). And Peter admonishes us, "Having a good conscience; that, whereas they speak evil of you, as of evildoers, they may be ashamed that falsely accuse your good conversation in Christ. For it is better, if the will of God be so, that ye suffer for well doing, than for evil doing" (1 Pet. 3-16-17). "But let none of you suffer as a murderer, or as a thief, or as an evildoer, or as a busybody in other men's matters. Yet if any man suffer as a Christian, let him not be ashamed; but let him glorify God on this behalf" (1 Peter 4:15-16; see the reference to persecution in verses 12-14).

---

[180] *Ibid.*, and Bernhard Kötting. "Darf ein Bischof in der Verfolgung die Flucht ergreifen?". *op. cit.*, pp. 221-226. Ibid also mentions further examples.

[181] Ibid, p. 224 and Alvyn Pettersen. "'To Flee or not to Flee': An Assessment of Athanasius's De Fuga Sua". *op. cit.* Athanasius had political and theolgoical reasons for his flight from the Arians. (pp. 31-33) and gave biblical examples for his theological considerations. He did, however, consider flight to be sometimes wrong. On his rethinking of the issue, see his article, 'De Vita Antonii' and his Letter at the Feast', *Ibid.*, pp. 37-40.

[182] Bernhard Kötting. "Darf ein Bischof in der Verfolgung die Flucht ergreifen?". *op. cit.*, pp. 221+226-227.

[183] See Adolf von Harnack. Die Mission und Ausbreitung des Christentums in den ersten drei Jahrhunderten. *op. cit.*, pp. 214-216.; Michael Slusser. "Martyrium III/1.". *op. cit.*, pp. 209.

33. Assistance for the Weak

Proposition: The Early Church occupied itself intensely with the fate of those who had failed under persecution,[184] but modern Christianity has ignored this still relevant issue. Almost all of the divisive movements in the first four centuries[185] (the Novitians, the Melitians in Egypt and the Donatists in Africa) originated in groups who either refused to reinstate lapsed believers (Latin 'lapsi' or 'traditores' – between 303-305; Greek 'parapeptokes'), even after repentance, or who annulled all the official acts of lapsed priests or bishops. The Early Church itself – and the major denominations – rejected the Donatist doctrine[186] and accepted the

---

[184] Adolf von Harnack. Die Mission und Ausbreitung des Christentums in den ersten drei Jahrhunderten. *op. cit.* pp. 214-216.; Michael Slusser. "Martyrium III/1.". *op. cit.* p. 209.

[185] Albert Ehrhard. Die Kirche der Märtyrer. *op. cit.* pp. 122-267 und Ivo Lesbaupin. Blessed are the Persecuted: The Early Church Under Siege. Orbis Books: Maryknoll (NY), 1987 [Original Portugiesisch]; Spire (Hodder & Stoughton): Sevenoaks (GB), 1988. pp. 41-43, which includes local schisms, following Gerhard Besier. "Bekenntnis - Widerstand - Martyrium als historisch-theologische Kategorie". pp. 126-147 in: Gerhard Besier, Gerhard Ringshausen (Ed.). Bekenntnis, Widerstand, Martyrium: Von Barmen 1934 bis Plötzensee 1944. Vandenhoeck & Ruprecht: Göttingen, 1986. p. 130.

[186] There is no comprehensive collection of the writings for and against Donatism, but see: Hans von Soden; Hans von Campenhausen (Ed.). Urkunden zur Entstehungsgeschichte des Donatismus. Kleine Texte für Vorlesungen und Übungen 122. de Gruyter: Berlin, 1950². 56 pp. Most of the literature on the movement is from the 19th c. and is in Latin, there are few modern studies and collections. See: Bernhard Kriegbaum. Kirche der Traditionen oder Kirche der Märtyrer? Die Vorgeschichte des Donatismus. Innsbrucker theologische Studien 16. Tyrolia-Verlag: Innsbruck, 1986; Hendrik B. Weijland. Augustinus en de kerkelijke tucht. J. H. Kok: Kampen, 1965; William H. C. Frend. The Donatists Church. Clarendon Press: Oxford, 1971¹; *Ibid.* & Oxford University Press: New York, 1985³; Emin Tengström. Donatisten und Katholiken: Soziale, wirtschaftliche und politische Aspekte einer nordafrikanischen Kirchenspaltung. Studia Graeca et Latina Gothoburgensia XVIII. EBA: Göteburg, 1964; Daniel Voelter. Der Ursprung des Donatismus, nach den Quellen untersucht und dargestellt. Mohr: Freiburg/Tübingen, 1883 (very critical of Augustin and the church); Ferdinand Ribbeck. Donatus und Augustinus oder der erste entscheidende Kampf zwischen Separatismus und Kirche. Bädeker: Elberfeld, 1858; Wilhelm Thümmel. Zur Beurteilung des Donatismus. M. Niemeyer: Halle, 1893 (emphasizes the difference of language and race). Still worth reading is: Chester D. Hartranft. "Introductory Essay". S. I-XXXV in: Aurelius Augustinus. The writings against the Manichaeans and against the Donatists (Ed. von J. R. King und Chester D. Hartranft). A Select Library of the Nicene and Post-Nicene Fathers of the Christian Church (Ed. von Philipp Schaff). Serie 1,

E. Behavior under Persecution

opinion of Augustine Aurelius[187] and Bishop Optatus[188] and the teachings of Scripture, that Christians who had given in to persecution could be received into the congregation when they had repented.[189]

Let us be merciful[190] towards those too weak to withstand, as Cyprian[191] was, and recognize the wisdom of avoiding persecution, and consider possibilities such as flight[192] or silence.

Peter is perhaps the best known example of a 'lapsi', who became weak out of fear for his life (Matt. 26:69-75; Mark 14:66-72; Luke 22:56-62; John 18:15-18+25-27: See also the warnings in Matt. 26:31-35; Mark 14:27-31; Luke 22:31-34; John 13:36-38). Peter formally denied his Lord ("Then began he to curse and to swear, saying, I know not the man. And immediately the cock crew." (Matt. 26:74=Mark 14:71), but repented and

---

Vol. 4 Wm. B. Eerdmans: Grand Rapids (MI), 1979 (Nachdruck von 1887) [see also www.ccel/fathers2npnf/ und auf CDROM Christian Classics Ethereal Library 1998. CCEL (Wheaton College: Wheaton, IL, 1998].

[187] *Ibid.*, pp. 130-131. The classical edition of Augustine's writings against the Donatists is: Aurelius Augustinus. Scripta contra Donatista. Corpus scriptorum ecclesiasticorum Latinorum 51. Tempsky: Wien, 1908. For an English edition, see: Aurelius Augustinus. The writings against the Manichaeans and against the Donatists (ed. by J. R. King and Chester D. Hartranft). A Select Library of the Nicene and Post-Nicene Fathers of the Christian Church (ed. by Philipp Schaff). Serie 1, Vol. 4 Wm. B. Eerdmans: Grand Rapids (MI), 1979 (repr. from 1887) [see also www.ccel/fathers2npnf/ und auf CDROM Christian Classics Ethereal Library 1998. CCEL (Wheaton College: Wheaton, IL, 1998)].

[188] The Latin edition of his book against the Donatists has been reprinted frequently since 1549. The last edition is: Optatus. De schismate Donatistarum. Ed. von Karl Ziwsa. Corpus scriptorum ecclesiasticorum Latinorum 26. Tempsky: Vindobonae, 1893; Reprint: S. Optati Milevitani libri VII septem ... The same series:. Johnson: New York, 1972; In English: Milevitanus Optatus. Against the Donatists. Translated Texts for Historians 27. Liverpool University Press: Liverpool, 1997; Optatus. The Work of St. Optatus Bishop of Milevis against the Donatists. no publisher: London, 1917; no German edition available, as far as I know.

[189] Bernhard Kriegbaum. Kirche der Traditionen oder Kirche der Märtyrer? *op. cit.* pp. 18-43. In his controversial discussion of the historical study of the Donatist movement, Kriegbaum demonstrates that the origins of Donatism are more complex than the mere issue of martyrdom.

[190] See: Patrick Johnstone. "Preparing 3rd World Believers for Church Growth under Persecution". *op. cit.*, p. 7 and Gerhard and Barbara Fuhrmann. "Versteckte Christen". Missionsbote (Allianz-Mission) 5/1983: 9-10.

[191] See: Michael Slusser. "Martyrium III/1.". *op. cit.*, p. 209; or Edelhard L. Hummel. The Concept of Martyrdom According to Siant Cyprian of Cartharrge. *op. cit.* for a more thorough study.

[192] See the article on flight above.

was received back into fellowship with the people of God. (See the end of the accounts above). Peter also shows us the close connection between fear of suffering and overconfidence. Note also that Jesus had already prayed for His disciples, "I pray not that thou shouldest take them out of the world, but that thou shouldest keep them from the evil" (John 17:15), and for Peter (Luke 22:31-32) that God would enable him to maintain his faith under persecution and personal failure.

34. Praying for the Persecutor

Proposition: Following Old Testament tradition (for example, Job 31:29; 42:8-9), the New Testament exhorts us to pray for God's grace for persecutors.

Jesus admonished the disciples, "Love your enemies, bless them that curse you, do good to them that hate you, and pray for them which despitefully use you, and persecute you" (Matt. 5:44, see also verse 45-48); "but I say unto you which hear, Love your enemies, do good to them which hate you, Bless them that curse you, and pray for them which despitefully use you" (Luke 6:27-28). Paul expresses the same commandment in similar words, "being reviled, we bless; being persecuted, we suffer it" (1 Cor. 4:12).

The most impressive testimony of a dying martyr is Jesus' prayer that God will have mercy on his persecutors. He prayed, "Father, forgive them; for they know not what they do" (Luke 23:34). The first Christian martyr, Stephan, prayed, "And he kneeled down, and cried with a loud voice, Lord, lay not this sin to their charge" (Acts 7:60). Both requests were heard, for some of the persecutors were later converted (the Roman officer in Luke 23:47; Paul in Acts 9:1-18). The history of the Church[193] contains many descriptions of dying martyrs such as Polycarp,[194] who pray for those who are tormenting them.[195]

---

[193] See: Eusebius von Caesarea. Kirchengeschichte. *op. cit.*, p. 245 [5. Book, Ch. 4, V.5].

[194] See: Martyrium des Polykarp 14,1-3 + 15,1 = pp. 12-15 in: Herbert Musurillo (Ed.). The Acts of Christian Martyrs. Clarendon Press: Oxford, 1972, 'Martyrium des Polykarp' pp. 2-21, also in Theofried Baumeister. Genese und Entfaltung der altkirchlichen Theologie des Martyriums. *op. cit.*, pp. 78-81, und in Eusebius von Caesarea. Kirchengeschichte. *op. cit.*, p. 212 [4. Book, Ch. 15, verse 33-35]. On the martyrdom of Polycarp, see: Hans-Werner Surkau. Martyrien in jüdischer und frühchristlicher Zeit. *op. cit.*, pp. 126-134 and the source documents. Eusebius von Caesarea. Kirchengeschichte. *op. cit.*, pp. 206-215 (4. Book, Ch. 14-15); see also

E. Behavior under Persecution

The modern Church has its own examples. In 1913, the Indonesian evangelist, Petrus Octavianus,[196] described a missionary in the Toradya area in Southern Celebes. Five tribe members wanted to kill him, but permitted him to pray first. He prayed aloud that they would be saved. Three of the murderers were banned to Java, were converted in prison and returned to Toradya, where they founded a church which later (1971) became the fourth largest church in Indonesia with over 200,000 members. Let us also not forget the five missionaries shot to death by the Aucas. Several of the murderers later became pillars of the Aucan church.[197]

35. Persecutors Become Converts

Proposition: **Many who began as persecutors of Christians have later become believers themselves.**

We have already seen two examples. The best known is, of course, Paul, who frequently referred to his former persecution of the church. (1 Cor. 15:9; Gal. 1:13+23; Phil 3:6; 1 Tim 1:13. See also Acts 9:4-5; 22: 4+7-8; 16:11+14-15). He describes himself as having been a "blasphemer, and a persecutor, and injurious" (1 Tim. 1:13), and writing about the reaction of Christians who had heard of his conversion, "But they had heard only, That he which persecuted us in times past now preacheth the faith which once he destroyed. And they glorified God in me" (Gal. 1:23-24). *When we pray for persecuted believers, we must include the persecutors*, who will either be converted or hardened because of the martyr's testimony. They will not be untouched.

Polycarp's letters, in which he represents his own view of martyrdom: "Die beiden Polykarp-Briefe". pp. 227-265 in: Joseph A. Fischer (Ed.). Die Apostolischen Väter. Kösel: München, 1981[8].

[195] See: Eusebius, Kirchengeschichte, 5, 2, 5-7 (Letter to the churches in Vienna and Lyon), in *Ibid.*, pp. 90-93 and in Eusebius von Caesarea. Kirchengeschichte. *op. cit.*, p. 246.

[196] Petrus Oktavianus. "Die Narde ausschütten". pp. 120-128 in: Otto Riecker (Ed.). Ruf aus Indonesien, Hänssler: Neuhausen, 1973[3] [1971[1]]. p. 126.

[197] Gruppe Elisabeth Elliot. Die Mörder - meine Freunde. CLV: Bielefeld, 1999 (Mrs. Elliot is the widow of one of the martyred missionaries).

F. Missions and Martyrdom

36. The Fruit of Martyrdom

Proposition: The blood of the martyrs is the seed of the Church. This well-known quotation from the Church Father Tertullian[198] has been passed down to us in the writings of Augustine and the Reformers. It forewarns the Roman emperors that their opposition will only enlarge the Church:[199] "The more you mow us down, the more we increase: the blood of Christians is a seed." ("semen est sanguis Christianorum"; *Apologia* 50:12ff. 'A seed of the church is the blood of the martyrs' is actually the more correct translation.[200])

Jesus, when warning His disciples of future persecution (Luke 21:12-21), had prophesied, "And it shall turn to you for a testimony,"[201] (Luke 21:13).[202] In the Epistle to the Philippians, Paul shows clearly that his imprisonment and suffering do not hinder the Gospel but further it (Phil. 1:12-26). "But I would ye should understand, brethren, that the things which happened unto me have fallen out rather unto the furtherance of the gospel" (Philippians 1:12).

The Early Church often referred to Jesus' words about His own death in John 12:24: "Verily, verily, I say unto you, Except a corn of wheat fall into the ground and die, it abideth alone: but if it die, it bringeth forth much fruit." One writer, for example, says, "Don't you see, that the more are executed, the more are added? This is not the work of man, but the power of God; these are the signs of His presence."[203] Martin Luther expressed the same idea in the following words, "Under persecution, Christianity

---

[198] On Tertullian' theology of martyrdom, see: William Carl Weinreich. Spirit and Martyrdom. *op. cit.*, pp. 223-272.

[199] Adolf von Harnack. Die Mission und Ausbreitung des Christentums in den ersten drei Jahrhunderten. *op. cit.*, pp. 506-510.

[200] Hans von Campenhausen. "Das Martyrium in der Mission". *op. cit.*, pp. 79-80.

[201] This testimony does not necessarily mean that people will be converted, but can also indicate a explicit testimony against the persecutor, even proof of his opposition to God.

[202] F. Kattenbusch. "Der Märtyrertitel". Zeitschrift für neutestamentliche Wissenschaft 4 (1903): 111-127, hier p. 112.

[203] Letter to Diognet 7,8-9, repr. in: Theofried Baumeister. Genese und Entfaltung der altkirchlichen Theologie des Martyriums. *op. cit.*, p. 103 (Nr. 40).

F. Missions and Martyrdom 69

grows, but where peace and quiet abound, Christians became lazy and apathetic."[204]

And indeed, the first organized persecution of the first congregation in Jerusalem only led to the dispersal of Christians into the whole Roman Empire! The first Gentiles were converted in Antioch, not by the apostles but by 'normal' Christians who had fled Jerusalem (Acts 7:54-8:8).[205] The International Congress on World Evangelization Lausanne (1974) noted, "Persecution is a storm that is permitted to scatter the seed of the Word, dispurse the sower and reaper over many fields. It is God's way of extending his kingdom."[206] Persecution has been one of the greatest factors in the spread of the Gospel of our Lord Jesus Christ.[207]

The fruit of persecution shows itself in different ways. Sometimes, believers are strengthened (Phil 1:12), and sometimes, the Gospel can be preached to people who might not hear it otherwise (for example, Phil. 1:13 "the whole Praetorian guard"). The dispersal of Christians spreads the Gospel into new areas (See Acts 11:19-21 and 8:1). Sometimes persecution makes the sermons and the witness of the believers more effective. In the first three centuries, soldiers and officers who became Christians were often in danger, but the number of believers in the military grew dramatically (beginning in the New Testament!).[208]

China is a modern example. We can not compute the number of Christians in China accurately, since government and official-church sources intentionally falsify the numbers. There is no census, and we have no registers of the home churches. In his German language news letter, "China Insight", Tony Lambert of the Overseas Mission Fellowship (former China Inland Mission), considered an expert on the statistics of Chinese Christianity,[209] came to the conclusion that his own figures are too low. After

---

[204] Martin Luthers Sämtliche Schriften. *op. cit.*, Vol. XIII, pp. 1078-1079.
[205] See especially Billy Kim. "God at Work in Times of Persecution (Acts 7:54-8:8)". pp. 57-59 in J. D. Douglas (Ed.). Let the Earth Hear His Voice: International Congress on World Evangelization Lausanne, Switzerland. World Wide Publ.: Minneapolis (MN), 1975.
[206] *Ibid.*, p. 57.
[207] *Ibid.* p. 58; See also B. Dyck. "Verfolgung fördert Gemeindewachstum". Dein Reich komme (Licht im Osten) 2/1983: 5 on Ethiopia, as an example.
[208] Adolf von Harnack. Die Mission und Ausbreitung des Christentums in den ersten drei Jahrhunderten. *op. cit.*, p. 580.
[209] See also: Tony Lambert. The Resurrection of the Chinese Church: A Unique Study of the Miraculous Survival of the Church in China. Hodder & Stoughton: London, 1991.

studying new state sources in 1997, he believes that the 18.7 to 39 million he had assumed for the year before, should be increased to 33 million, of whom 20 to 30 million are Evangelicals.[210] This would mean that China has the second largest Evangelical population of the world, after the USA (49 million). Brasil (13 million), Nigeria (5 million), Kenya (4 million) and South Korea (almost 4 million) have fewer – reason enough for Evangelical Christians to take more interest in that silent giant, the Chinese Church,.[211] *Idea* projects the number of Christians even higher for 1999.[212] Whereas there were approximately one million Protestants and three million Catholics in China in 1949, there are about 13 million Protestants in registered churches, 40-60 million Protestants in home churches, 4 million Catholics in the official Catholic church and 8 million underground Catholics.

Johan Candelin rightly said concerning the present situation worldwide, that it is not always true, that persecution produces churchgrowth, but in many countries in the world persecution grows because the fastes growing churches in the world exist in countries without religious liberty. [213] This has to kept in mind also.

37. Fruit is not Automatic

Proposition: Persecution does not automatically lead to church growth or to a purer, stronger faith.

The experience of the German Church under the Third Reich and under Communism, for example, has led to neither a more intense reflection about persecution nor to revival or church growth. Even when martyrdom

---

[210] See: Global Chinese Ministries. June 1999. pp. 1-2, distributed by ÜMG, 35325 Mücke, for more detailed statistics on the individual provinces.
[211] See: Bruder David, Dan Wooding, Sara Bruce. Gottes Schmuggler in China. R. Brockhaus: Wuppertal, 1981.
[212] Idea Spekrtum 40/1999: 9.
[213] Johan Candelin. "Persecution of Christians Today". S. 16-24 in: Konrad-Adenauer-Stiftung (Hg.). Persecution of Christian Today: Christian Life in African, Asian, Near East and Latin American Countries. Documentation October 28, 1999 Conference Venue ... Berlin. Konrad-Adenauer-Stiftung: Berlin, 1999 = Johan Candelin. "Christenverfolgung heute". S. 17-26 in: Konrad-Adenauer-Stiftung (Hg.). Verfolgte Christen heute: Christen in den Ländern Afrikas, Asiens, des Nahen Ostens und Lateinamerikas. Dokumentation 28. Oktober 1999 Internationale Konferenz ... Berlin. Konrad-Adenauer-Stiftung: Berlin, 1999, shortened version: Johan Candelin. "Mundtot Gemachten Stimme geben: Christenverfolgung heute". Confessio Augustana 1/2000: 13-18

F. Missions and Martyrdom

is fruitful, however, its results are never automatic, but always due to God's mercy.

Jesus' parable of the sower (Matt. 13:3-8+20-22) identifies persecution and pressure as just as dangerous to faith as wealth and egotism. Which is more hazardous to faith: persecution or wealth? Western Christians tend to glorify persecution, and believers under persecution tend to glorify liberty and wealth. Besides those who accept the Word of God and those who reject it, Jesus' parable identifies two further groups of people, who are both open to the Word, but fall away: "Behold, a sower went forth to sow; And when he sowed, some seeds fell by the way side, and the fowls came and devoured them up: Some fell upon stony places, where they had not much earth: and forthwith they sprung up, because they had no deepness of earth: And when the sun was up, they were scorched; and because they had no root, they withered away. And some fell among thorns; and the thorns sprung up, and choked them: But other fell into good ground, and brought forth fruit, some an hundredfold, some sixtyfold, some thirtyfold" (Matthew 13:3-8). "But he that received the seed into stony places, the same is he that heareth the word, and anon with joy receiveth it; Yet hath he not root in himself, but dureth for a while: for when tribulation or persecution ariseth because of the word, by and by he is offended. He also that received seed among the thorns is he that heareth the word; and the care of this world, and the deceitfulness of riches, choke the word, and he becometh unfruitful" (Matthew 13:20-22). The faith of the one suffers under persecution and pressure, the faith of the other is suffocated by worldly concerns and the deceit of wealth. That applies to us, as if it had been spoken in 2000 not 2000 years ago! Jesus neither glorifies persecution with its fears nor wealth with its worries. Both are serious trials for our faith. In both situations, we need to keep God's word and bring forth fruit.

Let us not become envious of others, but learn from them. We who enjoy liberty must learn from those who suffer, that Christianity is no 'fine weather' religion, but that we can endure under the most dreadful consequences. Besides, we can also employ our wealth and our time to serve the suffering family of faith. On the other hand, Christians under persecution can learn from us that peace and wealth alone do not bring happiness or make it easier to live biblical truth. Our faith does not depend on conditions, but only on the faithfulness of God, who fills us with His Holy Spirit, Who gives us the power to serve Him and to become more like Christ.

38. Martyrdom Accompanies World Missions

Proposition: Martyrdom is a part of world missions, for "Missions lead to martyrdom, and martyrdom becomes missions."[214]

Hans Campenhausen comes to this conclusion in his study of the Early Church. Jesus sent out the Seventy[215] and the Twelve with the words, "Behold, I send you forth as sheep[216] in the midst of wolves: be ye therefore wise as serpents, and harmless as doves. (Matt. 10:16; Luke 10:3. See the whole address on persecution[217]; Matt. 10:16-42.) Karl Rahner uses a similar formulation, "Church and missions affirm each other."[218] The universal spread of Christ's Church has always been accompanied with the blood of the martyrs and world missions are 'missions beneath the cross'."[219] Even more obvious are the less grievous forms of persecution. "As long as it preaches the Gospel, the Church will always confront rejection, persecution and death."[220] No wonder that, after leading him to Christ and calling him to become an evangelist, Ananaias warned Paul that his ministry would have an immense outcome, but would also bring the apostles immense suffering: "But the Lord said unto him (Ananaias), Go thy way: for he is a chosen vessel unto me, to bear my name before the Gentiles, and kings, and the children of Israel: For I will shew him how great things he must suffer for my name's sake" (Acts 9:15-16). Missiology must, therefore, pay more attention to the issue of persecution than it has done in the past, taking as our role models missiologists such as Karl Hartenstein[221]

---

[214] Hans von Campenhausen. "Das Martyrium in der Mission". *op. cit.*, p. 71.
[215] See Theofried Baumesiter. "Märtyrer und Verfolgte im frühen Christentum" *op. cit.*, p. 172.
[216] Luke even refers to them as lambs.
[217] Peter Mayer. "Zeugnis und Leiden des Jüngers Jesu - nach Matth. 10". pp. 2-16 in: Urgemeinde und Endzeitgemeinde - Missionarische Existenz in Zeugnis und Leiden: Vier Referate der Jahrestagung des Arbeitskreises für evangelikale Missiologie (AfeM). Idea Dokumentation 3/1988.
[218] Karl Rahner. Zur Tehologie des Todes, *op. cit.*, p. 93.
[219] Bruno Her, cited in: Ingrid Kastelan. "Verfolgung ist letztendlich Verheißung". idea 45/1977 (7.11.). pp. I-II, here p. I (on the AEM conference,"Gemeinde in Bedrängnis" 2.-6. Nov., 1977 in Burbach-Holzhausen).
[220] I. Bria. *op. cit.*, 268.
[221] See: Christof Sauer. Mission und Martyrium: Studien zu Karl Hartenstein und zur Lausanner Bewegung. *op. cit.*; Christof Sauer. "Die Bedeutung von Leiden und Martyrium für die Mission nach Karl Hartenstein". pp. 96-109 in: Fritz H. Lamparter (Ed.). Karl Hartenstein: Leben in weltweitem Horizont: Beiträge zu seinem 100. Geburtstag. edition afem - missions scripts 9. Verlag für Kultur und Wissenschaft Schirrmacher: Bonn, 1995; Karl Rennstich. "Urgemeinde und Endzeitge-

F. Missions and Martyrdom   73

and Georg Vicdeom,[222] who considered the suffering of missionaries and of the emerging church an integral element of their theology of missions.

39. The Martyr as 'Witness'; the 'Testimony' of the Martyrs

Proposition: The relationship between the Greek word family 'witness' ('martys') and the death of Christians for their faith, did not originate in the Early Church, but in The Revelation of John the Apostle, who speaks of "the souls of them that were slain for the word of God, and for the testimony (Greek 'Martyria') which they held" (Rev. 6:9) and of Antipas, who was murdered in Pergamon a "faithful martyr" (Rev. 2:13). The martyr is a witness to the sufferings of Christ, "the faithful witness" (Greek, 'martys'), (Rev. 1:5; 3:14).[223] The two witnesses in Chapter 11 die for their faith, and Revelations 17 describes the Whore of Babylon "drunken with the blood of the saints, and with the blood of the martyrs of Jesus" (verse 6). The close association between this Greek word family and the martyrdom of believers in Revelations is so obvious, that some believe the later meaning 'martyr' to have been intended,[224] although others disagree.[225] Hermann Strathmann, writing on Revelations 2:13, demonstrates the dilemma by pointing out that Antipas did not become a witness by dy-

---

    meinde: Missionarische Existenz in Zeugnis und Leiden." pp. 17-27 in: Urgemeinde und Endzeitgemeinde - Missionarische Existenz in Zeugnis und Leiden: Vier Referate der Jahrestagung des Arbeitskreises für evangelikale Missiologie (AfeM). Idea Dokumentation 3/1988. pp. 20-25.

[222] See: Georg Vicedom. Das Geheimnis des Leidens der Kirche. Theologische Existenz heute NF 111. Chr. Kaiser: München, 1963; Johannes Triebel. "Leiden als Thema der Missionstheologie": Der Beitrag Georg Vicedoms zum Thema im Kontext gegenwärtiger Stimmen. Jahrbuch für Mission 20 (1988): 1-20.

[223] I. Bria. "Martyrium". *op. cit.,* . 266.

[224] For example, Hans von Campenhausen. Die Idee des Martyriums in der Alten Kirche. *op. cit.,* 1936[1]; 1964[2]. pp. 42-46; Otto Michel. Prophet und Märtyrer. *op. cit.,* pp. 43-49; Walter Bauer. Griechisch-deutsches Wörterbuch zu den Schriften des Neuen Testaments ... Walter de Gruyter: Berlin, 1971[5]. Col. 977; 1988[6]. Col. 1002; See also: F. W. Danker. "Martyr". p. 267 in: Geoffrey W. Bromiley. (Ed.). The International Standard Bible Encyclopedia. Vol. 3. Wm. B. Eerdmans: Grand Rapids (MI), 1986. According to: Theofried Baumeister. "Märtyrer und Verfolgte im frühen Christentum". *op. cit.,* p. 170, the 2nd century Church interpreted the relevant texts in Revelations in this way.

[225] For example:. Johannes Beutler. "martyreo", "martyria", "martys" *op. cit.,* pp. 966-967; Allison A. Trites. The New Testament Concept of Witness. Society for New Testament Studies - Monograph Series 31. Cambridge University Press: Cambridge, 1977. pp. 154-174.

ing, but was killed because he was a witness.[226] Paul uses similar terms in Acts 22:20, "when the blood of thy martyr Stephen was shed." Even Theofried Baumeister is willing to accept this texts as the earliest usage of the term in this sense.[227] Stephan was executed because of his testimony, but Acts 22:20 relates the idea of death and testimony very closely.

Other texts relate martyrdom and witness, as well. In Hebrews 11:4, God gives the blood of Abel the 'testimony of righteousness'. In Luke 21:12-15, Jesus announces that a declaration of a persecuted believer in court would be counted as 'testimony' and that the Holy Spirit would provide the necessary wisdom. Both John (Rev. 1:5; 3:14) and Paul (frequently, but see: 2 Tim. 6:13; Col. 1:20-21; Phil. 2:8), affirm that Jesus witnessed and testified by His death. Many see a close connection between Jesus' 'good testimony' before Pilate (1 Tim. 6:13) and the term 'martyr'.[228]

In 1908, F. Kattenbusch[229] initiated an intense discussion[230] of the meaning of the term 'martys'. Did the New Testament use the Greek term for 'a witness' to refer to martyrs, or was this usage a later development?[231] In 1936, Hans von Campenhausen vehemently defended the idea that the Early Church had derived its double definition ('martys' as both 'witness' and 'martyr') from the New Testament.[232] Later critics of this view, such as

---

[226] Hermann Strathmann. "martys, martyreo, martyria, martyrion". *op. cit.*, p. 499.
[227] Theofried Baumeister. Die Anfänge der Theologie des Martyriums. *op. cit.*, pp. 31-32. According to: Theofried Baumeister. "Märtyrer und Verfolgte im frühen Christentum". *op. cit.*, p. 170, the 2nd century Church interpreted the relevant texts in Revelations in this way.
[228] Walter Bauer, Kurt und Barbara Aland. Griechisch-deutsches Wörterbuch zu den Schriften des Neuen Testaments ... Walter de Gruyter: Berlin, 1988^6. Sp. 999 = Walter Bauer. Griechisch-deutsches Wörterbuch zu den Schriften des Neuen Testaments ... Walter de Gruyter: Berlin, 1971^5. Col. 974 and Hermann Strathmann. "martys, martyreo, martyria, martyrion". *op. cit.*, p. 507.
[229] F. Kattenbusch. "Der Märtyrertitel". *op. cit.*, pp. 111-127; See also the next article by E. Hocedez. "Le concept de martyr". Nouvelle Revue Théologique 55 (1928): 81-99 + 198-208.
[230] Norbert Brox. Zeuge und Märtyrer. *op. cit.*, pp. 114-131; gives a detailed discription.
[231] F. Kattenbusch. "Der Märtyrertitel". *op. cit.*, pp. 112+114 concurs on the basis of Luke 21:13 and Hebrews 12:1, but only cautiously.
[232] Hans von Campenhausen. Die Idee des Martyriums in der Alten Kirche. Vandenhoeck & Ruprecht: Göttingen, 1964^2 [1936^1]. particularly. pp. 21-29+42-46 (In his Introduction in the 1964^2 edition, Campenhausen retreats somewhat, without giving any reasons and without revising his book. See: Hans von Campenhausen. "Das Martyrium in der Mission". pp. 71-85 in: Heinzgünter Frohnes, Uwe W. Knorr (Ed.). Die Alte Kirche. Kirchengeschichte als Missionsgeschichte 1. Chr.

F. Missions and Martyrdom

Norbert Brox,[233] understand 'witness' to mean 'a preacher who testifies'. Brox sees no connection between the idea of 'witness' and 'martyr' in the Greek term.[234] Most other writers adopt his view, even though few apply it consistently.[235]

'Preacher' is only one possible meaning for 'witness'. The Hebrew and Greek terms for a witness both originated in the legal sphere.[236] The Old Testament 'witness' was therefore always understood to be a witness in a law court, so that a martyr can be God's witness before mankind or a witness[237] in the Judgment against persecutors,[238] without having to be a 'preacher'. Nehemia 9:26 definitely portrays the prophets as witnesses for the prosecution, eliminated by the guilty Jews: "... they ... slew thy prophets which testified against them to turn them to thee." Judaism later adopt-

---

Kaiser: München, 1974; See also Ernst Günther. Martys: Die Geschichte eines Wortes. Bertelsmann: Gütersloh, 1941.

[233] Against von Campenhausen: Norbert Brox. Zeuge und Märtyrer. *op. cit.*, pp. 115-117 + 92-105 (on the references in Rev.) and Allison A. Trites. The New Testament Concept of Witness. *op. cit.* Allison A. Trites. "martys and Martyrdom in the Apocalypse". Novum Testamentum 15 (1973): 72-80; Johannes Beutler. Martyria: Traditionsgeschichtliche Untersuchungen zum Zeugnisthema bei Johannes. Frankfurter theologische Studien 10. Knecht: Frankfurt, 1972 (an excellent summary of Brox Ibid, pp. 32-33); Johannes Beutler. "martyreo", "martyria", "martys" *op. cit.*

[234] Norbert Brox. Zeuge und Märtyrer. *op. cit.*, pp. 230-236.

[235] For example,. Johannes Beutler. "martyreo", "martyria", "martys". *op. cit.* and Werner Stoy. Mut für Morgen. *op. cit.*, pp. 67-68.

[236] Hermann Strathmann. "martys, martyreo, martyria, martyrion". *op. cit.* 479.

[237] According to Gerhard Besier. "Bekenntnis - Widerstand - Martyrium als historisch-theologische Kategorie". *op. cit.*, p. 128, the distinction sometimes made between 'martyria', used in the synoptic Gospels to indicate the witness calling to conversion, and 'martyrion' the testimony against persecutors. (Mk 1:4 particularly; 6:11; Mt 24:14), is not always correct. See: Walter Bauer. Griechisch-deutsches Wörterbuch zu den Schriften des Neuen Testaments ... Walter de Gruyter: Berlin, 1971⁵.Col. 975-976 = Walter Bauer, Kurt and Barbara Aland. Griechisch-deutsches Wörterbuch zu den Schriften des Neuen Testaments ... Walter de Gruyter: Berlin, 1988⁶. Col. 1000-1001. On 'martys' in legal usage in Mk 14:63 = Mt 26:65, see: Hermann Strathmann. "martys, martyreo, martyria, martyrion". *op. cit.* p. 493. Both terms, 'martyrion' und 'martyria', were later used to refer to martyrdom.

[238] Norbert Brox. Zeuge und Märtyrer. *op. cit.*, pp. 27-29 finds the meaning 'witness for the prosecution' in the Last Judgment only in Matthew and Mark, and in James 5:3 to refer to earthly goods. Ethelbert Stauffer. Theologie des Neuen Testamentes. Bertelsmann: Gütersloh: 1941¹. p. 316, however, shows that the Old Testament and later Judaism were also familiar with the idea of the divine messenger as a witness for the prosecution int God's proceedings against mankind.

ed the idea: "At the same time, the death of the saints is a portentous testimony against the persecutors, which points beyond itself towards the future."[239]

The acts of the Pharisees and the Sadducees testify against them, Jesus tells us, "Wherefore ye be witnesses unto yourselves, that ye are the children of them which killed the prophets" (Matthew 23:31).[240] Thus, Scripture teaches both a testimony of words and a testimony of deeds. Jesus describes His own words as a testimony (John 5:36; 10:25; 10:37-38).[241] The martyr testifies not only in giving testimony, but also by his martyrdom.[242] In Luke 21:13, Jesus announces, "And it shall turn to you for a testimony."[243] The persecutors will either be further hardened, or will be brought to repentance by the martyr's testimony. God sometimes calls human beings as witnesses in His war against mankind, even against His own people. Otto Michel believes this idea to be the origin of the martyr idea in both the Old Testament and the New.[244]

Allison A. Trites defines five phases in the development of the term 'martys'. 1. The witness in legal proceedings. 2. A witness in legal proceedings who is executed because of his testimony. 3. Death as part of the testimony. 4. 'Martys'='martyr', but including the concept of 'witness'. 5. 'Martys'='martyr', but excluding the concept of 'witness'[245].

Trites assumes that the other members of the word family 'martys' were used in the first and second levels of development,[246] but that 'martys' itself had reached the third level at the end of New Testament time already.[247] This would mean that the term 'martys' did not yet have the meaning 'martyr', but was already intensely associated with it.[248]

---

[239] Ethelbert Stauffer. "Märtyrertheologie und Täuferbewegung". *op. cit.*, p. 545 on Judaism before Jesus' time.
[240] Johannes Beutler. "martyreo", "martyria", "martys". *op. cit.*, p. 959.
[241] Ceslas Spicq. Theological Lexicon of the New Testament. Hendrickson: Peabody (MA). [Original: Fribourg/CH, 1978/1982]. 3 Vols, Vol 2, pp. 447-452 ("martys").
[242] So especially Hans von Campenhausen. Die Idee des Martyriums in der Alten Kirche. Vandenhoeck & Ruprecht: Göttingen, 1936¹; 1964². p. 55.
[243] So especially F. Kattenbusch. "Der Märtyrertitel". *op. cit.*, p. 112.
[244] Otto Michel. Prophet und Märtyrer. *op. cit.*, p. 20.
[245] Allison A. Trites. "martys and Martyrdom in the Apocalypse: A Semantic Study". Novum Testamentum 15 (1973): 72-80, here pp. 72-73.
[246] *Ibid.* p. 77.
[247] *Ibid.* p. 80.
[248] *Ibid.* p. 77.

F. Missions and Martyrdom

I would agree with Oda Hagemeyer,[249] who concludes that the New Testament does not use the term to mean 'a martyr', but that its meaning is so closely connected with the testimony of faith, that we can already discover the early stages in the development of the later usage. Herman Strathmann writes, "The second century sees further development of the early stages apparent in the New Testament, above all in the work of the Johannic circle."[250] According to Strathmann, the New Testament usage meaning 'witness' is no more and no less than an earlier stage[251] in the development of the later meaning 'martyr'.

Brox has demonstrated that both the New Testament and the Early Church continue to employ 'martys' in its usual meaning 'witness'.[252] "Like 'martys', under the pressure of the Church's experience, the term 'martyria' also developed an affinity to cases in which death proved the witness's earnestness and his testimony. The term took on a martyrological coloration."[253]

It is not clear which document first applied the term explicitly to martyrdom. Theofried Baumeister, believes that the *Shepherd of Hermas* still lacks an appropriate term.[254] Clemens of Rome may connect oral testimony and martyrdom closely,[255] but without using the term 'martys' in that sense. He designates Peter as 'witness' or 'martyr' and reports, that, "after testifying, he achieved the place in glory due him."[256] Of Paul, Clemens writes, "... and gave testimony before the puissant; so he departed from this

---

[249] Oda Hagemeyer. "Theologie des Martyriums". Benediktische Monatsschrift 60 (1984) 309-315. here pp. 310-311.

[250] Hermann Strathmann. "martys, martyreo, martyria, martyrion". *op. cit.*, p 511.

[251] *Ibid.*, p. 508; similarly F. W. Danker. "Martyr". p. 267 in: Geoffrey W. Bromiley. (Ed.). The International Standard Bible Encyclopedia.Vol. 3. Wm. B. Eerdmans: Grand Rapids (MI), 1986 and Otto Hiltbrunner. "Martys". p. 1059-1060 in: Konrat Ziegler, Walther Sontheimer (Ed.). Der Kleine Pauly: Lexikon der Antike. 5 Vols. Vol. 3. dtv: München, 1979 [reprint 1975] mentions "Vorstufen".

[252] Norbert Brox. Zeuge und Märtyrer. *op. cit.*, pp. 196-230; See his summary, pp. 231-236.

[253] Hermann Strathmann. "martys, martyreo, martyria, martyrion". *op. cit.*, p. 507.

[254] Theofried Baumeister. Die Anfänge der Theologie des Martyriums. *op. cit.*, p. 257.

[255] Theofried Baumeister. Genese und Entfaltung der altkirchlichen Theologie des Martyriums. *op. cit.*, p. 45, Note. 6 on Klemens of Rom, (1.) Klemensbrief 5,4+7.

[256] (1.) Klemensbrief 5,4, "Der Klemensbrief". pp. 1-107 in: Joseph A. Fischer (Ed.). Die Apostolischen Väter. Kösel: München, 1981⁸ p. 31.

world."²⁵⁷ Does Clemens use 'testimony' to mean the apostles' declaration or their deaths?²⁵⁸

Sometime between Ignatius and the 'Martyrdom of Polycarp', Baumeister sees the inception of the classical martyr terminology. He considers the 'Martyrdom of Polycarp' (2.1), written in about 160 A. D.²⁵⁹ to be the first evidence of the usage of the term 'testimony' for martyrdom.²⁶⁰ The earliest universally accepted example, the usage in this document seems to reflect general usage. In the letter of the Churches from Vienne and Lyon, 177 A. D., this usage seems to have become common; Christ is called the "faithful and true martyr."²⁶¹

Ever since the second century, for a Christian to be executed for his faith was considered the highest form of persecution.²⁶² The Church distinguished between the 'confessor' (Lat. 'confessor', Gr. 'homologetes'),²⁶³ who was condemned to imprisonment for his faith, but still lived, and might even be released, and the martyr. Cyprian distinguished between martyrs, confessors who were tortured, and the 'faithful' (Lat. stantes'), who had not yet had the opportunity to prove their faith before the authorities.²⁶⁴ This distinction, which began to fade soon after Cyprian,²⁶⁵ is not incorrect. Indeed, it is helpful, but it no longer tallies with the New Testament terminology, which could designate not only Christians executed for their faith, but also those under threat of death or other sorts of persecution.

---

[257] (1.) Klemensbrief 5,7, *Ibid.*, p. 33.
[258] I consider the second alternative probable, since Peter achieves glory directly after his testimony; See also: F. Kattenbusch. "Der Märtyrertitel". *op. cit.*, p. 112 and Walter Bauer, Kurt and Barbara Aland. Griechisch-deutsches Wörterbuch zu den Schriften des Neuen Testaments ... Walter de Gruyter: Berlin, 1988⁶. Col. 999.
[259] Theofried Baumeister. Genese und Entfaltung der altkirchlichen Theologie des Martyriums. *op. cit.*, p. 75.
[260] Walter Bauer, Kurt and Barbara Aland. Griechisch-deutsches Wörterbuch zu den Schriften des Neuen Testaments ... Walter de Gruyter: Berlin, 1988⁶. Col. 999.
[261] Brief der Gemeinden von Vienne und Lyon (177 A. D.), in Theofried Baumeister. Genese und Entfaltung der altkirchlichen Theologie des Martyriums. *op. cit.*, p. 91; see also Eusebius von Caesarea. Kirchengeschichte. *op. cit.*, pp. 233-245 [5. Book, Ch. 2-3].
[262] Explicitly in The Shephard of Hermas, Parabel IX, 29; see: Theofried Baumeister. "Märtyrer und Verfolgte im frühen Christentum". *op. cit.*, p.169.
[263] Explicit in Eusebius von Caesarea. Kirchengeschichte. *op. cit.*, p. 244 [5. Book., Ch. 4, V.3]; See also Theofried Baumeister. "Märtyrer und Verfolgte im frühen Christentum". *op. cit.*, p. 170.
[264] See Johannes Herzog. "Märtyrer". *op. cit.*, p 167.
[265] *Ibid.*

F. Missions and Martyrdom

40. The Victory and Defeat of the Prophets Belong Together

Proposition: In both testaments, victories and miracles stand alongside defeats, persecution and death.[266]

The writer of Hebrews describes both the miracles and triumphs of the Old Testament prophets (Heb. 11:32-25) and their defeats and martyrdom (Heb. 11:35-38). The lives of Jesus and His disciples are no different, for He send them as He has been sent (John 17:18; 20:21). They partake in His sending, the power of His resurrection, His victory, His weakness and His martyrdom ('theologia crucis'). God liberates Peter in a miraculous way, for example (Acts 12:7-11), but permits James to be executed in the same wave of persecution (Acts 12:2). Jesus predicts Peter's martyrdom, but excepts John from it (Jon 21:15-23).[267] Jeremiah tells of his own deliverance in connection with the execution of Uriah (Jer. 26:23-24). It is up to God's wise sovereignty to decide which road His children must go. "Your will be done!" (Matt. 26:42; Luke 22:42; See also Matt 26:39, "but as thou wilt" or Acts 21:4, "The will of the Lord be done.").

God often sent angels to warn, protect or liberate the persecuted (for example: Jesus in His infancy, Matt. 2:13-15; Peter and John, Acts 5:19-20; Peter, Acts 12:11; Daniel's three friends, Dan. 3). Sometimes, He aids His children by miraculous earthquakes or quiets dangerous animals (Heb. 11:33-35; Acts 16:26; Daniel 6).

John considered himself a "companion in tribulation, and in the kingdom and patience of Jesus Christ" (Rev. 1:9) and thus preaches both persecution and the possibility of liberation, and the final triumph of the Church.

41. A Christian's Weakness is his strength

Proposition: The Christian's strength lies in his weakness, just as Jesus Christ's weakness meant His victory over the world and over Satan. This principle applies to the universal Church, as well as to the individual believer.

Paul often applied this truth, which John applied in Revelations to the whole Church, to himself personally. The book of Second Corinthians re-

---

[266] See the title of Herbert Schlossberg's book, Called to Suffer, Called to Triumph: 18 True Stories by Persecuted Christians. Multnomah: Portland (OR), 1990.
[267] See Otto Michel. Prophet und Märtyrer. *op. cit.* p. 27.

fers to this fact particularly often:[268] "And he said unto me, My grace is sufficient for thee: for my strength is made perfect in weakness. Most gladly therefore will I rather glory in my infirmities, that the power of Christ may rest upon me. Therefore I take pleasure in infirmities, in reproaches, in necessities, in persecutions, in distresses for Christ's sake: for when I am weak, then am I strong." (2 Corinthians 12:9-10). If this scripture presents Paul's 'infirmities' as his true 'glory', then it is even more evident in 2 Corinthians 11:23-30, in which Paul 'boasts' at ‚ministers of Christ' who rest upon the laurels of their own special gifts and successes: "Are they ministers of Christ? (I speak as a fool) I am more; in labours more abundant, in stripes above measure, in prisons more frequent, in deaths oft. Of the Jews five times received I forty stripes save one. Thrice was I beaten with rods, once was I stoned, thrice I suffered shipwreck, a night and a day I have been in the deep" (2 Cor. 12:23-25). He closes with the words, "Who is weak, and I am not weak? who is offended, and I burn not? 30 If I must needs glory, I will glory of the things which concern mine infirmities," (2 Cor. 12:29-30). Earlier in the letter (2 Corinthians 6:4-5), he refers to the persecution – not to his triumphs – as the verification of his office: "But in all things approving ourselves as the ministers of God, in much patience, in afflictions, in necessities, in distresses, In stripes, in imprisonments, in tumults, in labours ..."

This paradox suggests a completely new evaluation of a believer's suffering and apparent defeat, whether due to personal weakness or the opposition of the world around them. Paul thus writes, "And in nothing terrified by your adversaries: which is to them an evident token of perdition, but to you (a token) of salvation" (Philippians 1:28. See the context in verses 27-30.)

42. The Manifestation of the Children of God

Proposition: The 'manifestation of the children of God' (Rom. 8:10; see also verses 18-25), an important subject in the New Testament will occur at the Last Judgment, when God will reveal those who belong to Him and those who do not.

Our justification, a long-established legal fact, will be revealed to all men an all powers, to the visible and to the invisible world. "Beloved, now are we the sons of God, and it doth not yet appear what we shall be: but we know that, when he shall appear, we shall be like him; for we shall see him

---

[268] Theofried Baumeister. Die Anfänge der Theologie des Martyriums. *op. cit.*, pp. 169-176.

as he is" (1 John 3:2). Paul writes, "If ye then be risen with Christ, seek those things which are above, where Christ sitteth on the right hand of God. Set your affection on things above, not on things on the earth. For ye are dead, and your life is hid with Christ in God. When Christ, who is our life, shall appear, then shall ye also appear with him in glory" (Colossians 3:1).

For many reasons, Christians sometimes find it difficult to acknowledge the truth of the revelation of our glory and authority. We cannot bear the idea that there will be a day of judgment and vengeance, when all that has been done to believers will be proven and punished. Particularly hard to swallow is the thought that the appeals for justice made to God in the 'Psalms of Vengeance' or in Revelations (Rev. 6:10 for example) will be satisfied. But how can Christians deny a truth so often so clearly preached in the Bible? Many Christians have problems, because:

1. First of all, they no longer take God's wrath seriously.

2. They do not take their own legal standing seriously, for they judge what they are on the evidence of what they see and experience.

3. They have lost or repressed their hope in the final, visible victory of God and His Word.

4. They are only interested in their own private salvation, not in the rest of the world. They are interested neither in missions, the economy, politics or history.

The personal and cultural pessimism so evident in many Evangelical circles does not only cause confusion about the manifestation of the Last Judgment. We also no longer see any practical significance in prophecies concerning the future of Creation (Romans 8:15-39, for example). If we pay any attention to such prophecies at all, we relegate them to Eternity.

43. The Outcry for Justice

Proposition: Both the Old and the New Testaments repeatedly clamor for the punishment of those who persecute the Church, and continually warn that a dreadful judgment awaits those who oppose God and His Church (particularly Psalms 5, 7, 10; 35, 59, 69, 83, 109, 137, 139, 140). [269]

---

[269] Cornelis van der Waal. Het Verbondsmatig Evangelie. Buitjen & Schipperheijn: Amsterdam, 1990. pp. 144-149 = Cornelis van der Waal. The Covenantal Gospel.

This longing is most clearly expressed in the prayer of the martyrs in Revelation 6:10: "How long, O Lord, holy and true, dost thou not judge and avenge our blood on them that dwell on the earth?" This is not merely an appeal for personal revenge, nor does it demand any sort of practical, earthly activity or justify any sort of human force in word or deed. Christians know that God has already promised, "Vengeance is mine; I will repay" (Romans 12:19). Assured of God's vengeance, we can afford to bless those who persecute us (Romans 12:14)! This appeal for justice points to the future certainty that God will reveal those who were right and those who were wrong: "So that we ourselves glory in you in the churches of God for your patience and faith in all your persecutions and tribulations that ye endure: Which is a manifest token of the righteous judgment of God, that ye may be counted worthy of the kingdom of God, for which ye also suffer" (2 Thessalonians 1:4-5: see also verses 3-12).

May I remind you at this point, that a martyr (martys) is a witness, because he will testify against[270] his tormentors before God?[271]

God can, of course, punish the persecutors of His Church here and now. John's Revelation, for example, describes the earthly downfall of the Whore of Babylon. We need not fill a book with examples of God's temporal judgment of persecutors.[272]

44. Why are the Godless So Prosperous?

Proposition: The Old Testament often asks why the godless are so prosperous (especially Psalm 73:1-28; Jer. 12:1-4; Psal. 1-15; Job 21:6-16; Eccl. 8:10-14). This impassioned question requires a thorough biblical answer.

Jeremiah 12:1-4 is an excellent example. The prophet firsts asks humbly, "Righteous art thou, O LORD, when I plead with thee: yet let me talk with thee of thy judgments: Wherefore doth the way of the wicked prosper? wherefore are all they happy that deal very treacherously?" He asks, even

---

Inheritance Publ.: Neerlandia (CAN), 1990. pp. 127-131 and Werner Stoy. Mut für Morgen. *op. cit.*, pp. 50-51.

[270] In James 5:3, rust, an image for the transience of earthly goods, will testify against unbelief.

[271] Norbert Brox. Zeuge und Märtyrer. *op. cit.*, pp. 27-29, finds this idea especially in Matthew and Mark.

[272] Such as; Samuel Clarke. A Looking-Glass for Persecutors. W. Miller: London, 1674.

though he knows the answer very well, and relates it in the following verses. Three aspects are important:

1. He knows that the prosperity of sinners comes not from chance, but from God: "Thou hast planted them, yea, they have taken root: they grow, yea, they bring forth fruit: thou art near in their mouth, and far from their reins" (Jeremiah 12:2). The fact that, "Every good gift and every perfect gift is from above, and cometh down from the Father of lights" (James 1:17) is true for unbelievers, for God "maketh his sun to rise on the evil and on the good, and sendeth rain on the just and on the unjust" (Matthew 5:45; see also Acts 14:17).

2. Jeremiah demands that the godless receive the punishment they deserve, "pull them out like sheep for the slaughter, and prepare them for the day of slaughter" (Jeremiah 12:3).

3. In spite of the present prosperity of some unbelievers, he acknowledges the principle of curse and blessing pronounced in Deuteronomy 27-32. "How long shall the land mourn, and the herbs of every field wither, for the wickedness of them that dwell therein? the beasts are consumed, and the birds; because they said, He shall not see our last end" (Jeremiah 12:4).

The Psalm of Asaph (Psalm 73) provides another example Asaph nearly stumbled (verse 2), because he envied the prosperity of the wicked (verse 3). How can they do so well, although they mock God and achieve their wealth by wickedness (verses 4-15)? The psalmist struggles to understand (verse 16. See also verses 20.21), "Until I went into the sanctuary of God; then understood I their end" (verse 17), judgment (verses 16-20+27) desolation and terror, (verse 19). Asaph has not understood everything, but he concludes in verses 23 and 24, "Nevertheless I am continually with thee: thou hast holden me by my right hand. Thou shalt guide me with thy counsel, and afterward receive me to glory." Apparent external well-being is only secondary, for he concludes, "There is none upon earth that I desire beside thee" (verse 25).

Ecclesiastes deals with the same problem and comes to the same conclusion: "Let us hear the conclusion of the whole matter: Fear God, and keep his commandments: for this is the whole duty of man. For God shall bring every work into judgment, with every secret thing, whether it be good, or whether it be evil" (Ecclesiastes 12:13-14).

G. Contra a Religion of Prosperity

45. Christianity is not a Religion of Prosperity (Romans 5:1-5)

Proposition: Christianity is not a religion of prosperity which ignores problems and knows nothing of difficulties.

What is the value of a belief that has no answers for the difficulties of life? How much are its promises worth, if they cannot be confirmed in every day life? Biblical Christianity does not try to satisfy us with empty promises postponed til the hereafter, as wonderful as the 'hope of the glory of God' is (Rom. 5:2). Scripture's promises of peace and hope apply to here and now, in spite of all of life's darkness. When we take the appr. 165,000 Christians into account who die for their faith every year, if Christianity had no answers for the agony and darkness of this world, we would have to conclude that it is a failure.

In the Book of Romans, after discussing mankind's universal need for salvation in Christ, Paul introduces the problems, sufferings and difficulties of life (Romans 5:1-5), for Christianity is not simply a religion for the well-off.[273] "Therefore being justified by faith, we have peace with God through our Lord Jesus Christ: By whom also we have access by faith into this grace wherein we stand, and rejoice in hope of the glory of God. And not only so, but we glory in tribulations also: knowing that tribulation worketh patience; And patience, experience; and experience, hope: And hope maketh not ashamed; because the love of God is shed abroad in our hearts by the Holy Ghost which is given unto us" (Romans 5:1-5).

Note that Paul does not merely glory in the glory of God, as if the believer could only just manage to survive this life, but also rejoices in tribulations (verse 3), and finds spiritual meaning in the problems and sufferings of those who have been justified. Problems are to provide us with experience (verse 4), which augments our general and quite valid hope in the glory of God with a personal hope, won through patience and preservation, a hope which does not disappoint in spite of tribulation. Peace with God does not raise the believer above all problems! On the contrary, a Christian takes them more seriously as he experiences them with the gifts of peace and righteousness. Adolf Schlatter, writing about this text, says,

---

[273] As Martin frequently remarked. See: Walther von Loewenich. Luthers theologia crucis. Luther-Verlag: Bielefeld, 1982⁶.

G. Contra a Religion of Prosperity

"Besides future hope, Paul presents the Church's present, pressure, oppression, trials from the world around us. We have peace with God, but conflict and war with the world ... an inadequate glory, if it consisted only of hope ..."[274]

The patience and preservation described by Paul are not human achievements! Paul could only rejoice in the tribulations which produced hope, "because the love of God is shed abroad in our hearts by the Holy Ghost which is given unto us"; "because the love of God is shed abroad in our hearts by the Holy Ghost which is given unto us" (Romans 5:5). Schlatter expressed this in the following words, "The believer masters the difficulties of his position, for God provides him with His love."[275]

46. The Theology of Wealth-and-Health-Gospel is Questionable

Proposition: Romans 5:1-5 refutes doctrines which promise 'good' Christians only wealth, health and happiness without any problems or suffering.

Certainly, God can give all these things to those who obey His commandments, which serve the well-being of Creation. Indeed, He desires to do so and will (Mt 6,25-34), but according to His plan. This Christian 'Wealth-and-Health-Gospel', however, robs the believer of several elemental applications and results of his faith: patience, hope and confirmation; three things which Jesus Christ our Lord also had to learn as our role model (Heb. 5:8). How much more must we learn them!

Alfred Yeo begins the Evangelical Alliance's anthology on persecution in Asia with the words, "It is a fallacy to equte Christianity with health, wealth, success and smooth sailing."[276]

47. Denial and Suffering

Proposition: Denial[277] and suffering are central issues in Christian ethics and important elements of true faith and practice.

---

[274] Adolf Schlatter. Gottes Gerechtigkeit: Ein Kommentar zum Römerbrief. Calwer Verlag: Stuttgart, 1975⁵. p. 178.
[275] *Ibid.*, p. 179.
[276] Alfred Yeo. "Introduction". pp. 1-2 in: Bong Rin Ro (Ed.). Christian Suffering in Asia. Evangelical Fellowship of Asia: Taichung (Taiwan), 1989. p. 1.

Persecution is frequently accompanied by the deprivation of basic human needs such as food, clothing and housing (for example, 1 Cor. 4:11; 2 Cor. 6:5; 11:23-27; Phil. 4:12).

"Peter, who refused to believe that the Christ must suffer, was the first in the Church to be 'offended from the very beginning by the suffering Christ'."[278] Peter is the epitome of the Christian who flees unpleasantness, first denying his Lord's suffering ("Be it far from thee, Lord: this shall not be unto thee!" Matt. 16:22; Mark 8:32), then attempting to prevent it by force (Joh. 18:10), finally overestimating himself and failing (see above). Note, that this very Peter, who resisted the idea of suffering so strongly, later under Emperor Nero became one of the most courageous witnesses and martyrs of Jesus Christ!

48. Fight the Good Fight of Faith

Proposition: "Jesus promised His followers conflict and persecution, not peace."[279] Paul thus admonishes his colleague Timothy, "Fight the good fight of faith" (1 Tim. 6:12) and exhorts a persecuted congregation, "stand fast in one spirit, with one mind striving together for the faith of the gospel; And in nothing terrified by your adversaries: which is to them an evident token of perdition, but to you of salvation, and that of God. For unto you it is given in the behalf of Christ, not only to believe on him, but also to suffer for his sake; Having the same conflict which ye saw in me, and now hear to be in me" (Phil. 1:27-30).

49. Martyrdom is the Protest Against the Assault on the Soul.

Proposition: The suffering and death of the martyrs is the strongest protest of faith against the world's claim to power over not only the body, but also over the soul and conscience of mankind. The fear of God, the One Who has the power to destroy both body and soul in Hell, conquers the fear of those who can only destroy the body (Matt. 10:28).[280]

---

[277] Werner Elert. Das christliche Ethos: Grundlinien der lutherischen Ethik. Furche-Verlag: Hamburg, 1961². pp. 338-345, Chapter "Der Verzicht".
[278] Christof Sauer. Mission und Martyrium. *op. cit.*, p. 59, citing Dietrich Bonhoeffer.
[279] *Ibid.*, p. 98.
[280] Friedrich Graber. Der Glaubensweg des Volkes Gottes: Eine Erklärung von Hebräer 11 als Beitrag zum Verständnis des Alten Testamentes. Zwingli Verlag: Zürich, 1943. p. 262.

G. Contra a Religion of Prosperity

When we suffer persecution, Jesus exhorts us to "In your patience possess ye your souls" (Luke 21:19).

50. The Spectacle before the Invisible World

Proposition: "The martyr is observed and awaited in the invisible world."[281]

Paul considered the apostles a "spectacle unto the world, and to angels, and to men" (1 Cor. 4:9). From the heavenly places, the souls of the martyrs observe the fate of the Church, particularly the persecuted Church (Rev. 6:9-11), a "cloud of witnesses" (Heb. 12:1, see the connection to martyrdom in the martyr prophecies of the Old Testament and Jesus' sufferings in Heb. 11:39-12:2).[282] Being aware of those heavenly observers and remembering their martyrdom reminds us to look to Jesus' example (Heb. 12:1-2)!

51. The Vision of the Heavenly Places

Proposition: Persecution is of little value in comparison with eternal glory and God's rewards in Heaven. The Lord will reward longsuffering, faithfulness, faith[283] and hope, the virtues of the witness. These rewards correspond to the Biblical principle that the humble will be exalted by God (1 Pet. 5:6; James 4:10), as Jesus experienced, who "humbled himself, and became obedient unto death, even the death of the cross. Wherefore God also hath highly exalted him" (Phil 2:8-9). Revelations 20:4-6 presents the glorification of the martyrs, who rule with Christ after their death, as the final answer to the sufferings of Christ's Church, which John describes in Revelations so strikingly.[284]

---

[281] Christof Sauer. Mission und Martyrium. *op. cit.*, p. 112.
[282] See F. Kattenbusch. "Der Märtyrertitel". *op. cit.*, p. 114.
[283] The Greek word, 'pistis' can mean both 'faith/trust' and 'faithfulness/reliability'. See the distinction in 1 Pet. 1:5-9. It is used to mean 'faith' in 2 Thess. 1:3-4; Rev. 2:19; 14:12; 2 Tim. 3:10; 4:6-7, mentioned together with 'endurance' ('hypomone'). In Rev. 13:10, means 'Faithfulness', mentioned together with 'endurance'. Hope and endurance are linked in 1 Thess. 1:3 and Romans 15:5. Endurance and patience (Col. 1:11), and faith and suffering are all gifts of God (Phil 1:29)!
[284] Ulrich Kellermann. "Das Danielbuch und die Märtyrertheologie der Auferstehung". p. 51-75 in: J. W. Van Henten (Ed.). Die Entstehung der jüdischen Martyrologie. Studia Post-Biblica 38. E. J. Brill: Leiden, 1989. p. 65. Kellermann sees exact parallels between Dan. 7 and Revl 20 (pp. 65-66); see also Theofried Baumeister. Die Anfänge der Theologie des Martyriums. *op. cit.*, p 227.

Paul was quite familiar with the realities of missionary work, which is still accompanied by persecution, hate, physical suffering and grievous need, but knew that the difficulties and problems of the present are of no consequence in comparison with eternal glory (Rom. 8:18).[285] Not that the apostle denied the reality or significance of such difficulties. On the contrary, he acknowledged their importance, but considered them insignificant in comparison to the glory promised us in eternity. The relationship between present difficulties and future rewards might be compared with finances; our own personal income may be high, and of great importance to us, but in comparison to the billions required in the budget of the Federal government, our bank account is simply not noteworthy. In 2 Timothy 4:6-8, Paul contrasts his own future martyrdom (verse 6 "the time of my departure") with the heavenly reward (verse 8 "a crown of righteousness").

The Bible repeatedly promises rich divine rewards to believers who suffer persecution (Matt. 19:27-29). John's letters to the churches address the promise to "him that overcometh"[286] (Rev. 2:7+11+26; 3:5+12+21; 21:7). Many biblical writers comfort persecuted believers with this view of the heavenly goal. The writer of Hebrews writes, "Let us go forth therefore unto him without the camp, bearing his reproach. For here have we no continuing city, but we seek one to come" (Heb. 13:13-14). Future glory in heaven and hope of reward are frequently contrasted with earthly suffering. The tenor of Hebrew 12 is, that we should imitate Jesus, who willingly bore persecution for the sake of the heavenly compensation before Him (see also 1 Peter 1:11). Peter also writes, "But rejoice, inasmuch as ye are partakers of Christ's sufferings; that, when his glory shall be revealed, ye may be glad also with exceeding joy" (1 Peter 4:13). Clemens of Alexandria once said that Peter, "... having testified (i.e. suffered martyrdom) attained the appropriate place in glory."[287]

---

[285] In the letter about the martyrs of Lyon and Vienne (Eusebius Kirchengeschichte p. 234 [5. Book, Ch. 1, V.6]) the martyrs are portrayed as examples of the worthlessness of this life in comparison with future glory. See also William Carl Weinreich. Spirit and Martyrdom. *op. cit.*, pp. 205-206.

[286] Brother Andrew. "How Should Christians Regard Persecution?". p. 13-21 in: Brother Andrew (Ed.). Destined to Suffer? African Christians Face the Future. Open Doors: Orange (CA), 1979.

[287] (1.) Klemensbrief 5,4, in "Der Klemensbrief". p. 1-107 in: Joseph A. Fischer (Ed.). Die Apostolischen Väter. Kösel: München, 1981[8] p. 31.

G. Contra a Religion of Prosperity

Comfort during Persecution and future glory and rewards

Mark 10:29-30 "But he shall receive an hundredfold now in this time, houses, and brethren, and sisters, and mothers, and children, and lands, with persecutions; and in the world to come eternal life."

Luke 21:12-19 "But before all these, they shall lay their hands on you, and persecute you, delivering you up to the synagogues, and into prisons, being brought before kings and rulers for my name's sake. And it shall turn to you for a testimony. Settle it therefore in your hearts, not to meditate before what ye shall answer: For I will give you a mouth and wisdom, which all your adversaries shall not be able to gainsay nor resist. And ye shall be betrayed both by parents, and brethren, and kinsfolks, and friends; and some of you shall they cause to be put to death. And ye shall be hated of all men for my name's sake. But there shall not an hair of your head perish. 19 In your patience possess ye your souls."

Matt. 5:10-12 "Blessed are they which are persecuted for righteousness' sake: for theirs is the kingdom of heaven. Blessed are ye, when men shall revile you, and persecute you, and shall say all manner of evil against you falsely, for my sake. Rejoice, and be exceeding glad: for great is your reward in heaven: for so persecuted they the prophets which were before you."

Rom 8:35-37 "Who shall separate us from the love of Christ? shall tribulation, or distress, or persecution, or famine, or nakedness, or peril, or sword? As it is written, For thy sake we are killed all the day long; we are accounted as sheep for the slaughter. Nay, in all these things we are more than conquerors through him that loved us."

1 Cor. 15:30-31 "And why stand we in jeopardy every hour? I protest by your rejoicing which I have in Christ Jesus our Lord, I die daily."

Heb. 10:32-34 "But call to remembrance the former days, in which, after ye were illuminated, ye endured a great fight of afflictions; Partly, whilst ye were made a gazingstock both by reproaches and afflictions; and partly, whilst ye became companions of them that were so used. For ye had compassion of me in my bonds, and took joyfully the spoiling of your goods, knowing in yourselves that ye have in heaven a better and an enduring substance."

1 Pet. 4:13 "But rejoice, inasmuch as ye are partakers of Christ's sufferings; that, when his glory shall be revealed, ye may be glad also with exceeding joy."

> *Rev. 2:10* "Fear none of those things which thou shalt suffer: behold, the devil shall cast some of you into prison, that ye may be tried; and ye shall have tribulation ten days: be thou faithful unto death, and I will give thee a crown of life.'"

52. Scripture Does Not Restrict Persecution to the 'Last Days'

Proposition: The subject of persecution must not be limited to the discussion of Last Things,[288] or fall into disrepute when expectations of Christ's return are disappointed.[289] Scripture promises 'tribulation' and persecution to Christians of all times. So many generations believed the persecution of their times to be the harbinger of Christ's return.[290] Besides, the 'Great Tribulation'[291] is not the sole stage of history, nor does Scripture teach the doctrine of a Pre-Tribulation Rapture so unequivocally that we

---

[288] Unfortunately, the best German Evangelical work on the subject; Werner Stoy. Mut für Morgen: Christen vor der Verfolgung. Brunnen Verlag: Gießen, 1980², so strongly determined by the idea of the Second Return, that, after twenty years, it is outdated due to the fact that Communist Russia no longer dominates most Evangelical models. The same problem applies to; Larry W. Poland. The Coming Persecution. Here's Life Publ.: San Bernardino (CA), 1990, although this latter was published ten years later!

[289] Franz Stuhlhofer. 'Das Ende naht!': Die Irrtümer der Endzeitspezialisten. Brunnen: Giessen, 1992; Dwight Wilson. Armageddon Now!: The Premillenarian Respone to Russia and Israel Since 1977. Institute for Christian Economics: Tyler (TX), 1991² (repr. from Baker Book House: Grand Rapids (MI), 1977¹), pp. 86-122; Gary DeMar. Last Days Madness: The Folly of Trying to Predict When Christ Will Return. Wolgemuth & Hyatt: Brentwood (TN), 1991; Gary North. Rapture Fever: Why Dispensationalism is Paralyzed. Institute for Christian Economics: Tyler (TX), 1993; Otto Friedrich. The End of the World: A History. New York, 1982 (the most comprehensive historical study of the subject). For further examples of unfulfilled Evangelical models and predicitons, see; Timothy P. Weber. Living in the Shadows of the Second Coming: American Premillennialism 1875-1982. pp. 177-203; Joel A. Carpenter. The Renewal of American Fundamentalism. Diss.: Baltimore (MD), 1984. pp. 93-133.

[290] The best Protestant example is Martin Luther. Ethelbert Stauffer. "Märtyrertheologie und Täuferbewegung". *op. cit.*, p. 574 demonstrates the phenomenon amoung the Anabaptists.

[291] For an alternative view, see David Chilton. Die große Trübsal. Reformatorischer Verlag Beese: Hamburg, 1996 with appendix Thomas Schirrmacher. "Gründe für die Frühdatierung der Offenbarung vor 70 n. Chr." pp. 129-154: Engl. Original without the appendix: David Chilton. The Great Tribulation. Dominion Press: Fort Worth, Texas, 1987.

can depend on escaping persecution,[292] as many Western churches teach.[293] Horst Englemann writes, "When we apply Jesus' prophetic addresses (Matthew 24) to ourselves and not to any other time of salvation history, we realize that this accords with God's plan. As the Last Days approach (They began with the Resurrection of Christ: Acts 2:16ff; 1 Cor. 10:11b), the more intense the opposition to Christ and the pressure on Christians will become."[294]

The theology of martyrdom is especially central to the interpretation of prophetic texts. The prophets' message takes precedence over questions of chronology or direct fulfillment. The promise that martyrs persecuted on earth will reign with Christ must not be lost, for example, in the debate about the Millennium.

Horst Englemann[295] summarizes the five most important reasons which prevent Western Christians from studying the subject of persecution:

1. Geographic: "Such things will never happen here."

2. Historical: "That sort of thing never happens any more."

3. Theological: "We won't experience the Tribulation, because we will be raptured before it begins."

4. Spiritual: "There are so many Christians here, that we will be spared this kind of suffering."

5. Pragmatic: "We have so much else to worry about."

H. The State and Persecution

53. There are Many Kinds of Persecution

Proposition: The New Testament mentions many kinds of persecution as precursors of martyrdom.[296]

---

[292] Paul A. Marshall. Their Blood Cries out. *op. cit.*, pp. 157-160 ("In Search of Armageddon") with examples.

[293] *Ibid.*, pp. 159-160. Many of those who write about the Second Return, such as Dave Hunt, use the issue as background for their own warnings, but do little to assist persecuted Christians.

[294] Horst Engelmann. Gemeindestruktur und Verfolgung. *op. cit.*, p. 10.

[295] *Ibid.*, p. 29, based on Patrick Johnstone. "Preparing 3rd World Believers for Church Growth under Persecution". *op. cit.*, pp. 3-7 and Dan Kyanda. "The Attitude of the Prepared Christian". pp. 97-104 in: Brother Andrew (Ed.). Destined to Suffer? African Christians Face the Future. Open Doors: Orange (CA), 1979.

The first is mockery (Heb. 11:36) and scorn (Mark 9:12), which Jesus also addresses in the Sermon on the Mount: "Blessed are ye, when men shall revile you, and persecute you, and shall say all manner of evil against you falsely, for my sake" (Matt. 5:11). The Jews forbid Jesus to speak, spread rumors about Him, had Him illegally arrested, tortured and savagely executed – according to God's plan to exalt Him (Acts 2:22-36; Phil 2:6-11).[297] He was wounded for us (Isaiah 53:4-10).

Paul mentions daily dangers and wild animals as methods of persecution in 1 Corinthians 15:30-32. In 2 Corinthians 6:4-5, he writes, "But in all things approving ourselves as the ministers of God, in much patience, in afflictions, in necessities, in distresses, In stripes, in imprisonments, in tumults, in labours, in watchings, in fastings."

The Epistle to the Hebrews mentions various types of persecution suffered by first century believers: "But call to remembrance the former days, in which, after ye were illuminated, ye endured a great fight of afflictions; Partly, whilst ye were made a gazingstock both by reproaches and afflictions; and partly, whilst ye became companions of them that were so used. For ye had compassion of me in my bonds, and took joyfully the spoiling of your goods, knowing in yourselves that ye have in heaven a better and an enduring substance" (Heb. 10:32-34, see also the following verses). The Old Testament prophets endured more varied torments: "... others were tortured, not accepting deliverance; that they might obtain a better resurrection: And others had trial of cruel mockings and scourgings, yea, moreover of bonds and imprisonment: They were stoned, they were sawn asunder, were tempted, were slain with the sword: they wandered about in sheepskins and goatskins; being destitute, afflicted, tormented; (Of whom the world was not worthy:) they wandered in deserts, and in mountains, and in dens and caves of the earth" (Heb. 11:35-38). The diversity of methods is unlimited. Some 'less-serious' types, such as mockery, ostracism, mobbing and the public disparagement of Christians and their symbols and teachings are universal. These forms, although related to martyrdom in nature, must be distinguished from more serious methods such as physical injury, torture and execution, especially when the State is involved.

---

[296] John S. Pobee. Persecution and Martyrdom in the Theology of Paul. *op. cit.*, pp. 1-12.
[297] Tokunboh Adeyemo. "Persecution: A Permanent Feature of the Church". pp. 23-36 in: Brother Andrew (Ed.). Destined to Suffer? *op. cit.*, p. 25.

H. The State and Persecution

54. Martyr Terminology must not be Abused Politically

Proposition: We must avoid abusing martyr terminology politically and defining it in pious terms, since persecution can be due to Christian ethical or political positions.

Recent Catholic theology, particularly Liberation Theology, sometimes applies martyr terminology to political martyrs and resistance fighters.[298] On the one hand, it is quite proper that martyrdom sometimes has a concrete political aspect, above all when criticism of rulers initiates the persecution. Some Old Testament prophets such as Daniel or John the Baptist had clear political messages; even Jesus referred distinctly to politics, although the subject matter is only subsidiary. Athanasius, Thomas Becket, Dietrich Bonhoeffer, Martin Luther King – to mention a few – are quite properly described as martyrs.

Because the Anti-Christian state ('the beast') persecuted the "saints: here are they that keep the commandments of God, and the faith of Jesus" (Rev. 14:12), it will fail. Those who obey the Dragon will suffer the same fate (Rev. 12:17). The State perverts its charge when it penalizes those who obey God's commandments and believe on Christ (Note the sequence! The state is supposed to punish wickedness. Christians, who keep God's Law, should never come into conflict with the government!)

We must not, however, extend the terminology to make political resistance the criterion, so that the so-called martyr need not be a Christian at all, and his political ideas need not agree with Scripture.[299]

55. Against the Perfection of Power

Proposition: Christ's Church suffers, because its preaching of a perfect kingdom and judgement calls the excellence of human power into question.[300]

---

[298] Concilium 19 (1983) 3, especially. Karl Rahner. "Dimensionen des Martyriums: Plädoyer für die Erweiterung eines klassischen Begriffes". Concilium 19 (1983) 3: 174-176; Leonardo Boff. "Martyrium". Concilium 19 (1983) 3: 176-181; Johannes Baptist Metz, Edward Schillebeeckx. "Martyrium heute". Concilium 19 (1983) 3: 167-168; James Cone. "Martin Luther King". Concilium 19 (1983) 3: 230-236; all articles available in English in Johannes Baptist Metz, Edward Schillebeeckx (Ed.). Martyrdom Today. T. & T. Clark: Edinburgh & Seabury Press: New York, 1983.

[299] Gerhard Besier. "Bekenntnis - Widerstand - Martyrium als historisch-theologische Kategorie". *op. cit.*, pp. 139-143, enumerates various advocates of this objectable opinion.

Naturally, the State considers this doubt a challenge to its authority. The more authoritarian and nationalistic the government is, the more it fears the idea of a faith in Christ which transcends this world and its cultural and national boundaries.[301] The Book of Daniel sheds light on the issue, particularly in Nebuchadnezzar's dream (Dan. 2) and in Daniel's own visions (Dan. 7-12). Much of the subject matter of these dreams concern the persecution of believers.[302] Most Evangelical interpreters agree that the image seen by the king in Chapter 2 and the Four Beasts in Chapter 7 symbolize the sequence of world empires of the Babylonians (gold, lion), the Medes and the Persians (silver, bear), the Greeks (copper, panther) and the Romans (iron, the dreadful beast). Each vision repeats the promise that God will replace the Roman Empire with His own eternal Kingdom – a promise fulfilled in the New Testament Church. The whole book is permeated by the idea that, in spite of the power of the kingdoms of Daniel's day, God's Kingdom will survive them in eternity.

Nebuchadnezzar's dream ends when a stone from heaven destroys the image (Dan. 2:34-25), grows to become a 'great mountain', "and filled the whole earth" (Dan. 2:35, see vs. 45). Daniel comments, "And in the days of these kings (i.e. the Roman emperors) shall the God of heaven set up a kingdom, which shall never be destroyed: and the kingdom shall not be left to other people, but it shall break in pieces and consume all these kingdoms, and it shall stand for ever" (Dan. 2:44). The Age of Human Empires was to end with the Romans. Under Roman rule, the Kingdom of God would begin and grow to fill the whole earth. No one people, neither the Jews nor any of the other nations of any empire, would determine this Kingdom (as many interpret the phrase "the kingdom shall not be left to other people"). Jesus indeed founded His Kingdom during the period of the Roman Empire with the disciples and the church. He had often prophesied in many parables that this kingdom would grow to fill the earth (for example Matt. 13:24-35).

In the same way, Daniel sees the world empires symbolized by the beasts (Dan. 7:9-14 describes the vision, 7:17-27 the interpretation). God determines the end of these empires from His heavenly throne (Dan. 7:9-12), and their end comes, when the Son of Man (Dan. 7:13, a later designation of Jesus) enters Heaven (Jesus' Ascension) and receives "dominion,

---

[300] Based on Georg Vicedom. *Das Geheimnis des Leidens der Kirche. op. cit.*, p. 24.
[301] Patrick Johnstone. "Preparing 3rd World Believers for Church Growth under Persecution". *op. cit.*, pp. 3-4 considers Nationalism the worst opponent of the Body of Christ.
[302] *Ibid.*, p. 10.

H. The State and Persecution

and glory, and a kingdom, that all people, nations, and languages, should serve him: his dominion is an everlasting dominion, which shall not pass away, and his kingdom that which shall not be destroyed" (Dan 7:14) from God. "And the kingdom and dominion, and the greatness of the kingdom under the whole heaven, shall be given to the people of the saints of the most High, whose kingdom is an everlasting kingdom, and all dominions shall serve and obey him" (Dan. 7:27).

The prophet Daniel announces that God will replace Gentile kingdoms, as well as the Jewish Kingdom of God, with a Kingdom founded by the Messiah, a government which will not belong to any one nation, any one human ruler or any one religious group. Speaking of the Roman empire, the iron kingdom in Nebuchadnezzar's dream, Daniel writes, "And in the days of these kings shall the God of heaven set up a kingdom, which shall never be destroyed: and the kingdom shall not be left to other people, but it shall break in pieces and consume all these kingdoms, and it shall stand for ever," (Dan. 2:44). In another vision, the Messiah receives at this time "dominion, and glory, and a kingdom, that all people, nations, and languages, should serve him: his dominion is an everlasting dominion, which shall not pass away, and his kingdom that which shall not be destroyed" (Dan. 7:14). The statement that this eternal 'Kingdom' to be served and obeyed by all dominions, is to be "shall be given to the people of the saints of the most High" (Dan. 7:27) probably refers not the Jews but to the Church (as in Eph. 2:6; Luke 12:32; See also Eph. 1:20-21). The New Testament Church is thus not determined by any one nation; belonging to it transcends and overcomes all national borders. The fact that the People of God no longer corresponds to any nation-state, but belongs to all peoples, is a colossal provocation to human kingdoms and states.

56. Loyal Citizens

Proposition: Christians are loyal citizens, who seek the welfare of their state, country and people, but whenever the State tries to force them to dishonor God, they must obey God rather than man.[303]

---

[303] See; Edwin L. Frizen, Wade T. Coggins (Ed.). Christ and Caesar in Christian Missions. William Carey Library: Pasadena (CA), 1979, especially. Earle E. Cairns. "Under Three Flags". pp. 3-45; David H, Adeney. "The Preparation of Missionaries to Cope with Political Change". pp. 49-53; T. Grady Mangham. "Aftermath to Persecution". pp. 61-73; Abram J. Wiebe. "Special Problems with Islamic Governments": pp. 95-102.

The Church Father Tatian expressed this idea in the following words: "The Emperor commands me to pay taxes: I am prepared to pay. The Lord commands me to serve and to obey: I acknowledge that service. I must honor man in human fashion, but only God is to be feared ... Only when I am commanded to deny Him, will I disobey; then I would rather die ..."[304] Not surprisingly, the two most frequent statements in the records of cross-examinations during the Early Church period are, that the accused is a Christian, and that he emphasizes his loyalty to the State and its laws.[305] The Epistle to Diogenetes, written during this period, notes, "They love all – but are persecuted by all. We know nothing about them – and still condemn them ..."[306] and "Although they do good, they are punished as evildoers."[307]

God's plan for us is "peace, and not of evil" (Jer. 29:11), but these plans are closely related to the commandment, "And seek the peace of the city" (Jer. 29:7). This challenge concerns a heathen government, for it envisions Israel's exile in Babylon.

A Christian's behavior towards the State has two sides, for "We ought to obey God rather than men" (Acts 5:29; 4:19). On the one hand, we can refer to the Law of God in order to refute the State's claim to omnipotence. On the other, we obey our government, even when it overextends its mandate. We resist only when the authorities try to force us to disobey God's Law, or when we must defend the lives and rights of others. Because God commands it, a believer must pay taxes, however exorbitant, but we can still label the exaggerated tax rate tyranny. In the same way, we may protest against the increasing statistical registration made by our government (Such registrations have frequently been employed against Christians in times of persecution!), but still answer the questions made during a census.

It is, of course, difficult to conjecture in advance, to what extent we can cooperate with the government during periods of persecution, and when we must begin to resist. The deplorable conflicts between the registered and unregistered churches in the Soviet Union or in China stem from this problem. As Jesus said in His first address on persecution, "be ye therefore

---

[304] Tatian, Rede an die Griechen 4,1, in: Theofried Baumeister. Genese und Entfaltung der altkirchlichen Theologie des Martyriums. *op. cit.*, pp. 85+87 (Nr. 34).
[305] Gerhard Besier. "Bekenntnis - Widerstand - Martyrium als historisch-theologische Kategorie". *op. cit.*, pp. 129-130.
[306] Schrift an Diognet 5,11, in. Theofried Baumeister. Genese und Entfaltung der altkirchlichen Theologie des Martyriums. *op. cit.*, pp. 99 (Nr. 39).
[307] Schrift an Diognet 5,16, in. Theofried Baumeister. Genese und Entfaltung der altkirchlichen Theologie des Martyriums. *op. cit.*, pp. 101 (Nr. 39).

H. The State and Persecution

wise as serpents, and harmless as doves" (Matt. 10:16). Since this statement also applies to our relationship to the State, the individual must decide for himself, how long he can cooperate and when he must resist.[308]

Christians who still enjoy religious liberties must reconsider the issue in each individual case, whether our efforts for persecuted Christians really help or not. Many believers have been released from prison due to such endeavors, but sometimes interference from outside can cause damage. There is no patent solution; we must take the time to collect detailed information from local sources, study the situation in detail and think carefully before beginning to act. This is no new problem; the Church Fathers and the Reformers had to deal with it, too. Calvin once wrote to several suffering churches that he had not written earlier for fear of worsening their situation.[309]

57. Praying for a Peaceful Life

Proposition: Prayer is an essential tool: "I exhort therefore, that, first of all, supplications, prayers, intercessions, and giving of thanks, be made for all men; For kings, and for all that are in authority; that we may lead a quiet and peaceable life in all godliness and honesty. For this is good and acceptable in the sight of God our Saviour" (1 Tim. 2:1-3). Prayer is no pious excuse to avoid responsibility, so that we can lead quietist, pious lives! On the contrary, in prayer, the church interferes actively in politics, because we want to serve God in true peace.

1 Timothy 2:1-5 suggests that Paul is speaking specifically of prayer during worship. Prayer for authorities and for peace has thus always had a place in liturgy. Naturally, such prayer should not lead to a glorification of our leaders, but should oppose the injustice and discord of society, which particularly includes persecution of Christians and hindrances to the practice of our faith. The New Testament church in Jerusalem, for example, prayed that Peter be freed from prison: "And when they heard that, they lifted up their voice to God with one accord, and said, Lord, thou art God, which hast made heaven, and earth, and the sea, and all that in them is: Who by the mouth of thy servant David hast said, Why did the heathen rage, and the people imagine vain things? The kings of the earth stood up, and the rulers were gathered together against the Lord, and against his Christ (Psalm 21-2). For of a truth against thy holy child Jesus, whom thou

---

[308] Werner Stoy. Mut for Morgen, *op. cit.*, p.58.
[309] Calvin's Letter of the 10. June, 1552, in: Otto Michaelis. Protestantisches Märtyrerbuch. *op. cit.*, p. 218.

hast anointed, both Herod, and Pontius Pilate, with the Gentiles, and the people of Israel, were gathered together, For to do whatsoever thy hand and thy counsel determined before to be done. And now, Lord, behold their threatenings: and grant unto thy servants, that with all boldness they may speak thy word, By stretching forth thine hand to heal; and that signs and wonders may be done by the name of thy holy child Jesus. And when they had prayed, the place was shaken where they were assembled together; and they were all filled with the Holy Ghost, and they spake the word of God with boldness"(Acts 4:24-31). The church must not rely either on the government nor on resistance, but on the One Who rules all rulers.

58. Resisting the State

Proposition: We need a new evaluation of those who break State laws for the sake of the Gospel.[310]

Peter and the apostles preached the Gospel in spite of the State's prohibition (Acts 4:19-20; 5:29) and were frequently arrested and punished as a result (Acts 12:1-2; 12;3). In the face of Roman opposition, Christians referred to Jesus as Lord (Gr. 'kyrios') and king (in opposition to an imperial edict. Acts 17:6-7; 4:12). Israelite priests also opposed the kings who usurped clerical authority: "And they withstood Uzziah the king"(2 Chr. 26:18). The Egyptian midwives disobeyed Pharaoh's command to destroy the Israelite babies, and even lied in order to protect the children (Ex. 1:15-20). Moses' mother Jochebed saved her child illegally by a ruse, and lied to Pharaoh's daughter (Ex. 2:3-9). Rahab saved the Israelite spies by a ruse, when she resisted the king's command (Josh. 2). Rather than condemning their dishonesty, the New Testament presents them as role models of faith! (Heb. 11:31; James 2:25). Daniel and his friends often refuse to obey the commands of the rulers (Dan. 3:12+17, 6:13-14). Note that these example do not concern only idolatry or recantation of the Gospel, but any

---

[310] Bruder Andrew. "Wir brauchen eine neue Sicht der leidenden Kirche". Geöffnete Türen. Rundbrief Geöffnete Türen (Frutigen, Schweiz). Febr 1980. pp. 1-3, here p. 1-2 and W. Elwyn Davies. "When is it Legitimate to Disobey Government Edicts?". pp. 87-94 in: Edwin L. Frizen, Wade T. Coggins (Ed.). Christ and Caesar in Christian Missions. William Carey Library: Pasadena (CA), 1979. For a more detailed discussion, see: Brother Andrew. The Ethics of Smuggling. Coverdale House Publ.: London, 1974; for criticism of thise view, see: Greg L. Bahnsen. "Brother Andrew, The Ethics of Smuggling ...". The Journal of Christian Reconstruction 2 (1975/1976) 2 (Winter): Symposium on Biblical Law. pp. 164-169.

H. The State and Persecution

infringement of God's Law (murder, etc.). Such resistance assumes, however, that the State has required us to transgress against God's Law.

Particularly when two rules contradict each other, we notice that the values protected by the Law have differing priorities (Roman Catholic theology speaks of 'conflict of duty'). The clearest example is Peter's reply to the Jewish authorities who forbid the apostles to preach the Gospel: "But Peter and John answered and said unto them, Whether it be right in the sight of God to hearken unto you more than unto God, judge ye."(Acts 4:19). The divine commandment to preach the Gospel contradicted the divine law to obey the authorities. Daniel's friends stood in the same dilemma, but refused when Nebukadnezzar commanded them to worship his statue (Dan. 3). In the same way, Daniel refused to submit to Darius' command by altering his customary prayers, even though disobedience brought him into the lions' den. The ban on idolatry weighs more heavily than our duty to the State.

The Bible describes many ethical conflicts. In Mark 2:23-28 (= Matt. 12:1-7; Luke 6:1-5), Jesus justifies his disciples' plucking of grain on the Sabbath by referring to David, who was permitted to eat the Showbread, because he was starving (1 Sam. 21:4-7). The commandments to protect life and to circumcise were more important than the law of the Sabbath. In Matthew 12:5, Jesus asks, "Or have ye not read in the law, how that on the Sabbath days the priests in the temple profane the Sabbath, and are blameless?" He enumerates several biblical laws more important than the Sabbath law (the ministry of the priests, saving life, watering livestock, etc.). Jesus notes clearly that the priests desecrate the Sabbath, but remain "guiltless" in doing so (Matt. 12:5).

Reformed theology[311] has generally assumed that, when we are required to make a decision concerning God's commandments, there is always a right decision; to obey the higher law, which forms an exception to the lower,[312] which seems appropriate, since Biblical commandments infer that the individual can do right and good in every situation, and since Scripture gives us several examples of such ethical conflicts (see below). I know of

---

[311] E. g. John M. Frame. The Doctrine of the Knowledge of God: A Theology of Lordship. Presbyterian & Reformed: Phillipsburg (NJ), 1987. p. 137-139 "Hierarchies of Norms".

[312] Some non-Reformed theologians share this view, for example; Norman L. Geisler. "Graded Absolutism". pp. 131-137 in: David K. Clark, Robert V. Rakestraw. Readings in Christian Ethics. Vol. 1: Theory and Method. Baker Books: Grand Rapids, 1994; Norman L. Geisler. Christian Ethics. Baker: Grand Rapids, 1989. pp. 116-122 n. d.

no case in the Bible in which a person had no choice but to sin, and could only decide between a lesser offence and a more serious one. If a person became guilty by lying to save lives, the Bible would not later have portrayed this person as a role model for faith!

Lutheran theology, which deviates from Luther's own position, assumes that that a person is always culpable when he breaks the Law of God, although the higher commandment should be the criterion for such a decision. Walter Künneth, for example, considers the murder of a tyrant acceptable in certain extreme situations, but believes that the murderer still needs forgiveness for the sin.[313] Hans-Joseph Wilting has emphasized that the Lutheran position stems from the idea that the Christian, as a human being, is still a sinner, and thus never able to act sinlessly.[314] Luther himself, in opposition to the Catholic theologians of his day, considered a necessary lie not to be a sin.[315]

The idea that man must wait for a specific revelation from God or necessarily sin in an ethical collision, is not substantiated by Scripture, but developed out of theological systems which permit no other conclusion contradicting themselves. The Bible gives us no evidence that a person can be in a situation in which he absolutely cannot do God's will, but must necessarily commit a sin. I know of no attempt to justify this idea by referring to concrete Biblical examples. Was it really a sin, even a lesser offence, for Peter to refuse to obey the authorities who forbid him to obey God by preaching the Gospel? Did he sin by deeming the Great Commandment more important than obedience to the authorities?

Such ethical collisions are much more common than we think; they are part of everyday life. Every human being evaluates conflicting values every day. The very existence of the four covenant institutions (the family, the

---

[313] Walter Künneth. Der Christ als Staatsbürger. TVG. R. Brockhaus: Wuppertal, 1984. p. 96. The most detailed exposition on this view can be found in; Helmut Thielicke. Theologische Ethik. Vol. 2: Entfaltung, Part 1: Mensch und Welt. J. C. B. Mohr: Tübingen, 1959². pp. 56-327.

[314] See; Martin Honecker. Einführung in die Theologische Ethik. Walter de Gruyter: Berlin, 1990. p. 238 und Hans-Josef Wilting. Der Kompromiß als theologisches und als ethisches Problem. Patmos: Düsseldorf: 1975. pp. 11-46 on Helmut Thielicke und pp. 47-64 on Wolfgang Trillhaas. Since Wilting discusses only recent Lutheran theologians, other ideas on ethical conflicts are not considered.

[315] Axel Denecke. Wahrhaftigkeit: Eine evangelische Kasuistik. Vandenhoeck & Ruprecht, Göttingen, 1971. pp. 251-253 and William Walker Rockwell. Die Doppelehe des Landgrafen Philipp von Hessen. N. G. Elwert'sche Verlagsbuchhandlung: Marburg, 1904. pp. 178-180.

H. The State and Persecution

State, the Church, the Economy) leads to the necessity. From the moment I get up in the morning, I must decide how to fulfil my duties as husband, father, pastor, employer and citizen, and thus must continually assess the requirements of each role. I can seldom accomplish all duties at once, but all are still God's charge to me. Under normal conditions, we have enough time to satisfy the demands of our various responsibilities, and the consequences of our decisions have little weight. Not until dramatic situations arise, such as a threat to life, do we become painfully aware of this process.

Both work and rest are divine commandments. God gave us a pattern of six days for labor and one for reset, but it is up to me to decide when I work for pay and when I work for nothing, when I rest and when I sleep, and how much time I spend resting and working. Such decisions are not always invisible or easy. Every time that a customer deliberates which commodity he will buy, and considers how much money he needs for other financial responsibilities, he compares his options according to his value system, and automatically comes into a conflict of duty. The well-off have fewer such conflicts than those who lack sufficient wealth and who must decides which important needs he must ignore. The decision to purchase food for on's children instead of for himself is simply the resolution of a collision of values.

59. The Persecution of Christians Can Develop into Genocide

Proposition: The Persecution of Christians Can Develop into Genocide

The massacre of the Armenians[316] and the Assyrians[317] in Turkey is one example. In more recent times, the Islamic government of Sudan[318] has been threatening tribes who are partly Christian and partly animistic. The

---

[316] Wolfgang Gust. Der Völkermord an den Armeniern: Die Tragödie des ältesten Christenvolkes der Welt. Carl Hanser Verlag: München, 1993; see also the collection of documents by: Tessa Hofmann, Gerayer Koutcharian (Ed.). Völkermord, Vertreibung, Exil, Menschenrechtsarbeit für die Armenier 1979-1987. Gesellschaft für bedrohte Völker: Göttingen, 1987 and my review in Querschnitte 2 (1989) 4 (Oct-Dec): 8; and Caroline Cox, John Eibner. Ethnische Säuberung und Krieg in Nagorni Karabach. Christian Solidarity International: Binz (CH), 1993^1; 1995^2. pp. 20-31.

[317] Gabriele Yonan. Ein vergessener Holocaust: Die Vernichtung der christlichen Assyrer in der Türkei. Pogrom Taschenbücher 1018. Gesellschaft für bedrohte Völker: Göttingen, 1989.

[318] See; Cal R. Bombay. Let my People Go! The true Story of Present-Day Persecution and Slavery. Multnomah Publ.: sisters (OR), 1998.

annihilation of the Christian Armenians by the Moslem Turks and Kurds at the beginning of the Twentieth Century was one of the most massive massacres of modern history until the Third Reich tried to destroy the Jewish people. Turkey had begun slaughtering the Armenians in the Nineteenth Century, but the major wave of killing, which also included other Christian groups, took place prior to the First World War. Some two million Armenians were massacred by the Turks between 1877 and 1939. Denied by the Turkish government, the story has been ignored in Germany, who had trained the Turkish army, provided German officers, and played a passive role in the operation. In his excellent compilation of the documentation on the subject, in which he presents a detailed list of evidence, describesthe background and the results of the affair and investigates the German role, Wolfgang Gust, a reporter for *Spiegel*, insures that this savage massacre of the oldest Christian nation of the world (Conversion of the ruling family in 301 AD) by a Moslem state will not be forgotten. This volume is of immense relevance today, not only in reference to the war between Armenia and Aserbaidschan for the Caucasian Berg-Karabach, but also in reference to the constant ethnic cleansing carried out by Islamic states against Christian peoples (for example in southern Sudan).

60. The Persecution of Christians can be Part of Immense Mass Murders

Proposition: The Persecution of Christians has often been part of immense mass murders.

National Socialism and Communism are good examples. Both opposed the Christian faith violently and attacked other religions and nationalities as well. We have a fairly accurate estimate of the millions of victims to National Socialism,[319] but the victims of Communism have not been so well assessed. There are several reliable estimations of these numbers,[320] mostly from secular sources. These appraisals, of course, deal only with specific regions and times. A comprehensive statistic would have to first define which governments and movements should be defined as Communist. An excellent article by Jean-Pierre Dujardin in a 1978 edition of

---

[319] The most thorough compilation can be found in Wolfgang Benz (Ed.). Dimension des Völkermords: Die Zahl der jüdischen Opfer des Nationalsozialismus. Quellen und Darstellungen zur Zeitgeschichte 33. R. Oldenbourg: München, 1991.

[320] For a good summary of the history of perscution of Christians in the fomer East Block, see: Rudolf Freudenberger et. al. "Christenverfolgungen". *op. cit.*, pp. 51-62.

H. The State and Persecution

the Paris newspaper *Figaro* provides a thorough synopsis of the state of research and the available literature.[321] According to Dujardin, the number of victims in the Soviet Union was over 70,000,000. 24,000,000 died during Stalin's Terror, and 7,8000,000 during the annihilation of the Ukrainian people. At least 500,000 people died under the oppression of the East Block countries and the Baltic states. The number of victims of the People's Republic of China has been estimated at about 63,000,000 (by 1978), but the number of Soviet victims cannot be much lower. Other estimations are twice as high, but I have chosen to mention only the lower numbers. If we take the victims of the smaller states and areas, such as Cambodia[322] (2,500,00), we must add several millions. Another French work, the 1997 'Black Book of Communism'[323], which has become a standard reference, estimates the complete number of victims to Communism at about 95 million.[324]

61. Persecution of Christians under National Socialism

The persecution of Christians under National Socialism[325] demonstrates that such persecution is also possible in the West. Among the

---

[321] Jean-Pierre Dujardin. "N'oublions jamais ...". Figaro Nr. 7/78 vom 18. Nov., 1978 (German translation available from the Hilfsaktion Märtyrerkirche/Voice of Martyrs).

[322] Not including those who died after 1978. A more recent estimation ("Der rote Schrecken". Focus 48/1997: 168-170) arrives at the following numbers: China 65 Mill., USSR: 20 Mill., other Communist countries: 9,44 Mill.

[323] Stéphane Courtois et. al. (Ed.). The Black Book of Communism. Harvard University Press: Cambridge (MA) & London, 1999; Stéphane Courtois et. al. (Ed.). Das Schwarzbuch des Kommunismus: Unterdrückung, Verbrechen und Terror. Piper: München, 1998⁵ (French original 1997); See the review and summary in Eckhard Jesse. "Das Schwarzbuch des Kommunismus". Mut Nr. 374 (Oct 1998): 10-25.

[324] Stéphane Courtois et. al. (Ed.). Das Schwarzbuch des Kommunismus, *op. cit.*, p. 16.

[325] Rudolf Freudenberger et. al. "Christenverfolgungen". *op. cit*, pp 48-51; Walter Adolph (Ed.). Im Schatten des Galgens: Zum Gedächtnis der Blutzeugen in der nationalsozialistischen Kirchenverfolgung. Morus Verlag: Berlin, 1953 (only Catholic martyrs); Gerhard Besier, Gerhard Ringshausen (Ed.). Bekenntnis, Widerstand, Martyrium: Von Barmen 1934 bis Plötzensee 1944. Vandenhoeck & Ruprecht: Göttingen, 1986. pp. 11-165;. on Protestant martyrs, see; Margarete Schneider (Ed.). Paul Schneider - Der Prediger von Buchenwald. Hänssler: Neuhausen, 1981¹; 1996⁴; Rudolf Wentorf. Der Fall des Pfarrers Paul Schneider. Neukirchener Verlag: Neukirchen, 1989; Georges Casalis. "Theologie unter dem Zeichen des Martyriums: Dietrich Bonhoeffer". Concilium 19 (1983) 3: 236-240 = "Theology Under the Sign of Martyrdom: Dietrich Bonhoeffer". pp. 80-84 in: Jo-

millions of victims to National Socialism were 4,000 mostly Catholic clergymen. Three thousand pastors of the Bekennende Kirche (the Confessing Church) were imprisoned.[326]

I have chosen a fundamental work out of the flood of literature available, in order to clarify the problems involved in the discussion. Georg May's monumental book on the Catholic resistance to National Socialism and the Nazi attempts to eliminate the Roman Catholic Church[327] leaves the reader with a contradictory impression. On the positive side, note that:

On the basis of numerous original sources, May presents Nazism's views on the Catholic Church, the actions taken against the Church and the extent of Catholic resistance, which resulted in countless martyrs, particularly among the priests. The Catholic Church had many more martyrs than the Protestants.

May describes Hitler's own beliefs and his view of Christianity, which shows that National Socialism was itself a religion, and not just a political delusion.

May points out that the Protestant State Churches tend to falsify history by celebrating a few Protestant martyrs and rebels, which gives the impression that the religious resistance was Protestant, and that Protestant resistance was wide-spread. Particularly liberal, critical Christianity has tried to improve its reputation in this manner.

May's work also has its negative aspects, for he uses his book to prove the superiority of Catholicism over Protestantism.

He ignores the Catholic Church's compliance with Hitler, and gives the impression that the whole Church had opposed the Nazis rather than having any part in the party's success. In order to do so, May struggles to

---

hannes Baptist Metz, Edward Schillebeeckx (Ed.). Martyrdom Today. *op. cit.*, Georg Huntemann. Der andere Bonhoeffer. R. Brockhaus: Wuppertal, 1989; Christoph Strohm. Theologische Ethik im Kampf gegen den Nationalsozialismus: Der Weg Dietrich Bonhoeffers mit den Juristen Hans von Dohnanyi und Gerhard Leibholz in den Widerstand. Heidelberger Untersuchungen zu Widerstand, Judenverfolgung und Kirchenkampf im Dritten Reich 1. Chr. Kaiser: München, 1989; see also Hans-Joachim Ramm. Stets einem Höheren verantwortlich: Christliche Grundüberzeugungen im innermilitärischen Widerstand gegen Hitler. Hänssler: Neuhausen, 1996.

[326] Rudolf Freudenberger et. al. "Christenverfolgungen". *op. cit.*, p. 49.
[327] Georg May. Kirchenkampf- oder Katholikenverfolgung: Ein Beitrag zu dem gegenseitigen Verhältnis von Nationalsozialismus und christlichen Bekenntnissen. Christiana-Verlag: Stein am Rhein, 1991.

show that Hitler, who is known to have left the Catholic Church, had never been Catholic at all. May also fails to explain why Hitler was never excommunicated (The Protestant Church would have been just as lax in this respect).

May's harsh criticism of the Protestant Church fails to distinguish between the various camps, such as nominal Christians and convinced, practicing believers. Since his censure nowhere deals with Protestant doctrine, only with the reasons for the lack of resistance, his discussion gives Protestants no chance, and thus quenches even the self-critical deliberation of some people who might otherwise have taken May's warnings into consideration.

For Bible-believing Protestants, the book is a good example of the attitude of conservative Catholic theologians towards the goals of the Reformation, for May makes no attempt to distinguish between the Biblical justification of the Reformation and the liberal Cultural Protestantism of today. This is the book's major weakness: all the failures of the Protestant Church under National Socialism are blamed on Protestant doctrine, while the failings of Catholics are justified with the denial that such people were good, practicing Catholics. Prominent Protestant Nazis are quoted as if they were typical Protestants, but prominent Catholic Nazis are exposed as being only nominal Christians. In this way, May can pretend that all good Catholics resisted Hitler, while most Protestants supported him. It is unfortunate that this polemic apologetic intent makes the book, so subjective. It could otherwise become a standard work and its expert knowledge could offer Protestants so much.

I. Practical Compassion

62. When One Member suffers ...

Proposition: "Martyrdom calls for Christ's Church to Maintain Its Solidarity."[328]

The New Testament considers this solidarity an essential element of Christ's Law of Love, not an option for a single group of concerned believers. "Remember them that are in bonds, as bound with them; and them which suffer adversity, as being yourselves also in the body" (Heb. 13:3).

---

[328] Peter Beyerhaus. Die Bedeutung des Martyriums für den Aufbau des Leibes Christi. *op. cit.*, p. 140.

A Christian never suffers alone, but always as part of the Body of Christ : "And whether one member suffer, all the members suffer with it; or one member be honoured, all the members rejoice with it" (1 Cor. 12:26). Paul thus charges Timothy, "Thou therefore endure hardness, as a good soldier of Jesus Christ," (2 Tim. 2:3). He writes the Philippians, "Notwithstanding ye have well done, that ye did communicate with my affliction," (Phil 4:14). He suffers for the Ephesians' sake and considers his tribulations their glory (Eph. 3:13).

We must not allow our own comfortable situation to blind us to the problems of other Christians. Since this naturally requires a good system of communication, missionary societies, human rights organizations, international church connections, personal relationships with believers from other countries and international structures such as the World Evangelical Fellowship are absolutely necessary.

"A church which abandons its martyrs, never prays for them, never takes their part or cares for them, destroys not only the spiritual fellowship of the Body of Christ. It also betrays Christ, the Head of the Body, Who suffers with His members."[329] Speaking of His suffering followers and messengers, Jesus said, "Then shall the King say unto them on his right hand, Come, ye blessed of my Father, inherit the kingdom prepared for you from the foundation of the world: For I was an hungred, and ye gave me meat: I was thirsty, and ye gave me drink: I was a stranger, and ye took me in: Naked, and ye clothed me: I was sick, and ye visited me: I was in prison, and ye came unto me. ... Verily I say unto you, Inasmuch as ye have done it unto one of the least of these my brethren, ye have done it unto me" (Matt. 25:34-36+40: see verses 32-40 and 41-45).

Prayer is the first way to share others' burdens. "The supplication of the Church helps to save from death those emissaries of faith tested beyond their strength, who have despaired of life."[330] (2 Cor. 1:8-11; See also Phil 1:19). Practical compassion is the next part of our support, as the Book of Hebrews reminds us: "But call to remembrance the former days, in which, after ye were illuminated, ye endured a great fight of afflictions; Partly, whilst ye were made a gazingstock both by reproaches and afflictions; and partly, whilst ye became companions of them that were so used. For ye had compassion of me in my bonds, and took joyfully the spoiling of your goods, knowing in yourselves that ye have in heaven a better and an enduring substance" (Heb. 10:32-34; see verses 32-39). The writer of Hebrews

---

[329] *Ibid.*, p. 141.
[330] Christof Sauer. Mission und Martyrium, *op. cit.*, p. 108.

sees two sides of the struggle of suffering: some believers suffer directly, some suffer by sharing their sufferings. Some are persecuted, others become their 'companions'. Some lose their property, others have suffered with the prisoners. God expects us to feel personally affected by the sufferings of our brothers and sisters in Christ!

The Biblical commandment includes concrete social and political assistance.[331] Proverbs 24:11 admonishes us, "... deliver them that are drawn unto death, and those that are ready to be slain" and Proverbs 31:8 adds, "Open thy mouth for the dumb in the cause of all such as are appointed to destruction."

63. The Body's Intervention for its Martyrs Exposes Its Own Condition.

Proposition: "The Church's manner of dealing with martyrdom, whether we feel affected as a whole, and suffer with the suffering (1 Cor. 12:26) or whether we are apathetic about their tribulations, reveals the true state of the Church's fellowship."[332]

Christians privileged to live in countries with religious liberty must not rest upon their laurels, but must support their brothers and sisters in the faith. We only enjoy freedom of religion because others, not only Christians, have fought for it. God will reward our activities in Eternity, but they often result in earthly successes. Paul's model behavior in prison, which "But I would ye should understand, brethren, that the things which happened unto me have fallen out rather unto the furtherance of the gospel," (Phil 1:12) had results, for "many of the brethren in the Lord, waxing confident by my bonds, are much more bold to speak the word without fear" (Phil 1:14).

64. Communion is the Ideal Place to Remember Suffering Believers

Proposition: Communion (The Lord's Supper, the Mass) is the ideal place to recall those Christians who are persecuted for their faith, for

---

[331] Ravi Zacharias. "Christians are Compelled to Help". pp. 91-93 in: Nina Shea. In The Lion's Den: A Shocking Account of Persecution and Martyrdom of Christians Today and How We Should Respond. Broadman & Holman: Nashville (TN), 1997.

[332] Eduard Christen: " Martyrium III/2 *op. cit.*, p. 215.

both central aspects of the Body of Christ – fellowship and sacrifice – are closely related to martyrdom.

On the one hand, as Communion symbolizes Jesus' sacrifice of His body and blood, it focuses on His martyrdom. On the other hand, we also remember that all Christians are part of Christ's Body: "The cup of blessing which we bless, is it not the communion of the blood of Christ? The bread which we break, is it not the communion of the body of Christ? For we being many are one bread, and one body: for we are all partakers of that one bread" (1 Cor. 10:16-17). I cannot overemphasize Paul's admonition, "And whether one member suffer, all the members suffer with it; or one member be honoured, all the members rejoice with it" (1 Cor. 12:26). Thus I would urge congregations to find different ways to remember the persecuted when they celebrate Communion, whether during prayers of supplication, in the Introductory Words or by reading appropriate scriptures.

65. the Martyrs in Worship

Proposition: When the Body of Christ meets to worship, it should remember those who have suffered for Christ's sake and those who are still suffering.

Beginning with the Reformation, Protestant 'calendars of martyrs' have been available to assist us in our of the martyrs.[333] The first of these martyrologies, which refresh the liturgical memory of the blood witnesses of the past, was John Foxe's (1516-1587) 'Original Actes and Monuments of These Latter and Perillous Days' (1563), later known as 'The Book of Martyrs', which had great influence on the Anglicans, the Puritans, on the Reformed on the Continent[334] and on the *Evangelischen Namenskalen-*

---

[333] See above for Books of Martyrs of the various denominations. For a discussion of Protestant martyrologies, see also: A. G. Dickens, John M. Tonikn. The Reformation in Historical Thought. Harvard University Press: Cambridge (MA), 1985. pp. 39-57; Diana Wood (Ed.). Martyrs and Martyrologies. Papers Read at the ... Ecclesiastical History Society. B. Blackwell: Oxford, 1993; James Michael Weiss. "Luther and His Colleagues on the Lives of the Saints". The Harvard Library Bulletin 33 (1983): 174-195; Robert Kolb. For all the Saints. Changing Perceptions of Martyrdom and Sainthood in the Lutheran Reformation. *op. cit.*

[334] See Robert Kolb. For all the Saints. *op. cit.*, pp. 5-6; N. Norskov Olson. John Foxe and the Elizabethan Church. University of California Press: Berkeley, 1973; John T. McNeill. "John Foxe: Historiographer, Disciplinarian, Tolerationist". Church History 43 (1974): 216-229; William Haller. The Elect Nation: The Meaning and Relevance of Foxe's Book of Martyrs. Harper: New York, 1963; William Haller. "John Foxe and the Puritan Revolution". pp. 209-224 in: Richard Foster Jones

I. Practical Compassion 109

dar,[335] and is still being printed.[336] There are other good ways of recalling the martyrs to our memories, such as the ten statues of the martyrs of all confessions at Westminster Abbey in London.[337]

Worship of the martyrs, which arose in the first centuries[338] and is practiced in the Roman Catholic and Orthodox churches, is foreign to Protestantism, as it is non biblical, but it has served to keep the memories of persecution alive. To forget the saints and martyrs completely, is no alternative! Rather we should remember them as role models of faith,[339] and teach the church membership about them, in confirmation classes, for example. [340] In his Apology to the Augsburg Confession, Philipp Melanch-

---

(Ed.). The Seventeenth Century: Studies in the History of English Thought and Literature. Stanford: Standorf University Press, 1951.

[335] Evangelischer Namenkalender: Gedenktage der Christenheit. Evangelische Buchhilfe: Kassel, 1979 (16 pp.); Robert Lansemann. Die Heiligentage, besonders die Marien-, Apostel-, und Engeltage in der Reformationszeit ... Vandenhoeck & Ruprecht: Göttingen, 1939; see also the list in: Evangelisches Tagzeiten Buch. Vandenhoeck & Ruprecht: Göttingen, 1998⁴, and Frieder Schulz. "Das Gedächtnis der Zeugen: Vorgeschichte, Gestaltung und Bedeutung des Evangelischen Namenkalenders". Jahrbuch für Liturgik und Hymnologie 19/1975): 69-104.

[336] John Foxe. Book of Martyrs. W. Tegg: London, 1851 [1563]; John Foxe. Fox' Book of Martyrs. ed. by William Bryon Forbush. John C. Winston: Philadelphia (PN), 1926; newest edition: John Foxe. Foxe's Book of Martyrs and How They Found Christ: in Their Own Words. Christian Classic Series 3. World Press Library: Springfield (MO), 1998 [1563]; John Foxe. Foxe's Book of Martyrs. Thomas Nelson Publ.: Nashville (TN), 2000 [1563] (many other complete and abridged editions available).

[337] T. Melhuish. "The 20th Century Martys: Westminster Abbey". Church Building Nr. 53, 1998: 18ff and Peter Sandner. "Ökumene der Märtyrer: Neue Statuen an der Westminster Abbey in London". Diakrisis 20 (1999) 3: 149-155 and in more detail Andrew Chandler (Ed.). The Terrible Alternative: Christian Martyrdom in the Twentieth Century. Cassell: London, New York, 1998.

[338] Thomas Schirrmacher. "Die Entstehung der christlichen Heiligenverehrung in der Spätantike". Bibel und Gemeinde 90 (1990) 2: 166-175. Already in the Martyrium of Polykarp 22,1 [= p. 18-19 in: Herbert Musurillo (Ed.). The Acts of Christian Martyrs. Clarendon Press: Oxford, 1972, 'Martyrium des Polykarp' pp. 2-21] ca. 155-157 A. D. relates, that Polycarp's burnt body was worshippedn. After his death, worship services were held at his grave. [*Ibid.*, pp. 12-13].

[339] Martin Scharfe. "Der Heilige in der protestantischen Volksfrömmigkeit". Hessische Blätter für Volkskunde 60 (1969): 93-106.

[340] For Evangelical collections of biographies of modern martyrs, see: Haralan Popoff. Tortured for His Faith: A Epic of Christian Courage and Heroism in Our Day. Zondervan: Grand Rapids (MI), 1970¹; 1975²; Herbert Schlossberg. Called to Suffer, Called to Triumph: 18 True Stories by Persecuted Christians. Multnomah: Portland (OR), 1990.

ton gives three reasons for the commemoration of the martyrs and other saints:

1. We should thank God for the examples of His grace.

2. The martyrs' example should strengthen our faith.

3. We should follow the example of their faith, their love and their patience.[341]

For these reasons, the commemoration of the martyrs has always been part of worship in Protestant churches.[342] John Calvin added a prayer for the persecuted into his Geneva Order of Worship.[343]

66. Education on Persecution

Proposition: "Instruction about persecution is one of the fundamental dogmas in the young churches."[344]

"The best text book on persecution is the Bible."[345] As we have seen, many New Testament texts were written to prepare Christians for persecution or to encourage them under persecution. (Paul, for example,[346] followed Christ in martyrdom, as did most of the other New Testament writ-

---

[341] See the summary, *Ibid.*,p. 101 to Article 21 "Von der Anrufung der Heiligen" der Apologia der Confessio Augustana,. in: Horst Georg Pöhlmann et. al. (Ed.). Unser Glaube: Die Bekenntnisschriften der evangelisch-lutherischen Kirche. Ausgabe für die Gemeinde. GB Siebenstern 1289. Gütersloher Verlagshaus: Gütersloh, 1986. pp. 347-357 [Abschnitte 271-280].

[342] Robert Kolb. For all the Saints. Changing Perceptions of Martyrdom and Sainthood in the Lutheran Reformation. *op. cit.*, pp 148-158.

[343] Jean Calvin. Calvin-Studienausgabe. Vol. 2: Gestalt und Ordnung der Kirche. Neukirchener Verlag: Neukirchen-Vluyn, 1997. pp. 137-225 "Genfer Gottesdienstordnung (1542) mit ihren Nachbartexten", here p. 169; On Calvin's View of martyrdom, see also: Jean Calvin. Calvin-Studienausgabe. Vol. 3: Reformatorische Kontroversen. Neukirchener Verlag: Neukirchen, 1998. pp 267-367 'Gegen die Irrtümer der Anabaptisten' (1544), here pp. 366-367, and Hans Scholl's introduction,. pp. 267-277, here p. 271.

[344] Horst Engelmann. Gemeindestruktur und Verfolgung. *op. cit.*, p. 9.

[345] Preparing Believers for Suffering and Persecution: A Manual for Christian Workers. Hope: Bulawayo (Simbabwe), o. J. (ca. 1979). 15 pp. p. 6.

[346] John S. Pobee. Persecution and Martyrdom in the Theology of Paul. *op. cit.*, pp. 107-118.

I. Practical Compassion

ers.) We desperately need better literature[347] and more intensive Bible study material on the subject.[348]

As far as liturgy is concerned, there are many good ways to prepare Christians for persecution:[349] learning appropriate scripture texts by heart, songs, prayers, and sections of the worship service.[350] In many countries, Christians have bitterly regretted not being better prepared for persecution.[351]

"We also need a "new esteem for the power of prayer."[352] We could use the prayer of the Jerusalem Church, which led to Peter's miraculous liberation, as a model (Acts 4:23-31, based on Psalm 1:1-2).[353]

67. We Need Confessors

Proposition: The Church of Jesus Christ needs courageous saints and martyrs, men and women willing to confess their faith even whatever it costs – the hostility of society, the animosity of the State and of the religious groups, even the opposition of a misguided Church.

The experiences of the German Church under Nazism and Communism demonstrate this necessity. "From its very cradle, the Church has always been a confessing church."[354] If the Church does not confess its faith, it becomes easily deceived, and turns into a persecutor.

---

[347] Patrick Johnstone. "Preparing 3rd World Believers for Church Growth under Persecution". *op. cit.*, p. 6.
[348] In detail: Thomas Schirrmacher. Gottesdienst ist mehr: Plädoyer für eine liturgische Gottesdienstgestaltung. Theologisches Lehr- und Studienmaterial 2. Verlag für Kultur und Wissenschaft: Bonn, 1999.
[349] For good material for catechism, unfortunately out of date, see: Manfred Fermir. Christen in der Verfolgung. Anregungen: Arbeitshefte für den Religionsunterricht ... 3. R. Brockhaus, 1979.
[350] Preparing Believers for Suffering and Persecution: A Manual for Christian Workers. *op. cit.*, p. 6.
[351] For example in Korea, see Peter Pattison. Crisis Anaware: A Doctor Examines the Korean Church. OMF Books: Sevenoaks (GB), 1981. pp. 232-239.
[352] Bruder Andrew. "Wir brauchen eine neue Sicht der leidenden Kirche". *op. cit.*, pp. 1-3, here p. 2; see also: Bruder Andrew. And God Changed His Mind. Chosen Books: Old Tappan (NJ), 1990; Chosen Books: Grand Rapids (MI), 1999].
[353] William Carl Weinreich. Spirit and Martyrdom. *op. cit.*, pp. 32-34.
[354] Johannes Wirsching. "Bekenntnisschriften". pp. 487-511 in: Gerhard Krause, Gerhard Müller (Ed.). Theologische Realenzyklopädie. Vol. 5. Walter de Gruyter: Berlin, 1980. p. 487.

68. Perseverance is Essential

Proposition: **The ability to persevere under difficulties – particularly in the Church and in missions – is one of the most important marks of spiritual leadership and is an automatic preparation for persecution.**[355]

Because the fear of suffering, especially among the leadership, has such terrible consequences for the Body of Christ, perseverance should play a much greater role in theological training and in the choice of church workers. Because character development requires role models, this goal can only be achieved through the integration of teachers and students into local churches or into concrete organizations. Patience, perseverance and the willingness to sacrifice cannot be learned in class or by participation in short time projects, but only under long-term responsibility.

69. Church Structure and Persecution

Proposition: **In the planting of new churches, the leadership should try to develop structures which can withstand pressure and continue to fulfil their spiritual responsibilities under persecution.**[356]

Home churches[357] and cell groups are important,[358] because they function without a large organization.[359] We need more study on the subject.

---

[355] Patrick Johnstone. "Preparing 3rd World Believers for Church Growth under Persecution". *op. cit.*

[356] Horst Engelmann. Gemeindestruktur und Verfolgung. *op. cit.* und John S. Pobee. Persecution and Martyrdom in the Theology of Paul. *op. cit.* pp. 107-118 "Persecution and the Church". For Catholicism, see: Walbert Bühlmann. "Die Kirche als Institution in Situationen der Christenverfolgung". Concilium 19 (1983) 3: 217-220 = "The Church as Institution in the Context of Persecution". pp. 58-62 in: Johannes Baptist Metz, Edward Schillebeeckx (Ed.). Martyrdom Today. *op. cit.*

[357] Met Q. Castillo. The Church in Thy House. Alliance-Publishers: Malina (Philippinen), 1982 (in cooperation with Asia Theological Fellowship); Thomas S. Gosslin II. The Church without Walls. Hope Publ.: Pasadena, 1984.

[358] "Preparing 3rd World Believers for Church Growth under Persecution". *op. cit.*, p. 7 and Preparing Believers for Suffering and Persecution: A Manual for Christian Workers. Hope: Bulawayo (Simbabwe), n. d. (ca. 1979). 15 pp. p. 9 ("Every Christian home must become a church." Herbert Schlossberg. A Frangrance of Oppression: The Church and Its Persecutors. Crossway Books: Wheaton (IL), 1991. p. 161 considers congregationalists associations with small churches important.

[359] Preparing Believers for Suffering and Persecution. *op. cit.*, p. 9.

I. Practical Compassion

70. We Need Concrete Ideas

Proposition: **Awareness of the persecution of our brothers and sisters in Christ should become part of the everyday life of our churches. We must begin to make it an issue in all projects and work groups, but need concrete ideas to help realize this goal.**

- Let me conclude with a few ideas for the church leadership. Members can bring suggestions to the leadership's attention.

- As a child, I was always impressed by the devotional hall of the international center of the WEC in Bulstrode in London. I will never forget the pictures of the missionaries who have given their lives in Belgian-Congo (Zaire) for their faith.[360] Why not hang up similar pictures elsewhere? The missionaries who were shot to death by the Auca Indians were even portrayed on postage stamps![361]

- Pray for persecuted Christians every Sunday, or at least regularly, during worship. The prayer can be general, for a specific country or for a specific believer. Make this a customary part of your order of worship.

- Preach on the subject at least once a year. Also preach on 'The Price of Following Christ'. Good Scripture texts might be: Luke 21:12-15; Heb. 10:32-39; 1 Pet. 2:13-17; Matt. 5:10-16; 2 Thess. 1:3-12; Gal. 1:23-24; Mark 10:29.30; 2 Cor. 2:9-10; 2 Cor. 4:7-12; Rom. 8:35-39; John 15:18-21; Acts 16:13-34.

- Do not avoid scriptures which mention persecution or which describe the lives of martyrs such as Stephan, Paul or Jeremia. When preaching on a text which deals with persecution, include the issue in the sermon.

- Make sure that every prayer meeting in your congregation or area prays for at least one concrete need of some persecuted believer.

- Are there any Christians in your area from countries in which Christians are persecuted? Ask him to give a testimony. Perhaps a church member may be able to report on the subject after visiting such a country.

---

[360] See: Idoti und David M. Davies. With God in Congo Forests During the Persecution Under Rebel Occupation as Told by an African Pastor. Worldwide Evangelization Crusade: Bulstrode, Gerrards Cross (GB), 1971.
[361] See: Elisabeth Elliot. Die Mörder – meine Freunde. CLV: Bielefeld, 1999 (from the English).

- Cooperate with a mission board or human rights organization to prepare worship services, church meetings or cell group meetings on persecuted Christians.
- Take advantage of the International Day of Prayer for the Persecuted Church (IDOP) in November to hang up a presentation on persecution or to invite a guest speaker. Try to dedicate the preceding or following week to deepening awareness in youth groups, cell groups or prayer meetings.
- Give a church member the responsibility for informing the church regularly about persecution. (Use missionary journals or the Internet, etc to collect material).
- Make one church member responsible for issues such as human rights, religious liberty or the persecution of Christians. This person should make contact with the working groups of the church on the one hand, and with missionary societies and human rights organisations on the other.
- Provide your church with appropriate news letters or journals from missionary boards and human rights organisations.
- Organize occasional displays on the subject or reserve a space for it on the church bulletin board.
- Provide the congregation with a regular newsletter on the issue, add information to the church letter regularly or put on the church board.
- Write to persecuted Christians and their families and churches. Missionary societies and human rights organisations can provide you with addresses.
- Support petitions for persecuted Christians and write to governments and embassies.
- Write to your own politicians and to the embassies of involved countries. Write to embassies and politicians in these countries. Missionary societies and human rights organisations can provide you with addresses and information.
- Contact the representatives of your electoral district or other responsible community leaders and provide them with information on persecuted Christians.
- Encourage your denomination to get involved.
- At least once a year, donate the Sunday collection to an involved work group (in your denomination, many missionary societies, human rights organizations).

Appendix 1: Human Rights and Christian Faith

Published in Russian in the journal of the Academy of Science of Russia: POISK: Ezemedel'naja Vsesojuznaja Gazeta [Journal of the Russian Academy of Science]. Nr. 48 (446) 22.-28. November 1997. p. 13; reprinted in the news paper of the Russian Teacher's Association: Utschitjelskaja Gazeta (Russische Lehrerzeitung). No. 2 (9667) 3.1.1998. S. 21 + No. 3 (9668) 20.1.1998. p. 21 + No. 4 (9669) 3.2.1998. p. 22. Written for the Konferenz Evangelikaler Publizisten (Conference of Evangelical Journalists and Mediapeople) of the German Evangelical Alliance.

Man as Creation and Image of God

On December 10, 1948, the Soviet Union signed the General Declaration of Human Rights passed by the General Assembly of the United Nations. The declaration states that all human beings possess the same dignity (Article 1) and forbids all discrimination due to race, color, sex, language, religion or political conviction (Article 2). Because all men have the right to life and liberty (Article 3), both slavery (Article 4) and torture (Article 5) are prohibited. All are equal before the law and may be condemned only according to established law, only after being heard in a court of law (Articles 7-11). All are free to emigrate and to choose their place of residence (Article 13), and to request asylum in other countries (Article 14). Every human being is free to choose his spouse, and the family, as the "natural and basic unit in society', must be protected by the State and by society (Articles 16+26). The Declaration also demands the right of private property (Article 17), the right to liberty of conscience and religion, which includes the individual's right to change his faith (Article 18), the right of opinion and information (Article 19), the right to congregate and to form associations (Article 20), the right to vote (Article 21). Everyone has the right to security in social matters (Articles 22+25+28), to labor with just remuneration (Article 23) and to education (Article 26).

Closely related to the idea of human rights is the claim that all people have the same right to be treated as persons - whatever race, religion, sex, political persuasion or social or economic status they may be. What is the basis of human equality, if not the fact that all were equally created by God? Thus, a Christian argument for human rights must begin with the biblical account of Creation, "Let us make man in our image, after our likeness: and let them have dominion over the fish of the sea, and over the fowl of the air, and over the cattle, and over all the earth, and over every creeping thing that creepeth upon the earth. So God created man in his own image, in the image of God created he him; male and female created he them" (Gen. 1:26-27). The fact that Man was created in the image of God plays a major roll in the relationships of human beings to each other. Genesis 9:16, for example, requires murder to be punished, for it injures the image of God. "Whoso sheddeth man's blood, by man shall his blood be shed: for in the image of God made he man." (Genesis 9:6)

Creation exists for the glory of God and has its meaning from God. This fact holds all the more for the 'Crown of Creation', Mankind was created according to the divine order of Creation to fulfill the purpose given him by God. God made him ruler over the earth, but also gave him the responsibility for the preservation of the earthly creation. The psalmist writes, "Thou madest him to have dominion over the works of thy hands; thou hast put all things under his feet: All sheep and oxen, yea, and the beasts of the field;" (Psalm 8:6-7).

For this reason, human rights include only those privileges which God has given Man, no other rights which mankind may choose or claim for himself.

Christians may not, therefore, automatically identify the human rights catalogs formulated by western countries with those in the Bible. Scripture prescribes the right to an orderly court procedure according to clearly stated laws, to the hearing of witnesses, to judges who have not been bribed and to legal defense, as we will see. Such legal proceedings cannot, however, be automatically identified with Western jurisdiction. Supposing they could be—with which system? The German system, the British, the French, the American? We all know that these systems are quite different! There is plenty of room for a variety of legal systems which differ due to the cultural and historical traditions of their people, yet still guarantee human rights.

The Christian Roots of Human Rights

No one disputes the fact that human rights, given to protect the individual, are derived from Christian thought. The General Declaration of Human Rights of the United Nations, of December 10, 1948, clearly demonstrates its Christian roots. The bans on slavery and torture, the principle of equality before the law, the right to rest and recreation—as seen in the Sabbath or Sunday rest—come from Christian traditions and not by chance are the governments which confirm these rights and anchor them in their constitutions mostly in Christian countries. Even Karl Marx acknowledged this, for he rejected human rights as a product of Christianity (for example, Marx and Engels Works, Vol. 1).

No state and no legal system can survive without a minimum of common, and necessarily 'metaphysically' based values. A legal system assumes a value system, for law is derived from moral standards which exist prior to and outside itself.

The guarantee of human dignity assumes that Man is more than that which he perceives about himself. He cannot be comprehended by the means and methods of natural science. He is metaphysically open. The modern State, with its legal system, depends on requirements that it cannot itself guarantee.

Enlightenment or Forgiveness and Repentance?

According to the philosophies of the Enlightenment in the eighteenth century, which attempted to found human rights without God and against the Church, all Good, including human rights, could be derived from Nature and from Reason. Rousseau's identification of 'Reason' and 'Nature' is peculiar to Enlightenment thought. The attempt to base human rights on Nature has failed, however, for no one can agree on the meaning of 'Nature' or on how it's laws can be discovered. Wolfgang Schild, professor for penal law, writes, "The Enlightenment cannot and must not be the last word, our last word. Its rationality and functionality must be taken to its limits, for social life with a dignity worthy of Man is otherwise impossible. Even and particularly penal law cannot limit itself to rational means in order to achieve peace and order at any price: it requires the recognition of the human dignity - even of the felon - as its fundament and its limit."

The thought that human beings could be improved by education, and that human ills could be solved by intellectual enlightenment, is a basic problem of Greek philosophy, of Humanism and of the Enlightenment. The Humanist ideal of education owes its existence to the idea that morals could be raised through education, for it assumes that the individual does wrong only because he is ignorant or because he thinks wrongly, not because his will is evil and because he is incapable of doing good on his own strength. These philosophies try to reduce the ethical and responsible aspect of thought, words and deeds to the question of knowledge, which hold a man responsible, only when he knows what he is doing.

Yet we are surprised to learn that doctors smoke as much as laymen do, that people maintain unhealthy life-styles, and that women continually become pregnant in spite of a flood of information about birth control. We all know from our own lives, that knowing the right answer, even being convinced of it, in no way guarantees that we live accordingly. A politician who vehemently defends monogamy as the foundation of society in Parliament does not necessarily insist on marital fidelity in his private life, and is not immune to adultery or divorce.

The Bible teaches that human sin affects not only our thoughts, but also our whole being, and that above all, our wills, which are opposed to God, lead us to act and think falsely, so that more thought and consideration are in itself insufficient. We must clear up our old, sin-encumbered past. Christians believe that God Himself died in Man's place, when Christ died on the Cross for our lack of love and our egotism. When we acknowledge that we cannot save ourselves by our own strength and our own reason, but rely on Christ's fulfillment of our penalty, we can overcome our evil will by faith in Jesus, and renew our will and our mind according to God's will (Romans 1:20-25; 12:1-3). True renewal occurs when the power of God works in our inner selves; not through educational campaigns, but by God's love and forgiveness.

Human Rights Precede the State

Human dignity and human rights are part of man's being as God's creation. Thus, the State does not create human rights, it merely formulates and protects them. Since the right to life belongs to the very essence of the human being, man does not receive them from the government, and no government has the right to decide that its citizens have no more right to live, but can be executed at the ruler's whim. Nor does the State confer the right to have a family, for the State does not own the family, it merely acknowledges the duty implied in the order of Creation to protect marriage and the family.

There are, therefore, rights which existed prior to the State, and there are rights above the State, rights derived from nature, both from human nature and from the various types of human society. The government must respect these rights and accept the limitations implied by these natural, divinely given rights of the individual, the family, the employee (or the employer!) and other human social groups.

Since human rights are rooted in a moral code prescribed to the State, this code equally forbids a false appeal to human rights, because it also defends the human dignity of others. No one has the right to express his own personality through murder or arson, for example.

Human rights assume a State with limited powers and a law valid for all mankind, a law which limits the powers of government. Were this not so, man would indeed receive his rights from the State. The individual would then have only the rights and the claims to protection which his government assured. This is the socialist view, which leaves no place for criticism or correction of a State which has declared itself to be God.

The Meaning of Romans 13

The most important scripture about the role of the State is the thirteenth chapter of the Epistle to the Romans, which was written by the apostle Paul, who brought Christianity to Europe and Asia in the first century AD: "Let every soul be subject unto the higher powers. For there is no power but of God: the powers that be are ordained of God. Whosoever therefore resisteth the power, resisteth the ordinance of God: and they that resist shall receive to themselves damnation. For rulers are not a terror to good works, but to the evil. Wilt thou then not be afraid of the power? do that which is good, and thou shalt have praise of the same: For he is the minister of God to thee for good. But if thou do that which is evil, be afraid; for he beareth not the sword in vain: for he is the minister of God, a revenger to execute wrath upon him that doeth evil. Wherefore ye must needs be subject, not only for wrath, but also for conscience sake. For for this cause pay ye tribute also: for they are God's ministers, attending continually upon this very thing. Render therefore to all their dues: tribute to whom tribute is due; custom to whom custom; fear to whom fear; honour to whom honour." (Romans 13:1-7)

This text makes it clear that no one who opposes the State on principle can appeal to God's authorization. On the contrary: he is opposing God's law, and is rightly liable to legal proceedings (Rom. 13:2). Since the State has the duty to stem and to punish evil, Christians must do good, if they wish to avoid conflict. If a Christian does wrong, he is justly punished by the State. For the government, as God's minister, has the duty of vengeance (13:4). As a result, the Christian pays his taxes and gives government officials proper respect (13:6-7).

But the question is, who defines what is good or evil? Did Paul leave this up to the State? Can the State declare anything good and demand it from its citizens? No. When Paul spoke of goodness, he defined it according to God's will, and defined evil as that which was condemned by God's law. "Righteousness exalteth a nation: but sin is a reproach to any people." (Proverbs 14:34).

The Bible thus gives us clear limitations and directions for taxes, military service and the police. John the Baptist, for example, told the tax inspectors and the police (One body served both as police and as military): "Exact no more than that which is appointed you" and "Do violence to no man, neither accuse any falsely; and be content with your wages." (Luke 3:12-14).

From Paul's statements, we can derive two essential thoughts:

1. The government can judge only what people do, not what they think. It is responsible for good or evil 'works', with doing. It is not the duty of the State to control all sin, only those sins whose activity can be observed and which damage public order, which the State has the responsibility to maintain and to protect.

2. The State may not distinguish between Christians and other people, i.e. between believers in different faiths, as long as they pursue their beliefs in a peaceful manner. Since God forbids partiality in legal matters, Christians must be punished just as severely as unbelievers when they break the law. The State cannot distinguish between Christians and members of other religious groups, for it may judge only on the basis of deeds.

Human rights are protective; they serve not so much to define the privileges of the individual, as to limit the powers of the State and of other institutions which deal with the lives of individuals. For this reason, Paul limits the State's duties to specific aspects of life, rather than giving it the right to regulate and penalize all of man's thought and life.

The State is not to be identified with society, as the socialist governments have done ever since the French Revolution. In such states, all aspects of society including the family and the Church are subject to the government. Society is more than the State. The State does not have authority over all parts of society.

On the Separation of Church and State

Just as the State may not dominate a church or a religion, it may not itself be subject to any church or religion. The separation of Church and State does not contradict the Christian faith, but arises naturally out of it, for the Bible makes it the duty of the State to enable people to live in peace, whatever they believe. It is the responsibility of the Church and of religion to point to eternity, to provide moral stability and to encourage man's relationship to God.

The historian Eugen Ewig therefore speaks of the Old Testament Doctrine of Two Powers. Eduard Eichmann, also an historian, writing about the Old Testament division of powers between priest and king, "Along with the sacred Scripture, Old Testament views have become common property of the Christian West."

Jesus confirmed this separation in the words, "Render to Caesar the things that are Caesar's, and to God the things that are God's." (Mark 12:17). Because this rule comes from God, Who is above the emperor, the religious institutions of God on earth, the organized People of God, are not above the emperor. The first priority is obedience to God, Who determines and limits what belongs to Caesar. Caesar has no authority to determine or limit what belongs to God. This does not, however, mean that the ruler is dependent on the Church, for God has given him the responsibility for all the people in his realm, not only for the members of one religious group.

The separation of Church and State does not mean that their duties never overlap, or that neither institution needs the other. On the contrary, the Church may advise the government and teach it God's law, as Jehoida taught Jehoash. "And Jehoash did that which was right in the sight of the LORD all his days wherein Jehoiada the priest instructed him." (2 Kings 12:2). It is sad that the modern Church has given up this critical office and prefers to howl with the pack.

The separation of Church and State does not become a war against Christianity until the State forgets its obligation to God's law and begins to persecute the faith.

God Knows no Partiality

Centuries ago in the Bible, God made fair judicial proceedings a human right. A just judge is necessary to determine justice, and God is the prototype of the just judge (Deut. 10:17-18; Psalm 7:9+12; 9:5; 50:6. See also Psalm 75:3+8), "for the LORD is a God of judgment" (Isaiah 30:18). He is the defender of justice. Those who judge fairly act in God's Name. The Old Testament tells of the just king Jehoshaphat, "And said to the judges, Take heed what ye do: for ye judge not for man, but for the LORD, who is with you in the judgment. Wherefore now let the fear of the LORD be upon you; take heed and do it: for there is no iniquity with the LORD our God, nor respect of persons, nor taking of gifts." (2 Chronicles 19:6-7).

A judge must be aware of the fact that God is observing him and stands by the innocent: "To turn aside the right of a man before the face of the most High, to subvert a man in his cause, the Lord approveth not." (Lamentations 3:35-36).

For this reason the Bible has many directions concerning just, humane judicial proceedings. Prosecution, for example, requires at least two witnesses (Numbers 35:30; Deuteronomy 17:6; 19:15; Mat. 18:16; John 8:17; Heb. 10:28; 1 Tim 5:18), so that the accusation is brought by two or three witnesses (Deut 10:17-18). Violent witnesses are not to be heard (Psalm 35:11).

The judge's ruling must be completely impartial (Deut. 1:16; 2 Chr. 19:7; Prov. 18:5; 24:23; Job 13:10; Col. 3:25; Eph 6:9), for God is Himself impartial. (Deut 10:17-18). Only wicked judges are partial (Isa. 10:1-2; 3:9).

The ruling is to be made without prejudice (1 Tim. 5:21), after the judge has carefully examined all the evidence (Deut 17:4). "Execute true judgment," God says in Zecharia 7:9; so that the ruling need not be repealed.

"If there be a controversy between men, and they come unto judgment, that the judges may judge them; then they shall justify the righteous, and condemn the wicked." (Deuteronomy 25:1). Bribery must not influence the judge's opinion. "A wicked man taketh a gift out of the bosom to pervert the ways of judgment." (Proverbs 17:23). God is the great example. "For the LORD your God is God of gods, and Lord of lords, a great God, a mighty, and a terrible, which regardeth not persons, nor taketh reward:" (Deuteronomy 10:17). "Wherefore now let the fear of the LORD be upon you; take heed and do it: for there is no iniquity with the LORD our God, nor respect of persons, nor taking of gifts." (2 Chronicles 19:7)

Scripture generally approves of gifts, when given to delight or to help others. Sometimes, the Bible realizes, gifts may even be necessary, if people are to achieve valid goals. The wise teacher tells us, "A man's gift maketh room for him, and bringeth him before great men." (Proverbs 18:16) and "A gift in secret pacifieth anger: and a reward in the bosom strong wrath." (Proverbs 21:14). Should an innocent person be confronted with corrupt officials, he has no hope of achieving perfectly legal goals. If he has no opportunity of overcoming this corruption in any other way, he can get his rights with gifts. Only when he buys injustice, is he himself guilty of corruption. He who is forced to bribe others will certainly strive to eliminate corruption, particularly in the Church, or in other religious institutions.

For this reason, there must be no double standard, such as one set of laws for the wealthy and another for the peasants. The Old Testament required the same penal system for both nationals and for foreign residents: (Exodus 12:49). "Ye shall do no unrighteousness in judgment: thou shalt not respect the person of the poor, nor honour the person of the mighty: but in righteousness shalt thou judge thy neighbour." (Leviticus 19:15). Because God defends "the cause of the poor," (Prov. 29:7) and " the cause of the poor and needy." (Prov. 31:8), Proverbs 31:8-9 enjoins us, "Open thy mouth for the dumb in the cause of all such as are appointed to destruction. Open thy mouth, judge righteously, and plead the cause of the poor and needy."

The Bible thus measures the justice of a country by its protection of the weak. Not only the condition of the wealthy or the ruling class, but also the condition of the simple citizens is to be considered. Not only the condition of the State Church is significant, but also the condition of the smaller Christian groups. Not only the condition of the judges with money and power to defend their rights, is important, but also the condition of the poor, the widows and the orphans in court.

God is the Creator and the Lord of all mankind. He wishes us to treat with each other as His image and His creatures—human beings dealing with human beings, not animals with animals.

Appendix 2: Faith is a Human Right

Thomas Schirrmacher. "Glauben ist ein Menschenrecht". ai-Journal (Journal of Amnesty International Germany) 8/2000: 6-9

In many countries of the world, people still suffer persecution and discrimination, because they belong to a particular religion. Religious liberty and human rights are very closely related to each other – countries which restrict religious freedom normally transgress against other human rights, as well.

Donato Lama, a Catholic Philippino, had been working in Saudi Arabia for fifteen years, when policemen, searching his home in October 1995, found a photo of him at his devotions. Accused of evangelising, he was arrested and incarcerated without contact to the outside world, fettered and beaten. In December 1996, he was condemned to a year and a half prison and seventy lashes of the whip.

In its bi-annual statistic for 2000, the Christian organisation Open Doors designated Saudi Arabia the country with the least religious freedom. A 1999 report by the US government on religious liberty says of Saudi Arabia: "Freedom of religion does not exist. Islam is the official religion and all citizens must be Muslims. The Government prohibits the public practice of other religions. Private worship by non-Muslims is permitted. ... Under Shari'a (Islamic law), upon which the Government bases its jurisprudence, conversion by a Muslim to another religion is considered apostasy. Public apostasy is a crime punishable by death if the accused does not recant." (www.state.gov/g/drl/irf) Even if few are actually convicted for converting Moslems – such cases are seldom made public – this law breaks Article 18 of the Universal Declaration of Human Rights (UNO, 1948), which explicitly includes the right to change religion. Christians are particularly threatened by Saudi intolerance towards other religions. The majority of Christians in Saudi Arabia are foreign guestworkers. Catholic and Evangelical Philipinos, especially, are frequently swindled, and imprisoned for months, tortured and deported.

Article 18 of the Universal Declaration of Human Rights (UNO, 1948)

"Everyone has the right to freedom of thought, conscience and religion; this right includes freedom to change his religion or belief, and freedom, either alone or in community with others and in public or private, to manifest his religion or belief in teaching, practice, worship and observance."

Not only non-Moslems suffer persecution – Islamic groups which do not agree with the Hanbalic school, such as Shiites and the Islamic sects, are also attacked by the religious police 'Muttawwa'. Such persecution of religious groups other than the state religion occurs in many countries. Another universal trend can be observed in Saudi Arabia, as well. Cases dealing with religious liberty are frequently left up to the secret police instead of being taken to court.

In states which limit religious liberties, other human rights are frequently ignored, as well. There is a close relationship between the two. Millions suffer infringements of their human rights simply because they belong to a certain religious group.

Religious freedom is a fundamental human right. Article 2 of the Universal Declaration of Human Rights condemns discrimination due to race, color, gender, language, political convictions or religion. Article 18 defines the contents of freedom of thought, conscience and religion (see above).

Human rights and religious liberty have a common origin. The first human rights catalogues were composed in France in opposition to a tyrannical church. In the United States, they were drafted primarily by men who had fled religious persecution in Europe. The demand for religious liberty has thus strongly influenced the development of the idea of human rights.

For many years, the issue of religious freedom was overshadowed by the occupation with Communism. Since the fall of the Soviet Union, however, Islamic states which persecute their citizens on religious grounds have attracted attention.

Not only Christians are affected. The Baha'is suffer relentless persecution in many Islamic states. This new religion, which developed out of Shiite Islam, has been almost eradicated in Iran, the country of its origin. In other countries, such as Egypt, its members are oppressed in every way possible. In Turkmenistan, the Baha'is lost their registration in 1997, because they could no longer exhibit five hundred Turkmenien members, and are no longer allowed to hold worship services. In June 1999, the members of the Baha'i center, Ashgabat, were warned by government officials against distributing religious literature. The Baha'is represent the most heavily persecuted religious group in the world.

In Pakistan, blasphemy against Islam or Mohammed is punishable by death. Due to their beliefs, Christians are always in danger of being accused of blasphemy. In May of this year, the brothers Rasheed and Saleem Masih were condemned to thirtyfive years of prison and high fines, because they are alleged to have spoken of Islam and Mohammed disrespectfully.

The infringement of religous freedom, which takes on many forms, is not always carried out by the State. Religious people are especially opposed to groups different from the dominant faith of their society and governments often tolerate such persecution. India and Pakistan are examples. Ayub Masih has survived two attempts on his life after fanatic Moslems had sworn to kill him. All fourteen Christian families in his home village in Pakistan had to flee and hide. Ayub Masih is less afraid of the government than of Islamic extremists, since two Christians aquitted by the courts have already been murdered.

Countries without a state religion also persecute believers. In China, Christians have been arrested and condemned to long imprisonment. Members of Charismatic or unorthodox groups are condemned without due course of law to 're-education throug labor'. In July 2000, the religious group Falun Gong was outlawed. Since then, thousands have been arrested for practicing their faith or for protesting against the prohibition. Many have been condemned to prison for up to eighteen years. At the same time, the government has increased its supervision of other illegal religous groups, including Christian groups not belonging to the two churches officially sanctioned by the State. Outlawed groups include many Evangelical churches and Roman Catholic churches which do not wish to join the independent Chinese Catholic church. According to estimations, there are some sixty million Protestants in home churches and about eight million Roman Catholics in the undergrounds. In Tibet, where the Chinese authorities persecute Buddists, hundreds of Buddist nuns and monks are in prison.

In Cuba, Evangelical churches are frequently visited by the secret police, who want to prevent evangelistic activities. It is illegal to speak about the faith in public, church buildings may not be built or repaired, private meetings are not allowed. In spite of these difficulties, experts estimate that there are 10,000 home churches in Cuba. The Vietnamese government attacts native Christians in a massive propaganda campaign. A major target is the 150,000 to 300,000 Hmong who were converted in a revival beginning in 1985. The government wants to force these believers to return to their native religion, since the Vietnamese Constitution of 1992 limits religious liberty to the right to practice one's national religion.

One form of religious limitation is the forced registration of religious groups, such as in Turkmenistan. In its 'Concerns in Europe', Amnesty International reports a wave of police raids on Protestant churches. Adventist and Baptist worship services are interrupted, religious groups are dissolved and clergymen are fined. Officially registered religious groups enjoy liberty, but non-registered groups face all sorts of chicanery. To obtain registration, a group must overcome several hurdles. One problem is the requirement that the group include at least five hundred adult Turkmenish citizens as members. At the moment, only the Russian Orthodox Church and Sunni Moslems are approved. The Jehovah's Witnesses are also under pressure: a nineteen year old Witness, Kurban Sakirow was condemned to two years in prison in April of 1999, because he refused to serve in the military because of his faith.

Religious persecution does not always originate with the State. Especially in Latin American countries with drug mafias or guerilla armies, local bosses persecute believers. In Peru, Christians who protest against the mafia, the drug business or state terrorism, live in great danger. Seven hundred pastors have been murdered, and no one knows how many laymen have been killed. Many innocent Christians have also been imprisoned as terrorists.

Columbian Christians are also endangered. A liberation army kidnapped 150 participants in a Catholic mass in May of this year. Nineteen of these people have still not been released. Since Protestant free churches are often the only social institutions which refuse to pay protection money or to plant narcotics, the mafia murders their pastors and destroys their churches. Many Christians have fled into the cities, but revival in the endangered areas provides new victims.

Religiously motivated human rights activists and social workers are constantly threatened when they come to the aid of persecuted or discriminated minorities. In July, Amnesty International instituted a program to support Dionisio Vendresen, who has received several threats on his life. He is the regional coordinator of the ecclesiastical organisation 'Commisao Pastoral der Terra' (CPT) in the Brazilian state Paraná. The organisation combats the increasing violence in the region and aids victims of violence in legal matters.

As many Christian organisations are mainly involved with persecuted Christians, they are criticised for neglecting other religions. A debate in the German Parliament over the persecution of Christians degenerated into a dispute on the question of whether dealing with the persecution of Christians meant that members of other religions do not suffer persecution or whether Christians are more important than others. In realiy, protection of

Christians' rights to religious liberty has always increased the protects of others.

In the United States, the activities of Christian organisations have succeeded in creating a committee of representative of many religions and human rights organisations, which annually reports on the religious liberty in the whole world. Christian engagement thus serves all religions. The theology of all Christian confessions (with few exceptions) makes religious liberty for all beliefs a fundamental tenet of our faith. Religious persecution concerns not only Christians, but probably half of the victims are Christians.

Critics constantly insist that persecution is due to the intensive missionary work of Evangelicals in the Second and Third Worlds. As long as evangelistic efforts are carried out by persuasion in a peaceful way, they are protected by religious freedom The World Evangelical Alliance – the international umbrella organisation of Evangelicals – is quite aware that the present increase in persecution against Christians can be explained by the enormous growth of Evangelical churches due to missions in countries in which human rights infringements are common. The number of Chinese Christians has grown to about fifty five million. Religious liberty is inseparable from the right to evangelise. In Germany the law considers the right to the peaceful propagation of one's own faith (the right to missions) as a fundamental element of the right to one's own convictions.

All people world wide, whether religious or not, should join together to acheive religious liberty and human rights for all. Religious liberty cannot be disconnected and should be available to all. Where it is threatened, all suffer.

Appendix 3: A response to the high counts of Christian martyrs per year (2011)

First published as „A Response to the high counts of Christian martyrs per year". International Journal of Religious Freedom 4 (2011) 2: 9-13, https://www.iirf.eu/site/assets/files/92225/ijrf_vol5-2.pdf and as „A Response to the high counts of Christian martyrs per year". S. 37-42 in: William D. Taylor u. a. (Hg.). Sorrow and Blood. Pasadena (CA): William Carey Library, 2012. ISBN 978-0-87808-472-2

For many years one number has been provided every year to report on the annual number of Christian martyrs. This is provided by the "Status of Global Mission." The number is quoted by various institutions but only produced by one institution. At present it is most frequently quoted by the papal missions agency "Aid to the Church in Need". It reports 130,000 – 170,000 martyrs per year but does not conduct any of its own investigations.

This number is released every year in the *International Bulletin for Missionary Research*.[362] In 2010 the number stood at 178,000, for 2009 176,000,[363] and for 2011 it was corrected to 100,000.[364] As a yearly changing number people think it is the number of martyrs of the given year, but actually it is said to be the average number per year of the last full decade (eg 1990-2000, 2000-2010).

The commentary provided with the "Global Status of Mission" itself indicates that this number is the most quoted figure from this table.[365] A number of this magnitude is widespread through the books *World Christian Encyclopedia*, *World Christian Trends*, *Atlas of Global Christianity* and the electronic *World Christian Database*.

I find it difficult to criticize this number on account of its widespread use, particularly due to the facts that it comes from reputable researchers and good friends. However, as an academic I have too often had to answer

---

[362] www.internationalbulletin.org.
[363] "Status of Global Mission, 2011", see http://ockenga.gordonconwell.edu/ockenga/globalchristianity/resources.php.
[364] "Status of Global Mission, 2011." *International Bulletin of Missionary Research* 35 (1011) 1: 29, line 28; cf. Commentary "Christianity 2011: Martyrs and the Resurgence of Religion." Ibid., p. 28.
[365] Ibid., p. 28.

for such numbers before secular colleagues, politicians around the world, the German or European parliament, and journalists to just allow our institute (the International Institute for Religious Freedom) simply assume them.

Since by many secular, Christian, and among them also Evangelical[366] researchers and specialists the figure is 1. viewed to be too high, and 2. on the basis of numerous factors viewed to be a number that cannot even be collected, it would be desirable to have a precise account of the basis of comprehensive research upon which the number is compiled. Furthermore, it would be desirable to know which scientific standards are followed in the process and how research colleagues' conformity can be reviewed. All of this is not available – even the comprehensive presentation in *World Christian Trends* nowhere mentions the source of the data and which criteria were used in producing the estimates.[367]

But in the present media landscape in which we find ourselves, it is natural that someone with even a roughly estimated number has an advantage over an individual who says that the number cannot be reliably estimated at the present time.

The role of civil wars

According to the reports of its authors, the figure of 156,000 – 178,000 martyrs per year is an average number per year for the ten years 1990-2000.[368] In the process one has to recognize - without its being expressly stated - that the vast portion of the 1.6 million martyrs over a period of 10 years comes from the civil wars in southern Sudan and in Rwanda. Let us suppose one were to use even a broader definition of Christian persecution ("martyrs in the widest possible sense" [369]). Still, the extent to which Rwanda can be included at all, and the share of deaths in southern Sudan that can be traced back to the persecution of Christians by Muslims and not seen either affecting animists or originating with brutalizing southern Sudanese parties to the civil war, is at least disputed.

For the ten-year period 2000-2010, southern Sudan and Rwanda no longer count. The mammoth share of the amount of 10 x 100,000 comes under the civil war in the Democratic Republic of the Congo (DRC). Ad-

---

[366] Eg. http://www.persecution.net/faq-stats.htm.
[367] David Barrett, Todd Johnson. *World Christian Trends*. Pasadena (CA=: William Carey Library, 2001. chapter 16.
[368] "Christianity 2011: Martyrs and the Resurgence of Religion." Ibid., p. 28.
[369] Ibid., p. 28.

mittedly there were many Christians who died there, but that they died *because* they were Christians is not something that is defended by anyone in the literature. Let us suppose that there were 900,000 martyrs estimated for the DRC. The remaining 100,000 martyrs per year over 10 years would then move one far closer to an exceedingly lower number.

What I criticize above all is that nowhere is the composition of the figure presented according to countries. This would allow the main countries to be recognized and discussed, eg Congo. It would then be especially easy to see the one or two countries to which the high number could be traced back. I also criticize the fact that no discussion about these one or two difficult-to-classify-situations can occur.

Not every Christian who dies in a civil war like one in the Congo can simply be counted. An estimate is made about which portion of the Christians killed actually died as martyrs. This share then has to be discussed and justified. But instead of this, nowhere can it be found which portion was estimated, much less how the estimate was made. All that is said is that it is "a substantial proportion" of the 5.4 million in the Congo. A 10% increase in the number of martyrs in the Congo, however, would translate into an increase of the total number of 100,000 by 54,000 martyrs, a jump of over 50%! If 10% less than the unknown percentage in Congo were to be estimated, that would be 54,000 fewer annually, which means that the figure would shrink by over 50% from 100,000 to 46,000! This means that de facto the entire number of martyrs worldwide is decided by the estimate of the share of martyrs found among the victims of unrest in Congo.

Regarding definition

I see a general contradiction between the definition given by the Status of Global Mission, that martyrs are "believers in Christ . . . in a situation of witness," and the statement of "defining and enumerating martyrs in the widest possible sense."

An intra-Christian, theological definition will always be much tighter than a sociological one. As a sociologist of religion, I definitely see that a very broad number may be chosen that does not take into account whether the murdered Christian is a baby, a poor excuse for a churchgoer, or a sectarian of some sort. I personally consider the "situation of witness" to be unnecessary. If a church is blown up in Egypt and 20 people are killed in the process, this is considered Christian persecution even if the 20 people killed were only interested guests.

My broadest political definition would be the following: "Christians who are killed and who would not have been killed had they not been Christians." However, even if this definition is used as a basis, I would by far not come up to the 170,000 or 100,000 Christian martyrs per year.

More than 50 martyrs a day?

Events where 20 or 50 Christians killed are nowadays not only widely reported on in the Christian world. Rather, in some countries such as Germany this would as a rule even appear on the front page of newspapers. Experts who deal with the question of the persecution of Christians hear about this in any case. No one would say that this happens every day. However, even if we assume that there is an event with 50 murdered Christians every day, that would amount to an annual number of only 18,250. Given 20 murdered Christians per day would be 7,300 – a number which I consider more realistic.

It might be pointed out that there have been and are events that generate a higher yearly average than than 50 per day. Indeed that is true, but these are individual events spread out over years. I know of the following countries for which this applies in the recent years: Indonesia, India, Iraq, and Nigeria. The point is that these events hardly overlap with each other. Stated otherwise: In years past these horrible events have occurred selectively within a period of 1-3 years and in the years thereafter were superseded by other main events in other countries. Again stated alternatively: As a general rule, an event with more than 100 Christian martyrs in a country occurs one time a year somewhere in the world.

The strange numbers that arise when one simply makes a rough estimate is demonstrated when a grading is made in the 'World Christian Database' countries according to the annual number of martyrs, whereby the average over the last 50 years was taken (beginning in 1960).

In Denmark and Finland there are said to be 15 martyrs per year, while in Sweden there were 19, in Switzerland 20, in the Netherlands 39, in Australia 45, in Canada 76, in Great Britain 149, and, believe it or not, in Germany 192. In all of these Protestant countries, there are no known martyrs and under no circumstances 50 times the number given since 1960.

That the high numbers are difficult to comprehend and are traceable to liberal estimates of the share of Christian martyrs killed as a result of warfare and civil war also applies to the numbers for historic cases. Were there really 1,000,000 martyrs at the hands of the National Socialists? No researcher of National Socialism (among whom I count myself with two

Appendix 3: A response to the high counts of Christian martyrs ... 135

dissertations) would attest to that. Admittedly there were millions of Christians who died in World War II, not, however, because they were persecuted as Chrsitians. Among true Christian martyrs are those Christians who were killed on account of their Christian resistance or as clerics or representatives of religious communities. Their destiny has been thoroughly researched, their stories have been recorded in biographical encyclopedias, and a curriculum vitae is available for almost every such individual. This notwithstanding, there is still a total of only a few thousand and not 1 million.

Are there so many martyrs among the dead in civil wars and other warfare?

I want to make one further comparison which leads me to believe that both numbers, the 170,000 and the 100,000, can be questioned. According to statistics of the World Health Organization, there were 184,000 victims of warfare and civil war in 2004.[370] And the number of martyrs is supposed to be just as large, without experts' immediately being able to list the cases which comprise these numbers? One can list all warfare and civil war in a year and make it clear how this number of 184,000 victims is composed. If the number of martyrs is just as large, how can the events not be likewise listed and added together more or less in one's head? How does it happen that far too few large events come to mind even to the experts which would be able to explain the high numbers?

On the road to research an actual number for a previous year

How high, then, is the actual annual number of Christian martyrs? I have occupied myself with this for years and have probably discussed this with every known expert from all large denominations and beyond who has anything to say about it. Let me put to one side for the time being the sheer difficulty of producing a definition of "martyr". Even if a concrete definition is set, experts strongly differ with respect to individual countries. Were the 'missing Christians' of North Korea killed decades ago or are they still living in camps and currently being killed?

If one asks for the total number worldwide, practically no one wagers an estimate. Additionally, everyone agrees that an average is confusing. Ra-

---

[370] World Health Organisation. *The Global Burden of Disease*. Geneva: WHO, 2008. p. 74, see http://www.who.int/topics/global_burden_of_disease/en/. Comp. the information of 171,000 for 2002 in the map among the atlas collection representing the actual world: http://www.worldmapper.org/display_extra.php?selected=484.

ther, the number of martyrs strongly fluctuates from year to year. For that reason the number has to be newly ascertained every year. Anyway, whoever hears a statistic for 2010 assumes that this is not an average value for 1990-2000, but rather that some institution has concretely researched the number for 2010 and has documented or at least has realistically estimated it on the basis of reports.

Overall I am of the opinion that we are far from having a reliable report of the number of martyrs annually. The International Institute for Religious Freedom will continue to address this issue, and wants to contribute to a fair and open universal discussion.

What we need is a database in which for any year we could enter all the known, larger cases so that at the end of the year we not only have a useable estimate, but rather a situation where given the list everyone can investigate the estimate's resilience.

Appendix 4: Religious Freedom and the Persecution of Christians

This article appeared in the Evangelische Verantwortung, Issue 2/2013, the journal of the 'Protestant Working Group' of the CDU/CSU, the party of Germany's present chancellor

Spiegel magazine recently ran an article with the title "Merkel at the Church Assembly: 'Christianity is the most persecuted Religion'" upon the occasion of the German Chancellor's words of greeting at the Fall Synod of the Protestant Church in Germany (EKD). Many newspapers and commentaries were indignant. And the indignation about Merkel's statement appeared for many to be greater than that about the persecution of Christians itself. I would have at least expected statements in the media such as: "Indeed, the persecution of Christians is widespread around the world, and there are far too many Christians who die, but one should also think about . . ." The way it is left, however, gives the impression that the reaction would have been different if another religion besides Christianity had been mentioned.

I can above all not follow the argumentation which is often heard that such a statement is not permissible because it disparages other religions or means that their persecution is less evil. We continually say that the abuse of women occurs more frequently than the abuse of men. But with that statement we are not saying that the abuse of men is a good thing! Whoever detects that the frequency of desecration of Jewish graves is above-average does not thus find desecration of other graves to be a good thing or a less severe matter. And if there are rankings for democracy, freedom of the press, corruption, racism, hostility towards women and their victims, then why not for religious freedom and related victims? In my book *Racism* I document that globally the most widespread forms of racism are forms of racism against Jews, Sinti and Roma, and against dark-skinned individuals. However, in so doing I am not lessening expressions of racism towards others. "Every persecuted individual suffers - regardless of which religion he belongs to," stated Wenzel Michalski, the head of Human Rights Watch (HRW) in Germany). And in the newpaper *Die Welt* it was recently stated that the German Federal Government should work for the protection of all threatened minorities. But that is what this German administration is doing more than practically any other government in the world! At the last German Federal Parliament debate (Bundestag), I sat in the official visitors' gallery among Baha'i, Alevites, and Sufis who were thankful for the debate.

The German Chancellor Angela Merkel correctly stated in her welcoming words at the Synod that the global situation of religious freedom can generally be described as negative and also clearly stated that religious freedom is to be protected in Germany and around the world as "an elemental human right." Whoever accuses the Chancellor of only wanting to protect Christians did not listen to the Chancellor when she spoke at the Synod or any other time she has spoken on this topic.

As far as I am able to tell from looking at it, no one has said, in any case, that her statements are generally untrue. A number of people have said – and that would come closer to the truth – that we do not have enough data and that there should have been more restraint with respect to the available data or that here and there one should differentiate more. One can and should certainly wrangle more over this: For example, I myself have used scientific arguments to contradict the oft mentioned number of 100,000 Christian martyrs worldwide – this number is supposedly five to ten times too high. However, whoever doubts the statements made by the Chancellor as such should not deal with her short assertion but rather with the specialists and studies the Chancellor references in making such statements.

For instance one could look at the new comprehensive study entitled *Christianophobia* (Oxford 2012) by Rupert Shortt. The work contains the literal statement made by the Chancellor. One could take the August 2011 report of the PEW Forum on Religion & Public Life, "Rising Restrictions on Religion," according to which no religion experiences more oppression in more countries than Christians, namely in 130 countries, the updates for 2012 and 2013 give even higher numbers. One could look at publications of the International Institute for Religious Freedom, which I have the privilege to direct. While it is indeed Evangelical in its orientation, its accredited specialist journal, the *International Journal of Religious Freedom*, has authors from all religions as well as non-religious researchers who publish in it.

I am arguably not completely innocent, since in 2010 in my keynote speech at the 47th Federal Annual Meeting of the Protestant Working Group of the CDU/CSU (the CDU is Mrs Merkel's party) entitled "Persecution and Discrimination of Christians in the 21st Century" (see *Evangelische Verantwortung* 11+12, pp. 5-10), before which the German Chancellor gave a clear indication of support for religious freedom and expressed opposition to the persecution of Christians. I made similar statements which I still stand by. Moreover, the data which has been amassed on the state of religious freedom in the last three years support me on this. For that reason, I would like to briefly sketch the salient points.

Christianity on the sunny side and on the dark side of religious freedom

Christianity enjoys the sunny side of religious freedom more than the other large world religions, but the same applies to the dark side. No other large religious community has such a high percentage of members who live in a realm of religious freedom. That naturally has to do with the fact that almost all earlier "Christian" nations, i.e., nations with a majority Christian population, now grant religious freedom and are predominantly functioning democracies. A certain exception to the rule is seen in a number of Orthodox countries which find themselves in midfield between democracy and an autocratic state. For that reason, religious freedom is partially limited even if no one dies there for his or her faith.

On the other hand, there is no other large religious community which features such a high percentage of adherents who are continually affected by harassment all the way to threats made to life and limb. And even among the smaller religions there are only a few which have comparable percentages. For instance there are the Baha'i, who largely owe this situation to their founding in Iran and their strong expansion within the Islamic world, or to the Jehovah's Witnesses, whose conscientious objection to military service has led to their imprisonment in many places. And even for them the percentage of adherents *killed* does not seem to be higher than for Christianity at large.

Recently the PEW Foundation, located in Washington, has brought together all available international surveys on religious freedom in three studies from 2009, 2011, and 2012. In the process, they came to results similar to that of the Hudson Institute's Center for Religious Freedom, likewise located in Washington, and our International Institute for Religious Freedom: In 64 countries around the world, i.e., one third of all countries, there is no religious freedom or only a very limited form of religious freedom. Unfortunately, these 64 countries account for two-thirds or, more precisely, 70% of the world population. There were 24 countries involved where armed conflict resulted in more than 1,000 deaths and where religious affiliation played a central role. As a result, there were 18 million refugees worldwide.

Let us look more closely at the 64 countries with respect to the two largest world religions: The case of a large number of Muslims living in a non-Muslim country with limited religious freedom is only found in India. Conversely: A large number of Christians living in a country with a limited level of religious freedom where the majority of the population is Christian is only found in Russia.

If we disregard India and Russia for a moment, the difference between the situation faced by Christians and Muslims quickly becomes apparent: the remaining 700 million Muslims who live in countries with limited religious freedom or no religious freedom live in Islamic countries.

In contrast, the remaining 200 million Christians living in countries with limited religious freedom or no religious freedom live as minorities in non-Christian countries, spread out predominantly over communist countries and in Islamic countries (as well as in India).

This means that Muslims actually enjoy much less religious freedom than Christians. However, since most of them live in Muslim countries, they only notice this in those rare cases where they seek to break out of their religion, for instance if they wish to become atheists or Christians, or if they do not belong to religious orientations tolerated by the state or to spin-offs, as was the case for Shiites recently slain in Pakistan.

Christian Persecution without Parallel

In which sense does the frequency and massive extent of persecution of Christians justify our focusing especially on them with regard to this topic? Is it true that the persecution of Christian minorities around the world has taken on such a magnitude that the sheer numbers involved foist themselves upon us as far as the question of religious freedom is concerned?

It is at the same time difficult to lump everything in the world together or to define the point at which an individual begins to be persecuted or suffer discrimination. Does it already occur at the point when an individual only has the justified concern that his or her own church could be set on fire during a worship service, or does it only occur at that point when the church is actually set on fire? Is an individual only persecuted if religion is the sole reason for harassment, or is it also the case when religion is only one element among many?

Violence against Christians ranges from the murder of nuns in India to the torching of churches in Indonesia, the battering of priests in Egypt, and the torture of a recalcitrant pastor in Vietnam, all the way to children being

Appendix 4: Religious Freedom and the Persecution of Christians

cast out of their families in Turkey or Sri Lanka if they go to Christian worship services.

Hindu fundamentalism is also directed against Muslims. However, regarding the 50,000 affected Christians from the Indian state of Orissa (who were driven from their homes in 2008/2009, whereby some 500 people died, and with those remaining still living in tents), there is hardly a parallel to be found anywhere in the world.

Regarding the 100,000 Christians on the Maluka Islands of Indonesia who were displaced by force in 2000/2001 (whereby several thousand deaths occurred), there is at the present no parallel. In the Sudan and Nigeria there were many Christians who likewise died – as complicated as the detailed situation in these countries at the border between Islam and Christianity in Africa might be.

The displacement of hundreds of thousands of Christians from Iraq between the years 2007 and 2009 has no parallel in the religious world at the moment. Above all, at the current time, very unfortunately this is finding its continuation in Syria. This is due to the fact that this displacement is only one building block within a larger development. Before our eyes, the share of long-established Oriental and Catholic churches in core Islamic countries is drastically shrinking. Every time that I meet with the Ecumenical Patriarch of the Orthodox Church in Istanbul, he mentions a even smaller number of members of his church in Turkey where once millions of Christians lived. The Syrian-Orthodox patriarch reported something similar about Syria to me recently which is alarming, indeed also even to a lesser degree about about Lebanon. Even in Egypt, the sole core Islamic country in which an Oriental church has been maintained with millions of members, the most recent developments have led to fears that the centuries long truce has come to an end. Christians in Syria are suffering tremendously and their future looks dismal, regardless of which party wins.

Furthermore, practically every day we receive reports from churches which have been set on fire or have been bombed, whereby Christians die. They are seldom from Nepal, Sri Lanka, and India but more frequently from Pakistan and Indonesia and continually, however, from Egypt, Iraq, Syria, or Nigeria. And quite frequently the number of fatalities lies above 20, occasionally over 50. It is increasingly the case that such reports also make their way into the German media. As far as I know there is nothing comparable with respect to other religions. At most, the fatalities as a result of inner-Islamic conflicts could be mentioned.

Whoever wants to outdo these dramatic events of the 21st century by referring to historical events would have to go back to the persecution of Jews in the Third Reich or the bloody turmoil between Hindus and Muslims during the time of the founding of India and Pakistan or – again as part of the persecution of Christians – the mass murders conducted by Stalin or Mao.

Let me choose an additional example. In many countries it is dangerous to leave Islam, regardless of whether one goes in the direction of atheism, Baha'I, or into Islamic belief orientations which are viewed as sects. However, leaving Islam far most frequently occurs in the direction of the other large world religion, Christianity. The German magazine *Der Spiegel* has written: "Since the influence of fundamentalists has increased, the pressure on Christian minorities has intensified. The Protestant Church in Germany (EKD) holds Christians to be the most frequently persecuted faith community in the world: "Even more threatened than traditional Christians, however, are Muslims who convert to Christianity." Further, "Apostasy, that is, falling away from Islam, can be punishable by death according to Islamic law – and in Iran and Yemen, Afghanistan, Somalia, Mauretania, Pakistan, Qatar, and Saudi Arabia the death penalty still applies." Remarkably, "The Egyptian Minister of Religion defends the lack of a death penalty for converts from Islam Egyptian law – because apostasy from Islam is already the equivalent of high treason" (http://www.spiegel.de/spiegel/print/d-69174713.html).

Four negative Developments

In the following, four negative developments will be named, which are increasingly limiting religious freedom and in particular the freedom of Christians.

1. Fundamentalism

In what is undisputedly the first place – especially when it comes to Christians killed - one finds fundamentalism, in particular violent fundamentalist movements in Islam, Hinduism (above all in India), and in Buddhism (above all in Sri Lanka). The term fundamentalism no longer means a certain conservative view of the Holy Scriptures and also does not mean that which is propagated in many areas of the media. The well-established term fundamentalism found in academic sociology of religion does not refer to any movement that makes a truth claim. In that case there would almost only be fundamentalists in the world outside the West, and the most tolerant people would be those who have no religion or truth claim (reality deconstructs this argument). Instead, fundamentalism means wanting "to push through a truth claim by force" and in particular has been coined since 1979, when Ayatollah Khomeini forced his claim to truth upon all people and has forced that claim to the present day.

An individual who holds something to be absolutely right or wrong is not dangerous due to that fact. It first becomes a problem for the society when the idea is developed that he may force others to believe the same thing and do the same thing, and that the entire society has to function the way he considers to be right. And it is this sort of fundamentalism which has appeared in various world religions and which is responsible for the great number of Christian martyrs and for the victims representing other religions.

The main culprits are predominantly not governments or people groups. Rather, it is above all violent, fundamentalist movements, which in most cases fight against the governments of their countries of origin – Iran and Sri Lanka are likewise exceptions as are the Islamist movements in other countries tolerated or even supported by Saudi Arabia or Pakistan.

In addition to its direct influence, fundamentalism has set an additional devastating development into motion. This is due to the fact that precisely in heavily populated countries such as India, Indonesia, and Nigeria, in which the great world religions used to live together reasonably well in peace, fundamentalism stirs up unrest and fuels violence, as in the case of Hinduism in India or has often been the case with Islam in Indonesia. If relevant state authorities do not uncompromisingly move against it, a small minority within the religion – the number of such supporters of fundamentalism mostly ranges between 1 % and 5 % - can destabilize entire countries and can replace what has been a peaceful relationship among many millions of people with tension.

2. Religious Nationalism

Through globalization and the shifting of masses of people around the world, there are more and more countries where it is very difficult to maintain a sense of nationalism on common ancestry, common history, common language, or similar things. There are more and more countries and parties, which, in order to salvage nationalism or in order to gather the population behind them, have reached for the 'religion' card. A Turk is a Muslim, an inhabitant of Sri Lanka is Buddhist, an Indian is Hindu, and of late a Hungarian is best a Christian.

Religious Nationalism is not the fundamentalist variation which directly advocates violence. However, religious nationalism nevertheless is growing around the world, and belonging to a country is again often determined according to the majority religion. Religious nationalism is also the great danger in the 'Arabellion' occurring in Arab countries. The diverse Arab societies do not actually coalesce anything into one anymore. They are completely disjointed. That is why the following call is not unheard: "The only future that is possible for the country is one that is under the religious flag." In the process, however, all religious minorities and non-Muslims are ostracized or become second class citizens.

3. The displacement of long-established Christians from core Islamic countries

The third large development is the displacement of long-established Christians and Christian churches from core Islamic countries in the Islamic world. The Islamic world has in the meantime – with the exception of Southeast Asia – become almost completely devoid of Judaism; if the developments seen over the prior years continue, it will perhaps soon be Christian-free, with the exception of Southeast Asia.

The Example of Turkey: Overall in recent years there have only been few Christians who have been killed on account of their being Christian. The traditional Christian churches – for example the Greek Orthodox churches – are dying due to the relocation of young people and the educated. Young families have long since made their way to the West. When extrapolated for all the core Islamic countries, this is a dramatic development: With this type of Christianity, which if often linked to an ancient language (including the language Jesus used) and which preserves ancient cultural assets, it is not only churches which die out but old cultures as well. What the Copts pass on is largely Egyptian culture from the time before Islam conquered Egypt. The Copts pass on Christian culture prior to the time of Islam and Arabization and elements included in it from pre-Christian Egyptian culture.

This applies in a very similar manner to other religious minorities in the Islamic world, including Islamic minorities, such as the predominantly Turkish Alevites. They account for an estimated 13 % of the population of Turkey. However, they are not tolerated in Turkey, used to be severely persecuted, and new experience strong discrimination. Germany is their number one country of escape and destination. Since they do not hold to the Sharia and always grant more rights to women, they largely integrate themselves well in Germany. Similarly the Baha'I, originally from Iran, have more problems in all the core Islamic countries than do Christians due to discrimination, various disadvantages, and persecution. Many of them have, for that reason left, their home countries and headed in the direction of the West.

4. Limitations on religious freedom due to obligatory registration

The fourth global development to mention is the limitation on religious freedom due to obligatory registration. We have experienced an increasing problem in many countries around the world due to the fact that there are increasingly complex registration processes to deal with. It is above all the small religious communities which are under perpetual suspicion of being remotely controlled from outside the country, of conducting money laundering, or of being a danger to the internal peace of the country. In part, laws have been passed which apply to everyone, and that leads to a growing number of Christians around the world suddenly landing in the realm of illegality. The consequences are frequently that they are not allowed to own or lease buildings, that they are not able to offer theological training, that they have difficulty entering certain professions, are not able to work for the state, cannot study, and the like. Fortunately, the Special Rapporteur on freedom of religion or belief for the United Nations, Prof. Heiner Bielefeldt, has made the topic of registration a focal point for his activities.

From all of this it becomes clear: In a globalized world, the lack of religious freedom in other countries has an effect on us almost automatically: For example: at Coptic celebrations in December 2010 and January 2011 there were attacks on Coptic churches in Egypt with numerous fatalities. After that, there were serious threats against Coptic churches in Europe. What a lot of people miss is the following: A short time later, for the first time in many decades in Germany, worship services of an entire denomination took place under police protection! We live in a globalized world: Problems come to us.

Four positive Developments

At the same time, however, there are positive trends which are recognizable alongside the already described negative developments.

1. Ecumenical efforts against the persecution of Christians

The Global Example: In 2011 the Roman Catholic Church, the World Council of Churches, and the World Evangelical Alliance worked out a joint code of ethics for Christian mission: "Christian Witness in a Multi-Religious World." In this document it is set down that mission is always to respect the dignity of individuals and their human rights and must never employ force, state support, bribery, or psychological manipulation. This was the first joint document produced by these three largest Christian umbrella organizations, which together represent 95% of global Christianity. It is not coincidental that this document was produced by the distress of the persecution of Christians and is a response to anti-conversion laws around the world.

The Example of India and Bangladesh: In India the Catholic Church, the National Council of Churches, and the National Evangelical Alliance combined to form the umbrella organization named the National United Christian Forum in India and in Bangladesh named The United Forum of Churches Bangladesh. In the respective countries they are to approach government with a single voice and jointly serve to awaken attention to the discrimination and persecution of Christians

The Example of Germany: The central synod of the Protestant Church of Germany (EKD) has recently established a specific Sunday as a day of commemoration and persecuted Christians. The German Bishops' Conference has reactivated the day of commemoration for martyrs on the second Christmas holiday (Boxing Day, December 26), which up to the time of the fall of the wall between East and West Germany had played an important role. The Evangelical-Lutheran Church in Württemberg, according to its tradition was always interested in the issue of the suffering of persecuted Christians, uses the same date but also recommends the date used by the EKD. Since 1996 the German Evangelical Alliance has followed an international date at the beginning of November for a worldwide day of prayer for persecuted Christians. Despite the various dates, all the organizations have met more than once, determined that they are all pursuing the same concern, and have decided as a symbolic expression of solidarity to jointly look for a country to have as a focal point for each liturgical year.

2. Political efforts against the persecution of Christians

In the political realm there have been great strides of progress which have been utilized for the cause of religious freedom in countries which are not free. An absolutely unusual story comes from Sinyo Harry Sarundajang, who unfortunately is almost only known in Indonesia:

Following international pressure, Sarundajang was sent by the Indonesian President to North Sulawesi in 2002, where on Ambon Islad, or more specifically the so-called Malukus, thousands of Christians had been killed by a heavily armed, 300-man strong jihad army going by the name of "Laskar Jihad." The province had become ungovernable, and Christians were, however, also entangled in the problem because many of them had supported the island's efforts at independence. Sarundajang was sent there as the Executive Governor – together with a contingent of marines consisting of thousands of soldiers in order to bring peace and to prepare for a normal gubernatorial election. As a committed Christian, who had the reputation of being immune to corruption, he visited all the Muslim leaders privately at home without police protection (on his orders the army remained in their barracks and on the ships) and sought out discussions with them. In addition, he visited the Christian leaders and said to them: "For peace, however, I expect that you give up support for the plans for independence." A related book with this story was written by the spiritual father of Laskar Jihad, Attamimy, praising Sarundajang. It contains an unbelievable foreword by the founder and supreme commander of the jihad army, Ka'far Umar Thalib. He wrote: "If I had met such a Christian earlier, I would have never started our army." After meeting Sarundajang he dissolved his army, plain and simple.

The Example of Turkey: In 2007 two Turkish Christians and one German Christian were brutally murdered in the Turkish city of Malatya. An essential reason that the case was not dropped, but rather that the influential individuals behind the acts were sought, lies in the fact that the German Embassy monitored the case and sent a representative to each day in court.

The Example of South Africa: The African branch of the International Institute for Religious Freedom (IIRF), in cooperation with political institutions, has formulated a new religious freedom law for South Africa which in the meantime has been put before the President for review and assessment. In the Constitution of the Republic of South Africa religious freedom is indeed mentioned, but it also states that a later law with constitutional status should govern the particulars. Should this political undertaking be successful, it could function as an example for all of Africa south of the Sahara.

The Example of Pakistan: A man in Pakistan, who was threatened with the death penalty on account of converting to Christianity, was brought out of the country and received asylum due to the fact that the topic was increasingly dealt with on the ground – by Western embassies, among others.

3. Scholarship in the cause of religious freedom

Persecutors of Christians have, thanks to increased information and documentation by scholars, fewer and fewer excuses if they maintain that claims of persecution are invented or exaggerated. The following is also important: In addition to state institutions, which collect data, such as the US Department of State, there are institutions which retain their independence so that their results are impartial beyond the shadow of a doubt.

An additional example: The growing international journal entitled the *International Journal for Religious Freedom* (*IJRF*), accredited by the Department of Higher Education and Training in South Africa, initially had trouble finding authors who wanted to or could subject their articles to peer review. Nevertheless, the number of researchers in all branches of study who occupy themselves with the removal of religious freedom in various contexts is growing strongly around the world. For that reason, it is becoming easier and easier to find expert articles.

A further example: Two statisticians of religion, Brian J. Grim, known as a leading researcher in the PEW Forum study yielding the report entitled *Global Restrictions on Religion*, and Roger Finke, sociology professor and director of the Association of Religion Data Archives, show in their book *The Price of Freedom Denied*[371] just how much religious freedom contributes to the peace and the continued existence of a society. Their basic thesis is simple: In countries with religious freedom, there is much more social peace than in countries without religious freedom. A limitation on religious freedom is often the reason for violent conflicts in the first place. Religious homogeneity does not guarantee freedom from conflict. Rather, it encourages apparent tensions.

The example of the Oslo Declaration: The Oslo Coalition on Freedom of Religion or Belief has worked out the *Oslo Declaration Missionary Activity and Human Rights: Recommended Ground Rules for Missionary Activities* in order to stimulate a global discussion. With financial support of the Norwegian Ministry of Foreign Affairs, the text was developed by scholars from numerous specialized areas, domestic and international experts, and representatives of churches and practically all non-Christian religions in Norway. The Declaration, which was also signed by Muslim associations, defines peaceful missionary efforts as an essential part of religious freedom

---

[371] Brian J. Grim, Roger Finke. The Price of Freedom Denied: Religious Persecution and Conflict in the Twenty-First Century. Cambridge: Cambridge University Press, 2010.

and consequently as an elementary human right. Simultaneously, the document expressly emphasizes the rights of those who are missionized.

4. Human rights organizations for religious freedom

Traditional human rights organizations are taking a stronger stand against the persecution of Christians, the persecution of other religious minorities, and they see the right to religious freedom to be a human right equivalent to, for example, freedom of the press or the prohibition on torture. For example, the Society for Threatened Peoples has made religious ethnic minorities a topic, while the International Society for Human Rights has made the fate of individuals a focus. Even the largest human rights organization, Amnesty International, which for a long time only unwillingly made specifically religious problems a topic or often gave the topic of freedom of religion step-motherly treatment, has more frequently changed its course, as the 2012 annual report demonstrates.

Selected Bibliography on Persecution of Christians[372]

David H. Adeney. "The Preparation of Missionaries to Cope with Political Change". pp. 49-53 in: Edwin L. Frizen, Wade T. Coggins (Ed.). Christ and Caesar in Christian Missions. William Carey Library: Pasadena (CA), 1979

Tokunboh Adeyemo. "Persecution: A Permanent Feature of the Church". pp. 23-36 in: Brother Andrew (Ed.). Destined to Suffer? African Christians Face the Future. Open Doors: Orange (CA), 1979

Tokunboh Adeyemo. "Persecution: A Permanent Feature of the Church". Evangelical Ministries/Ministères Evangélique (Association of Evangelicals of Africa and Madagascar) Mar-Aug 1985: 3-9

Tokunboh Adeyemo. De gemeente zal altijd vervolgd worden. n.d.

Walter Adolph (Ed.). Im Schatten des Galgens: Zum Gedächtnis der Blutzeugen in der nationalsozialistischen Kirchenverfolgung. Morus Verlag: Berlin, 1953 (Catholic Martyrs)

M. Searle Bates. Glaubensfreiheit: Eine Untersuchung. Church World Service: New York, 1947

Brother Andrew. The Ethics of Smuggling. Coverdale House Publ.: London, 1974

Bruder Andrew mit John und Elizabeth Sherill. Der Schmuggler Gottes. R. Brockhaus: Wuppertal, 1977[1]; 1978[2]; 1979[3]; 1980[Tb1]; 1981[Tb2]; 1982[Tb3]; 1984[Tb4]; 1986[Tb5]; 1988[Tb6]; 1999[Tb7]

Brother Andrew. Is Life So Dear? Thomas Nelson: Nashville (TN), 1974; Kingsway Publications: Eastbourne (GB), 1985

Bruder Andrew. Kampf um Afrika: Was uns die Presse verschweigt. R. Brockhaus: Wuppertal, 1978 [Engl. original Battle for Africa. Revell: Old Tappan (NJ), 1977]

Brother Andrew (Ed.). Destined to Suffer? African Christians Face the Future. Open Doors: Orange (CA), 1979

Brother Andrew. "How Should Christians Regard Persecution?". pp. 13-21 in: Brother Andrew (Ed.). Destined to Suffer? African Christians Face the Future. Open Doors: Orange (CA), 1979

Bruder Andrew. "Wir brauchen eine neue Sicht der leidenden Kirche". Geöffnete Türen. Rundbrief Geöffnete Türen (Frutigen, Schweiz). Febr 1980. pp. 1-3

Brother Andrew. A Time for Heroes. Vine Books: Ann Arbor (MI), 1988

Brother Andrew, Verne Becker. The Unforgettable Story of a Man Who Discovered the Adventure of the Calling. Moorings: Nashville (TN), 1996

Bruder Andrew. Der Auftrag für Bruder Andrew. Leuchter: Erzhausen, 1999

Bruder Andrew. Da änderte Gott seine Absichten ... weil sein Volk zu beten wagte. Offene Grenzen: Prilly (CH), 1994, 1998 [Engl. original And God Changed His Mind. Chosen Books: Old Tappan (NJ), 1990; Chosen Books: Grand Rapids (MI), 1990, 1999]

---

[372] Titles on religios liberty or human rights are only included in exceptional cases.

Bruder Andrew. Für Sie persönlich: 40 Botschaften aus 40 Jahren Dienst für die verfolgte Kirche. Open Doors/Offene Grenzen: Prilly (CH), n. d. (1994)

Norbert Brox. Zeuge und Märtyrer: Untersuchungen zur frühchristlichen Zeugnis-Terminologie. Studien zum Alten und Neuen Testament 5. Kösel: München, 1961

Armenien: Völkermord, Vertreibung, Exil, Menschenrechtsarbeit für die Armenier 1979-1987. Ed. by Tessa Hofmann and Gerayer Koutcharian for the Coordinating Group, Armenien der Gesellschaft für bedrohte Völker: Göttingen, 1987

Aurelius Augustinus. Scripta contra Donatista. Corpus scriptorum ecclesiasticorum Latinorum 51. Tempsky: Wien, 1908

Aurelius Augustinus. The writings against the Manichaeans and against the Donatists (Ed. von J. R. King und Chester D. Hartranft). A Select Library of the Nicene and Post-Nicene Fathers of the Christian Church (Ed. von Philipp Schaff). Series 1, Vol. 4 Wm. B. Eerdmans: Grand Rapids (MI), 1979 (Repr. from 1887) (in the Internet ccel.wheaton.edu/fathers2/ speziell /npnf1-04/npnf1-04-48.htm and on CDROM Christian Classics Ethereal Library 1998. CCEL/Wheaton College: Wheaton (IL), 1998; Edition 2000 available)

Sergej S. Averincev. Die Solidarität in dem verfemten Gott: Die Erfahrung der Sowjetjahre als Mahnung für die Gegenwart und Zukunft. Ed. by Peter Stuhlmacher. J. C. B. Mohr: Tübingen, 1996. 46 pp.

Emmanuel S. A. Ayee. "Persecution: A Bible Study Guide". Evangelical Ministries/Ministères Evangélique (Association of Evangelicals of Africa and Madagascar) Mar-Aug 1985: 1925

Greg L. Bahnsen. "Brother Andrew, The Ethics of Smuggling ...". The Journal of Christian Reconstruction 2 (1975/1976) 2 (Winter): Symposium on Biblical Law. pp. 164-169

Ann Ball mit Paul Marx, Stephen Dunham. The Persecuted Church in the Late Twentieth Century. Maginificat Press: Avon (NJ), 1990 (40 Countries, Catholic point of view)

Cal R. Bombay. Let my People Go! The true Story of Present-Day Persecution and Slavery. Multnomah Publ.: sisters (OR), 1998 (on slavery and martyrdom in Sudan)

Met Q. Castillo. The Church in Thy House. Alliance-Publishers: Malina (Philippinen), 1982

Bruder David, Dan Wooding, Sara Bruce. Gottes Schmuggler in China. R. Brockhaus: Wuppertal, 1981

David B. Barrett. World Christian Encyclopedia. Nairobi etc.: Oxford University Press, 1982

David B. Barrett, Todd M. Johnson. "Annual Statistical Table on Global Mission: 1997". International Bulletin of Missionary Research 21 (1997) 1 (Jan): 24-25

David B. Barrett, Todd M. Johnson. "Annual Statistical Table on Global Mission: 1998". International Bulletin of Missionary Research 22 (1998) 1 (Jan): 26-27

David B. Barrett, Todd M. Johnson. "Annual Statistical Table on Global Mission: 1999". International Bulletin of Missionary Research 23 (1999) 1 (Jan): 24-25, [also reproduced in in World Evangelization (Lausanne Committee) April 1999]

Selected Bibliography on Persecution of Christians 153

David Barrett, George T. Kurian, Todd M. Johnson. World Christian Encyclopedia: A Comparative Survey of Churches and Religions in the Modern World. 2 Bände. Oxford University Press: New York, Oxford usw., 2001

David B. Barrett, Todd M. Johnson. "Annual Statistical Table on Global Mission: 1999". International Bulletin of Missionary Research 23 (1999) 1 (Jan): 24-25

David B. Barrett, Todd M. Johnson. "Annual Statistical Table on Global Mission: 2000". International Bulletin of Missionary Research 24 (2000) 1 (Jan): 24-25

David B. Barrett, Todd M. Johnson. "Annual Statistical Table on Global Mission: 2001". International Bulletin of Missionary Research 25 (2001) 1 (Jan): 24-25

Walter Bauer. Griechisch-deutsches Wörterbuch zu den Schriften des Neuen Testaments ... Walter de Gruyter: Berlin, 1971^5. Sp. 973-978; Walter Bauer, Kurt und Barbara Aland. Griechisch-deutsches Wörterbuch zu den Schriften des Neuen Testaments ... Walter de Gruyter: Berlin, 1988^6. Col. 998-1002

Hans F. Bayer. Jesus' Predictions of Vindication and Resurrection. J. C. B. Mohr: Tübingen, 1986

Theofried Baumeister. Martyr invictus: Der Märtyrer als Sinnbild der Erlösung in der Legende und im Kult der frühen koptischen Kirche. Forschungen zur Volkskunde 46. Regensberg: Münster, 1972

Theofried Baumeister. "Märtyrer und Verfolgte im frühen Christentum". Concilium 19 (1983) 3: 169-173 = "Martyrdom and Persecution in Early Christianity". pp. 3-8 in: Johannes Baptist Metz, Edward Schillebeeckx (Ed.). Martyrdom Today. *op. cit.*

Theofried Baumeister. Die Anfänge der Theologie des Martyriums. Münsterische Beiträge zur Theologie 45. Aschendorff: Münster, 1980 [Dissertation Die Anfänge der Märtyrertheologie. Münster, 1976]

Theofried Baumeister. Genese und Entfaltung der altkirchlichen Theologie des Martyriums. Traditio christiana 8. Peter Lang: Bern, 1991

Ludwig Bertsch SJ. "Predigtgedanken". pp. 11-15 in: Gebetstag für die verfolgte Kirche 1992. Arbeitshilfen 99. Sekretariat der Deutschen Bischofskonferenz: Bonn, 1992

Gerhard Besier, Gerhard Ringshausen (Ed.). Bekenntnis, Widerstand, Martyrium: Von Barmen 1934 bis Plötzensee 1944. Vandenhoeck & Ruprecht: Göttingen, 1986

Gerhard Besier. "Bekenntnis - Widerstand - Martyrium als historisch-theologische Kategorie". S. 126-147 in: Gerhard Besier, Gerhard Ringshausen (Ed.). Bekenntnis, Widerstand, Martyrium: Von Barmen 1934 bis Plötzensee 1944. Vandenhoeck & Ruprecht: Göttingen, 1986

Gerhard Besier. Pfarrer, Christen und Katholiken". Neukirchener Verlag: Neukirchen, 1992

Gerhard Besier. Der SED-Staat und die Kirchen. 3 Vols. Neukirchener Verlag: Neukirchen, 1993, 1995, 1995

Gerhard Besier. "Der SED-Staat und die evangelischen Kirchen". Beilage zum HMK-Kurier 5/1995. reproduced by: Hilfsaktion Märtyrer Kirche: Uhldingen, 1997. 12 pp.

Johannes Beutler. Martyria: Traditionsgeschichtliche Untersuchungen zum Zeugnisthema bei Johannes. Frankfurter theologische Studien 10. Knecht: Frankfurt, 1972

Johannes Beutler. "martyreo", "martyria", "martys" Col. 958-973 in: Exegetisches Wörterbuch zum Neuen Testament. 2 Vols. Vol. 2. W. Kohlhammer: Stuttgart, 1992²

Peter Beyerhaus. Die Bedeutung des Martyriums für den Aufbau des Leibes Christi (Eph. 1,22-23). Orthodoxe Rundschau 16 (1984): 4-24 (Special edition)

Peter Beyerhaus. Die Bedeutung des Martyriums für den Aufbau des Leibes Christi. Diakrisis 25 (1999) 3: 131-141

Peter Beyerhaus. Martyrdom - Gate to the Kingdom of Heaven". pp. 163-179 in: God's Kingdom and the Utopian Error. Tyndale: Wheaton (IL), 1992

Peter Beyerhaus. "Tödliche Gegnerschaft: Gottes Wort in der missionarischen Konfrontation". Confessio Augustana 1/2000: 7-12

Peter Beyerhaus. "Tödliche Gegnerschaft: Gottes Wort in der missionarischen Konfrontation". Confessio Augustana 1/2000: 7-12

Leonardo Boff. "Martyrium". Concilium 19 (1983) 3: 176-181 = "Martyrdom: An Attempt at Systematic Reflection". pp. 12-17 in: Johannes Baptist Metz, Edward Schillebeeckx (Ed.). Martyrdom Today. *op. cit.*

Dietrich Bonhoeffer. Nachfolge. Chr. Kaiser: München, 1950³; 1987¹⁶ [1937]; now under Dietrich Bonhoeffer Werke, Vol. 4. Gütersloher Verlagshaus: Gütersloh, 1989¹; 1994²

Herman Boonstra. "La Persecution: Formule de Dieu pour la Croissance". Evangelical Ministries/Ministères Evangélique (Association of Evangelicals of Africa and Madagascar) Mar-Aug 1985: 11-13

Daniel Boyarin. Dying for God: Martyrdom and the Making of Christianity and Judaism. Stanford University Press: Stanford (CA), 1999

Kevin Boyle, Juliet Sheen (Ed.). Freedom for Religion and Belief: A World Report. Rouledge: London/New York, 1997

Thieleman J. (= Janszoon) Van Bragt. The Bloody Theater of Martyrs Mirror of the Defenseless Christians. Mennonite Publ. House: Scottdale (SAU), 1951⁶·ᵉⁿᵍˡ·; Herald Press: Scottdale (USA), 1987¹⁵, 1998ᵍᵉᵇ [Dutch Original: Bloedig tooneel, ca. 1660]

I. Bria. "Martyrium". pp. 266-270 in: Karl Müller, Theo Sundermeier (Ed.). Lexikon missionstheologischer Grundbegriffe. D. Reimer: Berlin, 1987

Geoffrey W. Bromiley. "Persecute". pp. 771-774 in: Geoffrey W. Bromiley. (Ed.). The International Standard Bible Encyclopedia. Vol. 3. Wm. B. Eerdmans: Grand Rapids (MI), 1986

Walbert Bühlmann. "Die Kirche als Institution in Situationen der Christenverfolgung". Concilium 19 (1983) 3: 217-220 = "The Church as Institution in the Context of Persecution". pp. 58-62 in: Johannes Baptist Metz, Edward Schillebeeckx (Ed.). Martyrdom Today. *op. cit.*

Earle E. Cairns. "Under Three Flags". pp. 3-45 in: Edwin L. Frizen, Wade T. Coggins (Ed.). Christ and Caesar in Christian Missions. William Carey Library: Pasadena (CA), 1979

Hans von Campenhausen. Die Idee des Martyriums in der Alten Kirche. Vandenhoeck & Ruprecht: Göttingen, 1936¹; 1964²

Hans von Campenhausen. "Das Martyrium in der Mission". pp. 71-85 in: Heinzgünter Frohnes, Uwe W. Knorr (Ed.). Die Alte Kirche. Kirchengeschichte als Missionsgeschichte 1. Chr. Kaiser: München, 1974

Selected Bibliography on Persecution of Christians 155

Johan Candelin. "Christenverfolgung heute". pp. 17-26 in: Konrad-Adenauer-Stiftung (Ed.). Verfolgte Christen heute: Christen in den Ländern Afrikas, Asiens, des Nahen Ostens und Lateinamerikas. Dokumentation 28. Oktober 1999 Internationale Konferenz ... Berlin. Konrad-Adenauer-Stiftung: Berlin, 1999, Engl. Translation:
Johan Candelin. "Persecution of Christians Today". pp 16-24 in: Konrad-Adenauer-Stiftung (Ed.). Persecution of Christian Today: Christian Life in African, Asian, Near East and Latin American Countries. Documentation October 28, 1999 Conference Venue ... Berlin. Konrad-Adenauer-Stiftung: Berlin, 1999; (abridged version) Johan Candelin. "Mundtot Gemachten Stimme geben: Christenverfolgung heute". Confessio Augustana 1/2000: 13-18
Tony Carnes. "The Torture Victim Next Door: Hidden Victims of Religious Persecution Find Refuge in America". Christianity Today 44 (2000) 3: 70-72
Georges Casalis. "Theologie unter dem Zeichen des Martyriums: Dietrich Bonhoeffer". Concilium 19 (1983) 3: 236-240 = Georges Casalis. "Theologie unter dem Zeichen des Martyriums: Dietrich Bonhoeffer". Concilium 19 (1983) 3: 236-240
Andrew Chandler (Ed.). The Terrible Alternative: Christian Martyrdom in the Twentieth Century. Cassell: London, New York, 1998
Jonathan Chao. "Witness in Suffering". S. 43-54 in: Bong Rin Ro (Ed.). Christian Suffering in Asia. Evangelical Fellowship of Asia: Taichung (Taiwan), 1989
Michael I. Chorev. Ich schreibe euch, Kinder ...: Briefe aus dem Straflanger. Verlag Friedensstimme: Gummersbach, 1986
Eduard Christen. "Martyrium III/2.". S. 212-220 in: Gerhard Krause, Gerhard Müller (Ed.). Theologische Realenzyklopädie. Vol. 22. Walter de Gruyter: Berlin, 1992
Christen Asiens: zwischen Gewalterfahrung und Sendungsauftrag. EMW-Informationen Nr. 124 (Okt 2000). EMW: Hamburg, 2000. 61 S.
"Christenverfolgungen". Sp. 1115-1120 in: Josef Höfer, Karl Rahner (Ed.). Lexikon für Theologie und Kirche. Vol. 2. Herder: Freiburg: 1986 (repr. from 1958)
Christian Suffering and Persecution. Asian Perspectives, Heft 9. (The Declaration of the 4th ATA Theological Consultation in Hong Kong. Asia Theological Association (ATA): Taichung (Taiwan), 1984
Samuel Clarke. A Looking-Glass for Persecutors. W. Miller: London, 1674
Carsten Colpe. "Christenverfolgungen". pp. 1161-1164 in: Konrat Ziegler, Walther Sontheimer (Ed.). Der Kleine Pauly: Lexikon der Antike. 5 Vols. Vol. 1. dtv: München, 1979 [repr from 1975]
Chuck Colson. "Foreword". pp. ix-xii in: Nina Shea. In The Lion's Den: A Shocking Account of Persecution and Martyrdom of Christians Today and How We Should Respond. Broadman & Holman: Nashville (TN), 1997
James Cone. "Martin Luther King". Concilium 19 (1983) 3: 230-236 = "Martin Luther King: The Source for His Courage to Face Death". pp. 74-79 in: Johannes Baptist Metz, Edward Schillebeeckx (Ed.). Martyrdom Today. *op. cit.*
Max Conrat. Die Christenverfolgungen im römischen Reich: Vom Standpunkt des Kuristen. Scientia Verlag: Aalen, 1973 (repr. from Leipzig, 1897)
Felix Corley, John Eibner. In The Eye of the Romanian Storm: The Heroic Story of Pastor Lazlo Tokes. F. H. Revell: Old Tappan (NJ), 1990
Caroline Cox, John Eibner. Ethnische Säuberung und Krieg in Nagorni Karabach. Christian Solidarity International: Binz (CH), 1993[1]; 1995[2]

Stéphane Courtois et.al. (Ed.). The Black Book of Communism. Harvard University Press: Cambridge (MA) & London, 1999 = Stéphane Courtois u. a. (Ed.). Das Schwarzbuch des Kommunismus: Unterdrückung, Verbrechen und Terror. Piper: München, 1998⁵ (French Original 1997)

Asa Hollister Craig. Christian Persecutions. Burlington (WI), 1899 (Catholic Martyrs)

Scott Cunningham. Through Many Tribulations: The Theology of Persecution in Luke-Acts. Journal for the Study of the New Testament Supplement Series 142. Sheffield Academic Press: Sheffield (GB), 1997

Erwin Damson. Gezeichnet Mielke - Streng geheim! Hänssler Verlag: Holzgerlingen, 1999

F. W. Danker. "Martyr". pp. 267 in: Geoffrey W. Bromiley. (Ed.). The International Standard Bible Encyclopedia. Vol. 3. Wm. B. Eerdmans: Grand Rapids (MI), 1986

W. Elwyn Davies. "When is it Legitimate to Disobey Government Edicts?". pp. 87-94 in: Edwin L. Frizen, Wade T. Coggins (Ed.). Christ and Caesar in Christian Missions. William Carey Library: Pasadena (CA), 1979

Idoti und David M. Davies. With God in Congo Forests During the Persecution Under Rebel Occupation as Told by an African Pastor. Worldwide Evangelization Crusade: Bulstrode, Gerrards Cross (GB), 1971

Gerhard Dedeke. Die protestantischen Märtyrerbücher von Ludwig Rabus, Jean Crespin, und Adriaen van Haemstede und ihr gegenseitigen Verhältnisse. Diss.: Universität Halle-Wittenberg, 1924

A. G. Dickens, John M. Tonikn. The Reformation in Historical Thought. Harvard University Press: Cambridge (MA), 1985 (pp. 39-57 on Martyrologies)

Jean-Pierre Dujardin. "N'oublions jamais ...". Figaro Nr. 7/78, 18.11.1978

Friedrich Durst. "Afrikanische Christen zwischen Wachstum und Bedrängnis". Confessio Augustana 1/2000: 1925

B. Dyck. "Verfolgung fördert Gemeindewachstum". Dein Reich komme (Licht im Osten) 2/1983: 5

Günther Ebel, Reinier Schippers. "Persecution, Tribulation, Affliction". pp. 805-809 in: Colin Brown (Ed.). The New International Dictionary of New Testament Theology. Regency/Zondervan: Grand Rapids (MI), 1976. Vol. 2.

Günther Ebel, Reinier Schippers, Lothar Coenen. "Bedrängnis, Verfolgung". pp. 60-64 in: Lothar Coenen u. a. (Ed.). Theologisches Begriffslexikon zum Neuen Testament. Vol. 1. R. Brockhaus: Wuppertal, 1967

Albert Ehrhard. Die Kirche der Märtyrer: Ihre Aufgaben und ihre Leistungen. J. Kösel & F. Pustet: München, 1932

John Eibner (Ed.). Christen in Ägypten. Institut für religiöse Minderheiten in der islamischen Welt: Zürich, 1992. 40 pp. [Engl. Edition:]

John Eibner (Ed.). Christians in Egypt: Church under Siege. Institute for Religious Minorities in the Islamic World: Zürich, Washington, 1993]

Werner Elert. Das christliche Ethos: Grundlinien der lutherischen Ethik. Furche-Verlag: Hamburg, 1961². pp. 338-345 (Ch. "Der Verzicht")

Elisabeth Elliot. Die Mörder - meine Freunde. CLV: Biefelfeld, 1999 (from the English)

Selected Bibliography on Persecution of Christians 157

Horst Engelmann. Gemeindestruktur und Verfolgung. Theologische Untersuchungen zu Weltmission und Gemeindebau (Ed. by Thomas Schirrmacher and Hans-Georg Wünch). AG Weltmission und Gemeindebau: Lörrach, 1981

"Erklärungen zu Übergriffen auf Christen". pp. 27-30" in: Christen in der indischen Nation. Informationen Nr. 121 (Sept 1999). Evangelisches Missionswerk in Deutschland: Hamburg, 1999

Evangelischer Namenkalender: Gedenktage der Christenheit. Evangelische Buchhilfe: Kassel, 1979 (16 pp.)

Evangelisches Tagzeiten Buch. Vandenhoeck & Ruprecht: Göttingen, 1998[4]

"Facing the Fire: Christians Under Persecution". Crossroads (Middle East Christian Outreach) Nr. 70: March 1988: 2-9

Gernot Facius. "'In unserem Jahrhundert sind die Märtyrer zurückgekommen'". Die Welt vom 18.11.1999. pp. 12

Manfred Fermir. Christen in der Verfolgung. Anregungen: Arbeitshefte für den Religionsunterricht ... 3. R. Brockhaus, 1979

C. J. Fick. Die Märtyrer der Evangelisch-Lutherischen Kirche. Vol. 1. Niedner: Saint Louis (USA), 1854

Mark Finley, Steven R. Mosley. Unshakable Faith: How to Stand Fast in the Worst of Times. Pacific press Publ.: Boise (ID), 1996. 75 pp. (Adventist point of view)

H. A. Fischel. "Martyr and Prophet: A Stufy in Jewish Literature". Jewish Quarterly Review 37 (1946/47): 265-280+363-386

Walter Flick. "Verfolgung ohne Ende. Idea-Spektrum 49/2000: 22-23

George Fox. Cain against Abel: Representing New-England's Church-Hirarchy in Opposition to Her Christian Protestant Dissenters. o. V.: London (?), 1675. 48 pp.

John Foxe. Book of Martyrs. W. Tegg: London, 1851 [1563]

John Foxe. Fox' Book of Martyrs. Ed. byWilliam Bryon Forbush. John C. Winston: Philadelphia (PN), 1926

John Foxe. Fox's Book of Martyrs and How They Found Christ: in Their Own Words. Christian Classic Series 3. World Press Library: Springfield (MO), 1998 [1563]

John Foxe. Fox's Book of Martyrs. Thomas Nelson Publ.: Nashville (TN), 2000 [1563]

John Foxe. Fox's Book of Martyrs. Thomas Nelson Publ.: Nashville (TN), 2000 [1563]

Freedom of Religion: A Report with Special Emphasis on the Right to Choose Religion and Registration Systems. Forum 18: Oslo, 2001 (auch zum Downloaden unter www.normis.no, dann unten auf "Forum 18" klicken)

William H. C. Frend. Martyrdom and Persecution in the Early Church: A Study of a Conflict from the Maccabees to Donatus. Basil Blackwell: Oxford, 1965; Anchor Books: Garden City (NY), 1967

William H. C. Frend. The Donatists Church. Clarendon Press: Oxford, 1971[1]; ibid. & Oxford University Press: New York, 1985[3]

Rudolf Freudenberger u. a. "Christenverfolgungen". pp. 23-62 in: Gerhard Krause, Gerhard Müller (Ed.). Theologische Realenzyklopädie. Vol. 8. Walter de Gruyter: Berlin, 1981

Hellmuth Frey. Die Botschaft des Alten Testamentes. Calwer Verlag: Stuttgart, 1938

Gerhard und Barbara Fuhrmann. "Versteckte Christen". Missionsbote (Allianz-Mission) 5/1983: 9-10
P. G. "Reacting to Persecution". Seedbed 14 (1999) 2: 12-17
P. G. "Helping Victims of Anti-Christian Persecution". Seedbed 14 (1999) 2: 18-26
F. W. Gaß. "Das christliche Märtyrerthum in den ersten Jahrhunderten, und dessen Idee". Zeitschrift für die historische Theologie 29 (1859) 323-392 + 30 (1860) 315-381
Gebetstag für die verfolgte Kirche. Arbeitshilfen 13. Sekretariat der Deutschen Bischofskonferenz: Bonn, 1980
Gebetstag für die verfolgte Kirche 1984. Arbeitshilfen 35. Sekretariat der Deutschen Bischofskonferenz: Bonn, 1984
Gebetstag für die verfolgte Kirche 1985. Arbeitshilfen 38. Sekretariat der Deutschen Bischofskonferenz: Bonn, 1985
Gebetstag für die verfolgte Kirche 1986. Arbeitshilfen 43. Sekretariat der Deutschen Bischofskonferenz: Bonn, 1986
Gebetstag für die verfolgte Kirche 1987. Arbeitshilfen 49. Sekretariat der Deutschen Bischofskonferenz: Bonn, 1987
Gebetstag für die verfolgte Kirche 1988. Arbeitshilfen 58. Sekretariat der Deutschen Bischofskonferenz: Bonn, 1988
Gebetstag für die verfolgte Kirche 1989. Arbeitshilfen 63. Sekretariat der Deutschen Bischofskonferenz: Bonn, 1989
Gebetstag für die verfolgte Kirche 1990. Arbeitshilfen 78. Sekretariat der Deutschen Bischofskonferenz: Bonn, 1990
Gebetstag für die verfolgte Kirche 1991. Arbeitshilfen 85. Sekretariat der Deutschen Bischofskonferenz: Bonn, 1991
Gebetstag für die verfolgte Kirche 1992. Arbeitshilfen 99. Sekretariat der Deutschen Bischofskonferenz: Bonn, 1992
Gebetstag für die verfolgte Kirche 1993: China. Arbeitshilfen 105. Sekretariat der Deutschen Bischofskonferenz: Bonn, 1993
Gebetstag für die verfolgte Kirche 1994. Arbeitshilfen 119. Sekretariat der Deutschen Bischofskonferenz: Bonn, 1994
"Der geistliche Kampf um Korea". Beilage zum HMK-Kurier M 11403. reproduced by Hilfsaktion Märtyrer Kirche: Uhldingen, 1997. 4 pp.
Peter Gerlitz. "Martyrium I: Religionsgeschichte". pp. 197-202 in: Gerhard Krause, Gerhard Müller (Ed.). Theologische Realenzyklopädie. Vol. 22. Walter de Gruyter: Berlin, 1992
Ken R. Gnanakan. "A Biblical Perspective on Suffering" pp. 23-30 in: Bong Rin Ro (Ed.). Christian Suffering in Asia. Evangelical Fellowship of Asia: Taichung (Taiwan), 1989
Medardo Ernesto Gómez. Fire against Fire: Christian Ministry Face-to-Face with Persecution. Augsburg Publ.: Minneapolis (MN), 1990 [Original: Fuego contra fuego. Ediciones Liberación: (El Salvador), 1990] (Lutheran point of view)
André Grabar. Martyrium: Recherches sur le culte des reliques et l'art chrétien antique. Collège de France: Paris, 1943; Variorum Prints, 1972 (repr. from Paris, 1946)

Selected Bibliography on Persecution of Christians 159

Friedrich Graber. Der Glaubensweg des Volkes Gottes: Eine Erklärung von Hebräer 11 als Beitrag zum Verständnis des Alten Testamentes. Zwingli Verlag: Zürich, 1943

Myrna Grant. Gib nicht auf, Wanja! Die Geschichte des Iwan Moissejew. R. Brockhaus: Wuppertal, 1988[5]

Brad Stephan Gregory. Salvation at Stake: Christian Martyrdom in Early Modern Europe. Harvard Historical Studies 134. Harvard University Press: Cambridge (MA), 1999

Hermann Gröhe. "Einführung". pp. 11-15 in: Konrad-Adenauer-Stiftung (Ed.). Verfolgte Christen heute: Christen in den Ländern Afrikas, Asiens, des Nahen Ostens und Lateinamerikas. Dokumentation 28. Oktober 1999 Internationale Konferenz ... Berlin. Konrad-Adenauer-Stiftung: Berlin, 1999, English translation:

Hermann Gröhe. "Introduction". pp. 11-15 in: Konrad-Adenauer-Stiftung (Ed.). Persecution of Christian Today: Christian Life in African, Asian, Near East and Latin American Countries. Documentation October 28, 1999 Conference Venue ... Berlin. Konrad-Adenauer-Stiftung: Berlin, 1999

Hermann Gröhe. "Unsere Solidarität ist gefordert: Verfolgung von Christen in aller Welt". Evangelische Verantwortung 3/2000: 1-3

Ernst Günther. Martys: Die Geschichte eines Wortes. Bertelsmann: Gütersloh, 1941

Robert Gundry. Matthew: A Commentary on His Handbook for a Mixed Church Under Persecution. Wm. B. Eerdmans: Grand Rapids, 1982[1]; 1994[2]

Wolfgang Gust. Der Völkermord an den Armeniern: Die Tragödie des ältesten Christenvolkes der Welt. Carl Hanser Verlag: München, 1993

Ernst Haag. "Die drei Männer im Feuer nach Dan. 3:1-30". pp. 20-50 in: J. W. Van Henten (Ed.). Die Entstehung der jüdischen Martyrologie. Studia Post-Biblica 38. E. J. Brill: Leiden, 1989

Ferdinand Van der Haeghen (Ed.). Bibliographie des martyrologes protestantes Néerlandais. Nyhoff: LaHaye, 1890

Oda Hagemeyer. "Theologie des Martyriums". Benediktische Monatsschrift 60 (1984) 309-315

William Haller. "John Foxe and the Puritan Revolution". pp. 209-224 in: Richard Foster Jones (Ed.). The Seventeenth Century: Studies in the History of english Thought and Literature. Stanford: Standorf University Press, 1951

William Haller. The Elect Nation: The Meaning and Relevance of Foxe's Book of Martyrs. Harper: New York, 1963

Abram & Maria Hamm. Die Wege des Herrn sind lauter Güte. Verlag Friedensstimme: Gummersbach, 1985 (Soviet Union)

Peter Hammond. Faith under Fire in Sudan. Frontline Fellowship: Newlands (South Africa), 1996

Peter Hammond. In the Killing Fields of Mozambique. Frontline Fellowship: Newlands (South Africa), 1998

Adolf von Harnack. Die Mission und Ausbreitung des Christentums in den ersten drei Jahrhunderten. VMA-Verlag: Wiesbaden, n. d. repr from1924[4])

Hermann Hartfeld. Glaube trotz KGB. Verlag der Liebenzeller Mission: Bad Liebenzell, 1986 (abridged edition)

Chester D. Hartranft. "Introductory Essay". pp. I-XXXV in: Aurelius Augustinus. The writings against the Manichaeans and against the Donatists (Ed. by J. R. King and Chester D. Hartranft). A Select Library of the Nicene and Post-Nicene Fathers of the Christian Church (Ed. von Philipp Schaff). Series 1, Vol. 4 Wm. B. Eerdmans: Grand Rapids (MI), 1979 (repr from 1887) (Internet www.ccel/fa thers2npnf/ CDROM Christian Classics Ethereal Library 1998. CCEL (Wheaton College: Wheaton (IL), 1998)

Kim Hyun Hee. Die Tränen meiner Seelen. BasteiLübbe: Bergisch Gladbach, 1994[1]; Stephanus Edition: Uhldingen, 1997[2] (with Christian confession); Brunnen: Gießen, 1999[3] (Korea)

James C. Hefley, Marti Hefley, James Hefley. By Their Blood: Christian Martyrs of the Twentieth Century. Baker Book House: Grand Rapids (MI), 1994

Franz Kardinal Hengsbach. "Vorwort". pp. 5-6 in: Gebetstag für die verfolgte Kirche 1991. Arbeitshilfen 85. Sekretariat der Deutschen Bischofskonferenz: Bonn, 1991. p. 6: "Die Geschichte der Kirche ist auch die Geschichte ihrer Verfolgung."

J. W. Van Henten (Ed.). Die Entstehung der jüdischen Martyrologie. Studia Post-Biblica 38. E. J. Brill: Leiden, 1989

J. W. Van Henten. The Maccabean Martyrs As Saviours of the Jewish People: A Study of 2 and 4 Maccabees. Supplements to the Journal for the Study of Judaism 57. E. J. Brill: Leiden (NL), 1997

Johannes Herzog. "Märtyrer". S. 166-167 in: Friedrich Keppler (Ed.). Calwer Kirchenlexikon. Vol. 2. Calwer Verlagsb.: Stuttgart, 1941

Chua Wee Hian, Frank Saphir Khair-Ullah, Subodh Sahu. "Evangelism in the Hard Places of the World". pp. 464-473 in J. D. Douglas (Ed.). Let the Earth Hear His Voice: International Congress on World Evangelization Lausanne, Switzerland. World Wide Publ.: Minneapolis (MN), 1975

Otto Hiltbrunner. "Martys". pp. 1059-1060 in: Konrat Ziegler, Walther Sontheimer (Ed.). Der Kleine Pauly: Lexikon der Antike. 5 Vols. Vol. 3. dtv: München, 1979 [repr. from 1975]

Norman H. Hjelm (Ed.). Out of the Ashes: Burned Churches and the Community of Faith. NelsonWord: Nashville (TN), 1997

E. Hocedez. "Le concept de martyr". Nouvelle Revue Théologique 55 (1928): 81-99 + 198-208

Karl Holl. "Die Vorstellung von Märtyrer und die Märtyrerakte in ihrer geschichtlichen Entwicklung" [1914]. pp. 68-102 in: Karl Holl. Gesammelte Aufsätze zur Kirchengeschichte. Vol. 2: Der Osten. J. C. B. Mohr, 1928

Edelhard L. Hummel. The Concept of Martyrdom According to Siant Cyprian of Carthage. The Catholic University of America Studies in Christian Antiquity 9. The Catholic University of America: Washington, 1946

Georg Huntemann. Der andere Bonhoeffer. R. Brockhaus: Wuppertal, 1989

Arthur F. Ide. Martyrdom of Women: A Study of Death Psychology in the Early Church. Tangelwuld Press: Las Colinas (TX), 1985[1]; 1998[2]

Isaac Ienington. Concerning Persecution. Robert Wilson: London, 1661. 31 pp. (on the Quakers)

Informationsmappe Verfolgte Kirche heute. (Mattias Menzinger, Ed.). Kirche in Not/Ostpriesterhilfe: München, 1999

Dave Jackson, Neta Jackson. On Fire for Christ: Stories of Anabaptist Martyrs, Retold from Martyrs Mirror. Herald Press: Scottdale (USA), 1989
Patrick Johnstone. "Preparing 3rd World Believers for Church Growth under Persecution". Worldwide Thrust (WEC USA) Nov/1978: 3-7
Ephraim Kanarfogel. "Martyrium II: Judentum". pp. 202-207 in: Gerhard Krause, Gerhard Müller (Ed.). Theologische Realenzyklopädie. Vol. 22. Walter de Gruyter: Berlin, 1992
Kalman J. Kaplan, Matthew B. Schwartz (Ed.). Jewish Approaches to Suicide, Martyrdom, and Euthanasia. Jason Aronson: Northvale (NJ), 1997
Ingrid Kastelan. "Verfolgung ist letztendlich Verheißung". idea 45/1977 (7.11.). pp. I-II Konferenz der AEM "Gemeinde in Bedrängnis" 2.-6.11.1977 Burbach-Holzhausen
F. Kattenbusch. "Der Märtyrertitel". Zeitschrift für neutestamentliche Wissenschaft 4 (1903): 111-127
Philip Makau Kavuo. "Unchain My Brethren". Evangelical Ministries/Ministères Evangélique (Association of Evangelicals of Africa and Madagascar) Mar-Aug 1985: 14-15
Ulrich Kellermann. "Das Danielbuch und die Märtyrertheologie der Auferstehung". pp. 51-75 in: J. W. Van Henten (Ed.). Die Entstehung der jüdischen Martyrologie. Studia Post-Biblica 38. E. J. Brill: Leiden, 1989
Robert. A Kelly. "The Suffering Church: A Study of Luthers Theologia Crucis". Concordia Theological Quarterly 50 (1986): 3-17
Billy Kim. "God at Work in Times of Persecution (Acts 7:54-8:8)". pp. 57-59 in J. D. Douglas (Ed.). Let the Earth Hear His Voice: International Congress on World Evangelization Lausanne, Switzerland. World Wide Publ.: Minneapolis (MN), 1975
Nargaret Kirk. Zähle die Tage meiner Flucht. R. Brockhaus: Wuppertal, 1995 (Zentralcelebes)
Festo Kivengere. The Spirit is Moving. Africa Christian Press: Nairobi (Kenia) & Lagos: London, 1976
Festo Kivengere. Ich liebe Idi Amin: Uganda heute, Triumph der Liebe mitten in Leiden und Verfolgung. Hänssler: Neuhausen, 1978[1]; 1979[3]
Festo Kivengere. I Love Idi Amin: The Story or Triumph under Fire in the Midst of Suffering and Persecution in Uganda. Marshall, Morgan and Scott: London, 1977; Revell: Old Tappan (NJ), 1977
Festo Kivengere. Revolutionary Love. African Evangelistic Enterprise: Nairobi (Kenia), 1981
Max Klingberg (Hg.). Märtyrer heute. Schulte & Gerth: Asslar, 2000
Hubertus Knabe. Die unterwanderte Republik - Stasi im Westen. München: Propyläen, 1999
Rudolf Knopf, Gustav Krüger (Ed.). Ausgewählte Märtyrerakten. Sammlung ausgewählter kirchen- und dogmengeschichtlicher Quellenschriften 3. J. C. B. Mohr: Tübingen, 1929; revised by Gerhard Ruhbach Ibid., 1965 (Original texts in Greek and Latin)
O. Knoch. "dioko". Col. 816-819 in: Horst Balz, Gerhard Schneider (Ed.). Exegetisches Wörterbuch zum Neuen Testament. 2 Vols. Vol. 1. W. Kohlhammer: Stuttgart, 1992[2]

Bernhard Kötting. "Darf ein Bischof in der Verfolgung die Flucht ergreifen?". pp. 220-228 in: Ernst Dassmann (Ed.). Vivarium: Feschrift Theodor Klauser zum 90. Geburtstag. Jahrbuch für Antike und Christentum, Ergänzungsband 11. Aschendorff: Münster, 1984

Robert Kolb. For all the Saints. Changing Perceptions of Martyrdom and Sainthood in the Lutheran Reformation. Mercer University Press: Macon (GA), 1987

Konrad-Adenauer-Stiftung (Hg.). Persecution of Christian Today: Christian Life in African, Asian, Near East and Latin American Countries. Documentation October 28, 1999 Conference Venue ... Berlin. Konrad-Adenauer-Stiftung: Berlin, 1999 = Konrad-Adenauer-Stiftung (Hg.). Verfolgte Christen heute: Christen in den Ländern Afrikas, Asiens, des Nahen Ostens und Lateinamerikas. Dokumentation 28. Oktober 1999 Internationale Konferenz ... Berlin. Konrad-Adenauer-Stiftung: Berlin, 1999 (both to be ordered for free at KAS, Rathausallee 12, 53757 St. Augustin, Fax 02241/246648, email: zentrale@kas.de)

Sergei Kourdakov. Vergib mit Natascha. Felsenverlag: Ulm, 1996[14]

Bernhard Kriegbaum. Kirche der Traditionen oder Kirche der Märtyrer? Die Vorgeschichte des Donatismus. Innsbrucker theologische Studien 16. Tyrolia-Verlag: Innsbruck, 1986

Dan Kyanda. "The Attitude of the Prepared Christian". pp. 97-104 in: Brother Andrew (Ed.). Destined to Suffer? African Christians Face the Future. Open Doors: Orange (CA), 1979

Daniel Kyanda. "Mission and Persecution". Arbeitspapier der gleichnamigen Arbeitsgruppe auf der World Consultation on Frontier Mission, Edinburgh 1980. unpublished

Lactantius. De mortibus persecutorum. Ed. by J. L. Creed. Clarendon Press: Oxford, 1984

Martin Lange, Reinhold Iblacker (Ed.). Christenverfolgung in Südamerika: Zeugen der Hoffnung. Herder: Freiburg, 1980 (Catholic point of view) [Engl. translation:]

Martin Lange, Reinhold Iblacker (Ed.). Witnesses of Hope: The Persecution of Christians in Latin America. Orbis Books: Maryknoll (NY), 1981

Robert Lansemann. Die Heiligentage, besonders die Marien-, Apostel-, und Engeltage in der Reformationszeit ... Vandenhoeck & Ruprecht: Göttingen, 1939

Klaus-Reiner Latk. Stasi-Kirche. Stephanus Edition: Uhldingen, 1992

H. Last. "Christenverfolgung II (juristisch)". Col. 1208-1228 in: Reallexikon für Antike und Christentum. Vol. 2. Hirsemann: Stuttgart, 1954

Ivo Lesbaupin. Blessed are the Persecuted: The Early Church Under Siege. Orbis Books: Maryknoll (NY), 1987 [Original Portuguese]; Spire (Hodder & Stoughton): Sevenoaks (GB), 1988 (Cath.; pp. 1-61 On the Early Church, pp. 62-95 on Rev. The rest concerns present application)

"A Letter to the Churches in Asia". Asia Theological News 14 (1988) 3: 4-5

Gabriele Martina Liegmann. Eingriffe in die Religionsfreiheit als asylerhebliche Rechtsgutverletzung religiös Verfolgter. Nomos: Baden-Baden, 1993

Marc Lods. Confesseurs et Martyrs: Successeurs des prophètes dans l'église des trois premiers siècles. Cahiers Théologique 41. Delachaux & Niestle: Neuchatel, 1958

Walther von Loewenich. Luthers theologia crucis. Luther-Verlag: Bielefeld, 1982[6]. especially pp. 135-144

Selected Bibliography on Persecution of Christians 163

Eduard Lohse. Märtyrer und Gottesknecht. Forschungen zur Religion und Literatur des Alten und Neuen Testamentes 64 (NF 46). Vandenhoeck & Ruprecht: Göttingen, 1955

Bob und Penny Lord. They Died for Christ. Journeys of Faith: Westlake Village (CA), 1993

Martin Luthers Sämtliche Schriften. Ed. by Joh. Georg Walch. Verlag der Lutherischen Buchhandlung H. Harms: Groß Oesingen, 1986 (repr from 1910^2). Vol. XXIII (Register). Col. 1889-1890 See: "verfolgen", "Verfolger", "Verfolgung"

John T. McNeill. "John Foxe: Historiographer, Disciplinarian, Tolerationist". Church History 43 (1974): 216-229

"Märtyrer". Sp. 587-592 in: Kurt Galling (Ed.). Die Religion in Geschichte und Gegenwart. Vol. 3. J. C. B. Mohr: Tübingen, 1986^3 (repr from 1960^3)

Märtyrbuch: Denckwürdige Reden vnnd Thaten vieler H. Märtyrer ... L. König: Basel, 1597

"Märtyrer Christi in unserem Jahrhundert". Themenheft Diakrisis 20 (1999) 3: 129-192

T. Grady Mangham. "Aftermath to Persecution". pp. 61-73 in: Edwin L. Frizen, Wade T. Coggins (Ed.). Christ and Caesar in Christian Missions. William Carey Library: Pasadena (CA), 1979 (Examples, Vietnam and Chad)

Paul A. Marshall. Their Blood Cries out: The Untold Story of Persecution against Christians in the Modern World. Word: Dallas, 1997

Paul Marshall. "Persecution of Christians in the Contemporary World". International Bulletin of Missionary Research 22 (1998) 1 (Jan): 2-8

Paul A. Marshall (Hg.). Religous Freedom in the World: A Global Report on Freedom and Persecution. Broadman & Holman Publ.: Nashville (TN), 2000

Paul Marshall. "The Current State of Religious Freedom". International Bulletin of Missionary Research 25 (2001) 2: 64-66

Martyrs and Martyrdom in the Coptic Church. Saint Shenouda the Archimandrite Coptic Society: Los Angeles (CA), 1984

Peter Mayer. "Zeugnis und Leiden des Jüngers Jesu - nach Matth. 10". pp. 2-16 in: Urgemeinde und Endzeitgemeinde - Missionarische Existenz in Zeugnis und Leiden: Vier Referate der Jahrestagung des Arbeitskreises für evangelikale Missiologie (AfeM). Idea Dokumentation 3/1988

James Dabney McCabe. Cross or Crown: The Sufferings and Triumphs of the Heroic Men and Women who were Persecuted for the Religion of Jesus Christ. National Publ.: Cincinnati (USA), 1874

T. Melhuish. "The 20th Century Martys: Westminster Abbey". Church Building Nr. 53, 1998: 18ff

Johannes Baptist Metz, Edward Schillebeeckx. "Martyrium heute". Concilium 19 (1983) 3: 167-168

Johannes Baptist Metz, Edward Schillebeeckx (Ed.). Martyrdom Today. T. & T. Clark: Edinburgh & Seabury Press: New York, 1983

Otto Michel. Prophet und Märtyrer. Beiträge zur Förderung christlicher Theologie 37 (1932), Vol. 2. Bertelsmann: Gütersloh, 1932

Otto Michaelis. Protestantisches Märtyrerbuch: Bilder und Urkunden der evangelischen Märtyrerkirche aus vier Jahrhunderten. J. F. Steinkopf: Stuttgart, 1917

Robert Miner. Die Verkündigung des Evangeliums in Nordafrika. Theologische Untersuchungen zu Weltmission und Gemeindebau (Ed. by Thomas Schirrmacher und Hans-Georg Wünch). AG für Weltmission und Gemeindebau für Weltmission und Gemeindebau: Lörrach, 1981

Ivan Vasiljevitch Moisejev. Eine Märtyrergeschichte. Aktionskomitee für verfolgte Christen: Rheinbach, 1982[5]

Helmut Moll (Ed.). Zeugen für Christus: Das deutsche Martyrologium des 20. Jahrhunderts. 2 Vols. i. A. der Deutschen Bischofskonferenz. Schöningh: Paderborn, 1999

Jacques Moreau. Die Christenverfolgung im römischen Reich. de Gruyter: Berlin, 1971

Andrea Morigi, Vittori Emanuele Vernole, Priscilla di Thiene. Die Religionsfreiheit in den Ländern mit überwiegend islamischer Bevölkerung. Schriftenreihe von 'Kirche in Not/Ostpriesterhilfe'. KIN/OPH: München/Luzern/Wien, 1999 (Cath.)

Lorenz Müller. Islam und Menschenrechte. Diss. Hamburg, 1996

Herbert Musurillo (Ed.). The Acts of Christian Martyrs. Clarendon Press: Oxford, 1972

Wolfgang Nauck. "Freude im Leiden". Zeitschrift für neutestamentliche Wissenschaft 46 (1955): 68-80

Heinrich Öhler. "Christenverfolgungen". pp. 333 in: Friedrich Keppler (Ed.). Calwer Kirchenlexikon. Vol. 1. Calwer Verlagsb.: Stuttgart, 1937

Petrus Oktavianus. "Die Narde ausschütten". pp. 120-128 in: Otto Riecker (Ed.). Ruf aus Indonesien, Hänssler: Neuhausen, 1973[3] [1971[1]]

Bernardo Olivera. How Far to Follow? The Martyrs of Atlas. St. Bebes: Petersham (MA), 1997

N. Norskov Olson. John Foxe and the Elizabethan Church. University of California Press: Berkeley, 1973

Milevitanus Optatus. Against the Donatists. Translated Texts for Historians 27. Liverpool University Press: Liverpool, 1997

Optatus. The Work of St. Optatus Bishop of Milevis against the Donatists. O. V.: London, 1917

Optatus. De schismate Donatistarum. Ed. von Karl Ziwsa. Corpus scriptorum ecclesiasticorum Latinorum 26. Tempsky: Vindobonae, 1893; Nachdruck: S. Optati Milevitani libri VII septem ... dies. Reihe. Johnson: New York, 1972

Lutz E. von Padberg. Die Christianisierung Europas im Mittelalter. Reclam: Stuttgart, 1998

Peter Pattison. Crisis Anaware: A Doctor Examines the Korean Church. OMF Books: Sevenoaks (GB), 1981. pp. 232ff; 239

Helen Penfold. Remember Cambodscha. OMF Books: Sevenoaks (GB), 1979

Alvyn Pettersen. "'To Flee or not to Flee': An Assessment of Athanasius's De Fuga Sua". pp. 29-42 in: W. J. Sheils (Ed.). Persecution and Toleration. Papers Read at the ... Ecclesiastical History Society. B. Blackwell: Oxford, 1984

Giancarlo Politi Pime. "Märtyrer in China (I)". China heute 19 (2000) 1/2 (197/198): 27-35 (kath.)

Jan Pit. Ready for the End Battle. Open Doors: Johannesburg (South Africa), n.d. (ca. 1980), New edition:

Jan Pit. Persecution: It Will Never Happen Here? Open Doors: Orange (CA), 1981

Selected Bibliography on Persecution of Christians 165

Jan Pit (Ed.). Jeden Tag geborgen: 366 Andachten verfolgter Christen. Hänssler: Neuhausen, 1998
Jan Pit, Dan Wooding. Laos, No Turning Back: The True Story of Lungh Singh. Marshalls: Basingstoke (UK), 1985
John S. Pobee. Persecution and Martyrdom in the Theology of Paul. Journal for the study of the New Testament Supplement Series 6. JSOT Press: Sheffield, 1985
Larry W. Poland. The Coming Persecution. Here's Life Publ.: San Bernardino (CA), 1990
Haralan Popoff. Tortured for His Faith: A Epic of Christian Courage and Heroism in Our Day. Zondervan: Grand Rapids (MI), 1970^1; 1975^2
"Prepare for Sufferings Says a Letter to Asia's Churches". Evangelical World May 1988: 1-2
Preparing Believers for Suffering and Persecution: A Manual for Christian Workers. Hope: Bulawayo (Simbabwe), n. d. (ca. 1979). 15 pp.
Alfred de Quervain. Die Heiligung. Ethik Erster Teil. Evangelischer Verlag: Zollikon, 1946^2 [1942^1]. pp. 151-221 (Ch. III. "Das Kreuz im christlichen Leben")
Ludwig Rabus. Der Heiligen ausserwoehlten Gottes Zeugen, Bekennern vnd Martyrern ... 8 Vols. Balthasar Beck: Straßburg, 1552 & Samuel Emmel: Ibid., 1554-1558
Ludwig Rabus. Historien der Märtyrer ... 2 Vols. Josias Rihel: Straßburg, 1571 & 1572
Hugo Rahner. Die Märtyrerakten des zweiten Jahrhunderts. Zeugen des Wortes 32. Herder: Freiburg, 1954
Karl Rahner. Zur Theologie des Todes. Quaestiones disputatae 2. Herder: Freiburg, 1958, bes. "Exkurs über das Martyrium". pp. 73-106 [Ibid 1965^5]
Karl Rahner. "Dimensionen des Martyriums: Plädoyer für die Erweiterung eines klassischen Begriffes". Concilium 19 (1983) 3: 174-176 = "Dimensions of Martyrdom: A Plea for the Broadening of a Classical Concept". pp. 9-11 in: Johannes Baptist Metz, Edward Schillebeeckx (Ed.). Martyrdom Today. op. cit.
Hans-Joachim Ramm. Stets einem Höheren verantwortlich: Christliche Grundüberzeugungen im innermilitärischen Widerstand gegen Hitler. Hänssler: Neuhausen, 1996
Andreas Rapp (Hg.). Sie starben für Jesus. Brunnen: Basel, 2000 (Indien)
Gerhard Rauschen. Frühchristliche Apologeten und Märtyrerakten. 2 Vols. Bibliothek der Kirchenväter. Kösel: Kempten, n. d.
Bo Reicke. "The Inauguration of Catholic Martyrdom According to St. John the Divine". Augustinum (Rom) 20 (1980): 275-283
Karl Rennstich. "Urgemeinde und Endzeitgemeinde: Missionarische Existenz in Zeugnis und Leiden." pp. 17-27 in: Urgemeinde und Endzeitgemeinde - Missionarische Existenz in Zeugnis und Leiden: Vier Referate der Jahrestagung des Arbeitskreises für evangelikale Missiologie (AfeM). Idea Dokumentation 3/1988
Ferdinand Ribbeck. Donatus und Augustinus oder der erste entscheidende Kampf zwischen Separatismus und Kirche. Bädeker: Elberfeld, 1858
John Richard. "Preparing for Suffering". Asia Theological News 14 (1988) 3: 8-9
Donald W. Riddle. "From Apokalypse to Martyrology": Anglican Theological Review 9 (1927): 260-280

Bong Rin Ro. "Need for a Theology of Suffering". Asia Theological News 14 (1988) 3: 2-3
Bong Rin Ro (Ed.). Christian Suffering in Asia. Evangelical Fellowship of Asia: Taichung (Taiwan), 1989
Bong Rin Ro. "Christian Suffering - A Historical Perspective". pp. 55-75 in: Bong Rin Ro (Ed.). Christian Suffering in Asia. Evangelical Fellowship of Asia: Taichung (Taiwan), 1989
Bernard Ruffin. The Days of Martyrs: A History of the Persecution of Christians from Apostolic Times to the Time of Constantine. Our Sunday Visitor: Huntington (IN), 1985
Gerhard Ruhbach. "Christenverfolgung/-en".pp. 368-371 in: Helmut Burkhardt, Uwe Swarat (Ed.). Evangelisches Lexikon für Theologie und Gemeinde. Vol. 1. Brockhaus: Wuppertal, 1992
Gerhard Ruhbach. "Märtyrer" und "Märtyrerakten". pp. 1303 in: Helmut Burkhardt, Uwe Swarat (Ed.). Evangelisches Lexikon für Theologie und Gemeinde. Vol. 2. Brockhaus: Wuppertal, 1993
John Rutherford. "Persecution". pp. 23-24 in: James Orr (Ed.). The International Standard Bible Encyclopedia. 5 Vols. Vol. 4. Wm. B. Eerdmans: Grand Rapids (MI), 1957 [1939]
J. C. Ryle. Fünf Märtyrer: Treu bis in den Tod. CLV: Bielefeld, 1995
Nijole Sadunaite. Gottes Untergrundkämpferin: Vor Gericht - Erinnerungen - Briefe. Christiana-Verlag: Stein am Rhein, 1985 (Catholic point of view)
Aud Saeveräs. Der lange Schatten der Macht: Augenzeugenbericht. Brunnen: Gießen, 1993 (Ethiopia)
Peter Sandner. "Ökumene der Märtyrer: Neue Statuen an der Westminster Abbey in London". Diakrisis 20 (1999) 3: 149-155
Christof Sauer. Mission und Martyrium: Die Bedeutung Karl Hartensteins für die evangelikale Suche nach einer Theologie des Martyriums. Ev. Buchhandlung: Wiesbaden, 1991. 56 pp. (also:)
Christof Sauer. Mission und Martyrium: Studien zu Karl Hartenstein und zur Lausanner Bewegung. edition afem - missions scripts 5. Verlag für Kultur und Wissenschaft Schirrmacher: Bonn, 1994
Christof Sauer. "Die Bedeutung von Leiden und Martyrium für die Mission nach Karl Hartenstein". S. 96-109 in: Fritz H. Lamparter (Ed.). Karl Hartenstein: Leben in weltweitem Horizont: Beiträge zu seinem 100. Geburtstag. edition afem - missions scripts 9. Verlag für Kultur und Wissenschaft Schirrmacher: Bonn, 1995
Francis Schaeffer. Helft den Christen im Sowjetblock! Schwengeler: Berneck, 1983 [Engl.: The Responsibility of Free Christians Concerning the Persecuted Christians in the Soviet Bloc]
Martin Scharfe. "Der Heilige in der protestantischen Volksfrömmigkeit". Hessische Blätter für Volkskunde 60 (1969): 93-106
Winrich Scheffbuch. "Christenverfolgung". pp. 108-110 in: Evangelisches Gemeindelexikon. R. Brockhaus: Wuppertal, 1986
Christine Schirrmacher. "Human Rights and the Persecution of Christians in Islam". Chalcedon Report No. 375 (Oct 1996): 13-15
Christine Schirrmacher. "Menschenrechte und Christenverfolgung in der islamischen Welt". Querschnitte 12 (1999) 4/5 (Apr/Mai): 1-8

Christine Schirrmacher. "Menschenrechte und Christenverfolgung in der islamischen Welt". S. 24-35 in: Max Klingberg (Hg.). Märtyrer heute. Schulte & Gerth: Asslar, 2000

Christine Schirrmacher. "Wenn Muslime Christen werden - Glaubensabfall und Todesstrafe im Islam". S. 36-49 in: Max Klingberg (Hg.). Märtyrer heute. Schulte & Gerth: Asslar, 2000

Thomas Schirrmacher. "Vorwort". in: Horst Engelmann. Gemeindestruktur und Verfolgung. Theologische Untersuchungen zu Weltmission und Gemeindebau (Ed. by Thomas Schirrmacheraund Hans-Georg Wünch). AG Weltmission und Gemeindebau: Lörrach, 1981

Thomas Schirrmacher. "Vorwort" in: Robert Miner. Die Verkündigung des Evangeliums in Nordafrika. Theologische Untersuchungen zu Weltmission und Gemeindebau (Ed. by Thomas Schirrmacher and Hans-Georg Wünch). AG für Weltmission und Gemeindebau für Weltmission und Gemeindebau: Lörrach, 1981

Thomas Schirrmacher. "Armenien". Querschnitte 2 (1989) 4 (Oct-Dec): 8

Thomas Schirrmacher. Marxismus - Opium für das Volk? Schwengeler: Berneck (CH), 1990[1]; VKW: Bonn, 1997[2]

Thomas Schirrmacher. "Die Entstehung der christlichen Heiligenverehrung in der Spätantike". Bibel und Gemeinde 90 (1990) 2: 166-175

Thomas Schirrmacher. "Gründe für die Frühdatierung der Offenbarung vor 70 n. Chr." pp. 129-154 in: David Chilton. Die große Trübsal. Reformatorischer Verlag Beese: Hamburg, 1996

Thomas Schirrmacher. "Christlicher Glaube und Menschenrechte" (Russisch). POISK: Ezemedel'naja Vsesojuznaja Gazeta [Journal of the Russian Akadems of Science]. Nr. 48 (446) 22.-28. November 1997. p. 13

Thomas Schirrmacher. "Christlicher Glaube und Menschenrechte" (Russian). Utschitjelskaja Gazeta (Russische Lehrerzeitung). No. 2 (9667) 3.1.1998. p. 21 + No. 3 (9668) 20.1.1998. p. 21 + No. 4 (9669) 3.2.1998. p. 22

Thomas Schirrmacher. "Gründe für die Frühdatierung der Offenbarung vor 70 n. Chr." Anstöße Nr. 17. pp. 1-4 (Beilage zu Neues vom Euroteam 1/1998

Thomas Schirrmacher. "Wenn einer leidet ... leiden alle mit? Solidarität mit verfolgten Christen praktisch". Confessio Agustana 1/2000: 37-39

(Thomas Schirrmacher). Weltweiter Gebetstag für verfolgte Christen. Deutsche Evangelische Allianz: Stuttgart, 1998. 12. pp.

(Thomas Schirrmacher). Weltweiter Gebetstag für verfolgte Christen. Deutsche Evangelische Allianz: Stuttgart, 1999. 12. pp.

Thomas Schirrmacher. "Christlicher Glaube und Menschenrechte". Querschnitte 12 (1999) 3 (Mrz): 1-6

Thomas Schirrmacher. "Glauben ist ein Menschenrecht" (Titel). ai-Journal 8/2000: 6-9

Thomas Schirrmacher. "Wenn einer leidet ... leiden alle mit? Solidarität mit verfolgten Christen praktisch". Confessio Agustana 1/2000: 37-39

(Thomas Schirrmacher). Weltweiter Gebetstag für verfolgte Christen. Deutsche Evangelische Allianz: Stuttgart, 2000. 12. S.

Thomas Schirrmacher. "Jährlich 165.000 christliche Märtyrer". S. 18-23 in: Max Klingberg (Hg.). Märtyrer heute. Schulte & Gerth: Asslar, 2000

(Thomas Schirrmacher). Weltweiter Gebetstag für verfolgte Christen. Deutsche Evangelische Allianz: Stuttgart, 2001. 24. S.

Thomas Schirrmacher. Mission und Menschenrechte. RVB: Hamburg, 2001

Thomas Schirrmacher. Menschenrechte in Europa in Gefahr. RVB: Hamburg, 2001

Thomas Schirrmacher. "Anmerkungen zum Verhältnis evangelikaler Mission zum Kampf gegen Menschenrechtsverletzungen". Evangelikale Missiologie 17 (2001) 2: 65-75

Adolf Schlatter. Die Märtyrer in den Anfängen der Kirche. Beiträge zur Förderung christlicher Theologie 19 (1915), Vol. 3. Bertelsmann: Gütersloh, 1915

Herbert Schlossberg. Called to Suffer, Called to Triumph: Eighteen True Stories by Persecuted Christians. Multnomah: Portland (OR), 1990 (examples from 18 countries)

Herbert Schlossberg. A Frangrance of Oppression: The Church and Its Persecutors. Crossway Books: Wheaton (IL), 1991

Wilhelm Schneemelcher. "Christenverfolgungen". Col. 257-260 in: Hermann Kunst, Siegfried Grundman (Ed.). Evangelisches Staatslexikon. Kreuz Verlag: Stuttgart, 1966[1]

Wilhelm Schneemelcher. "Christenverfolgungen". Col. 324-327 in: Hermann Kunst (Ed.). Evangelisches Staatslexikon. Kreuz Verlag: Stuttgart, 1975[2]

Margarete Schneider (Ed.). Paul Schneider - Der Prediger von Buchenwald. Hänssler: Neuhausen, 1981[1]; 1996[4]

Hans-Joachim Schoeps. "Die jüdischen Prophetenmorde". pp. 126-143 in Hans-Joachim Schoeps. Aus frühchristlicher Zeit. J. C. B. Mohr: Tübingen, 1950

Frieder Schulz. "Das Gedächtnis der Zeugen: Vorgeschichte, Gestaltung und Bedeutung des Evangelischen Namenkalenders". Jahrbuch für Liturgik und Hymnologie 19 /1975): 69-104

Andreas Schwerd. Lateinische Märtyrerakten. Humanitas christiana 1. Kösel: München, 1960

Nina Shea. In The Lion's Den: A Shocking Account of Persecution and Martyrdom of Christians Today and How We Should Respond. Broadman & Holman: Nashville (TN), 1997

W. J. Sheils (Ed.). Persecution and Toleration. Papers Read at the ... Ecclesiastical History Society. B. Blackwell: Oxford, 1984

Olaf Sild. Das altchristliche Martyrium in Berücksichtigung der rechtlichen Grundlage der Christenverfolgung. Bergmann: Dorpat, 1920

Wolfgang Simson. Häuser, die die Welt verändern. C & P Verlag: Emmelsbüll, 1999. S. 188-211

Reinhard Slenczka. "Kirche unter dem Kreuz: Martyrium heißt nicht Leiden, sondern Zeugnis!". Confessio Augustana 1/2000: 41-48

Michael Slusser. "Martyrium III/1.". pp. 207-212 in: Gerhard Krause, Gerhard Müller (Ed.). Theologische Realenzyklopädie. Vol. 22. Walter de Gruyter: Berlin, 1992

F. Graeme Smith. Triumph in Death: The Story of the Malagasy Martyrs. Evangelical Press: Welwyn (GB), 1987; 1994[Tb]

Josiah Smith. Jesus Persecuted in His Disciples: A Sermon Preached in Charlestown, South-Carolina, anno Dom. 1742. S. Kneeland & T. Green: Boston, 1745. 22 pp.

Selected Bibliography on Persecution of Christians 169

Lacey Baldwin Smith. Fools, Martyrs, Traitors: The Story of Martyrdom in the Western World. A. A. Knopf: New York, 1997; Northwestern University Press: Evanston (IL), 1999[Tb] (Christian and secular Märtyrer)

Howard A. Snyder. The Community of the King. IVP: Downers grove (IL), 1977

Howard A. Snyder. Die Gemeinschaft des Gottesvolkes. Bundes-Verlag: Witten, 1979

Hans von Soden; Hans von Campenhausen (Ed.). Urkunden zur Entstehungsgeschichte des Donatismus. Kleine Texte für Vorlesungen und Übungen 122. de Gruyter: Berlin, 1950². 56 S.

Jonah Spaulding. A Summary History of Persecution from the Crucifiction of Our Saviour to the Present Time. S. K. Gilman: Hallowell (ME), 1819

William Spring. Simbabwe, verbranntes Land. Stephanus Edition: Uhldingen, 1987

Ethelbert Stauffer. "Märtyrertheologie und Täuferbewegung". Zeitschrift für Kirchengeschichte 52 (1933): 545-598

Ethelbert Stauffer. Theologie des Neuen Testamentes. Bertelsmann: Gütersloh: 1941¹; 1947⁴; 1948⁵ (in 1941¹ especially pp. 164-167+314-317)

Hans Dieter Stöver. Christenverfolgung im römischen Reich. Bechtermünz: Eltville am Rhein, 1990

Georg Stoll. "Gefahr für Leib und Leben". Stadt Gottes: Familienzeitschrift der Steyler Missionare 122 (1999) 9 (Sept): 8-10

Christoph Strohm. Theologische Ethik im Kampf gegen den Nationalsozialismus: Der Weg Dietrich Bonhoeffers mit den Juristen Hans von Dohnanyi und Gerhard Leibholz in den Widerstand. Heidelberger Untersuchungen zu Widerstand, Judenverfolgung und Kirchenkampf im Dritten Reich 1. Chr. Kaiser: München, 1989

Werner Stoy. Mut für Morgen: Christen vor der Verfolgung. Brunnen Verlag: Gießen, 1980²

Hermann Strathmann. "martys, martyreo, martyria, martyrion". pp. 477-520 in: Gerhard Kittel (Ed.) Theologisches Wörterbuch zum Neuen Testament. 10 Vole. W. Kohlhammer: Stuttgart 1990 (repr. from 1933-1979). Vol. IV [1942]

Hans-Werner Surkau. Martyrien in jüdischer und frühchristlicher Zeit. Vandenhoeck & Ruprecht: Göttingen, 1938

Harry W. Tajra. The Trial of Paul. Mohr Siebeck: Tübingen, 1989

Harry W. Tajra. The Martyrdom of St. Paul: Historical and Judicial: Context, Traditions, and Legends. Wissenschaftliche Untersuchungen zum Neuen Testament 67. Mohr Siebeck: Tübingen, 1994

Emin Tengström. Donatisten und Katholiken: Soziale, wirtschaftliche und politische Aspekte einer nordafrikanischen Kirchenspaltung. Studia Graeca et Latina Gothoburgensia XVIIIEBA: Göteburg, 1964

Merill Tenney. "Persecution". pp. 403 in: Everett F. Harrison. Baker Dictionary of Theology. Baker Book House: Grand Rapids (MI), 1975

Wilhelm Thümmel. Zur Beurteilung des Donatismus. M. Niemeyer: Halle, 1893

Doan van Toai. Der vietnamesische Gulag. Kipenheuer & Witsch: Köln, 1979 [Orig. Paris, 1979]

"A Theology of Suffering". Themenheft Asia Theological News 14 (1988) 3

Aron A. Toews. Mennonite Martyrs: People Who Suffered for Their Faith: 1920-1940. Kindred Press: Winnipeg (CAN) & Hillsboro (KS), 1990. [German original of 1949 on microfilm? in Library of Congress, Washington] (Mennonites in der Soviet Union)

Lazlo Tokes, David Porter. The Fall of Tyrants. Crossway Books: Wheaton (IL), 1990 (Romania)

Tortured for Christ. Themenheft Evangelical Ministries/Ministères Evangélique (Association of Evangelicals of Africa and Madagascar) Mar-Aug 1985

Johannes Triebel. "Leiden als Thema der Missionstheologie": Der Beitrag Georg Vicedoms zum Thema im Kontext gegenwärtiger Stimmen. Jahrbuch für Mission 20 (1988): 1-20

Allison A. Trites. "martys and Martyrdom in the Apocalypse": A Semantic Study. Novum Testamentum 15 (1973): 72-80

Allison A. Trites. The New Testament Concept of Witness. Society for New Testament Studies - Monograph Series 31. Cambridge University Press: Cambridge, 1977

Eberhard Troeger. "Verachtung, Bachteile - Unrecht, Tod? Christsein in islamischen Ländern". Confessio Augustana 1/2000: 29-33

Josef Tson. Suffering, Martyrdom, and Rewards in Heaven. University Press of America: Lanham/New York, 1998 [Diss. Heverlee (B), 1996]

Joseph N. Tylenda. Jesuit Saints and Martyrs. Loyola University Press: Chicago 1984[1]; Loyola Press: Chicago, 1998[2]

United Nations Information Organisation (London, England). Religious Persecution. H. M. Stationery Office: London, 1942. 24 pp.

www.state.gov/www/global/human_rights/irf/irf_rpt/1999/index.html (Bericht der US-Regierung zur Religionsfreiheit)

United States. Congress. House. Committee on Foreign Affairs. Religious Persecution as a Violation of Human Rights: Hearings and Markup before the Committee on Foreign Affairs and its Subcommittee on Human Rights and International Organizations, House of Representatives, Ninetyseventh Congress, second session, on H. Con. Res. 100,378,428,433, and 434, H. Res. 269, S. Con. Res. 18, February 10, March 23, May 25, July 27 and 29, August 5 and 10, September 23, December 1 and 14, 1982. U.S. G.P.O.: Washington, 1983. 948 pp.

United States. Congress. House. Committee on Foreign Affairs. Subcommittee on International Security, International Organizations, and Human Rights. Religious persecution: Hearings before the Subcommittee on International Security, International Organizations, and Human Rights of the Committee on Foreign Affairs, House of Representatives, One Hundred Third Congress, first and second sessions, October 28, 1993 and March 9, 1994. U.S. G.P.O., Supt. of Docs., Congressional Sales Office: Washington, 1994. 173 pp.

United States. Congress. Senate. Committee on Foreign Relations. S. 1868, the International Religious Freedom Act of 1998: Hearings before the Committee on Foreign Relations, United States Senate, One Hundred Fifth Congress, second session, May 12 and June 17, 1998. U.S. G.P.O., Supt. of Docs., Congressional Sales Office: Washington, 1998. 136 pp.

Selected Bibliography on Persecution of Christians 171

United States. Congress. House. Committee on International Relations. Freedom from Religious Persecution Act of 1977: Hearing before the Committee on International Relations, House of Representatives, One Hundred Fifth Congress, first session ... U.S. G.P.O.: Washington, 1977

United States. Congress. House. Committee on International Relations. H.R. 2431, Freedom from Religious Persecution Act: markup before the Committee on International Relations, House of Representatives, One Hundred Fifth Congress, second session, March 25, 1998. U.S. G.P.O., Supt. of Docs., Congressional Sales OfficeWashington, 1998. 237 pp.

United States. Congress. House. Committee on International Relations. Subcommittee on International Operations and Human Rights. Victims of religious persecution around the world: hearing before the Subcommittee on International Operations and Human Rights of the Committee on International Relations, House of Representatives, One Hundred Fifth Congress, second session, June 16, 1998. U.S. G.P.O., U.S. G.P.O. Supt. of Docs. Congressional Sales Office: Washington, 1998. 92 pp.

United State. Congress. House. Committee on International Relations. Subcommittee on International Operations and Human Rights. H. R. 2431, to establish an Office of Religious Persecutions Monitoring, to Provide for the Imposition of Sanctions against Countries Engaged in a Pattern of Religious Persecution, and for other Purposes: Markup before the Subcommittee on Internaional Operations and Human Rights of the Committee on International Relations, House of Representatives, One Hundred Fifth Congress, first session, September 18, 1997. U.S. G.P.O., Supt. of Docs., Congressional Sales Office: Washington, 1998. 110 pp.

United States. Congress. House. Committee on International Relations. Subcommittee on International Operations and Human Rights. Persecution of Chistians worldwide: hearing before the Subcommittee on International Operations and Human Rights of the Committee on Internatioinal Relations, House of Representatives, One Hundred Fourth Congress, second session, February 15, 1996. U.S. G.P.O., Supt. of Docs., Congressional Sales Office: Washington, 1996. 232 pp.

U. S. Department of State. Annual Report on International Religious Freedom, published by the the Bureau for Democracy, Human Rights, and Labor on Sept. 9. 1999. http://www.state.gov/www/golbal/human_rights/irf/irf_rpt/index.html

U. S. Department of State. Annual Report on International Religious Freedom, veröffentlicht vom the Bureau for Democracy, Human Rights, and Labor am 9.9.1999. http://www.state.gov/www/golbal/human_rights/irf/irf_rpt/index.html

U. S. Department of State. Annual Report on International Religious Freedom, veröffentlicht vom the Bureau for Democracy, Human Rights, and Labor am 5.9.2000. www.state.gov/g/drl/irl, dann 5.9.2000 anklicken

Urgemeinde und Endzeitgemeinde - Missionarische Existenz in Zeugnis und Leiden: Vier Referate der Jahrestagung des Arbeitskreises für evangelikale Missiologie (AfeM). Idea Dokumentation 3/1988

Georg Vicedom. Das Geheimnis des Leidens der Kirche. Theologische Existenz heute NF 111. Chr. Kaiser: München, 1963

Georgii Petrovich Vins. Chronique de la persécution religieuse. Éditions des Catacombes: Courbevoie (F), 1975

Georgii Petrovich Vins. Testament from Prison. Ed. by Michael Bordeaux. D. C. Cook Publ.: Elgin (IL), 1975

Georgii Petrovich Vins. Three Generations of Suffering. Hodder & Stoughton: London, 1976

G. P. Wiens [= Georgii Petrovich Vins]. Zeugnis vor der Kommission für Sicherheit und Zusammenarbeit in Europa 7 Juni 1979. Missionswerk Friedensstimme: Cologne, n.d. [1979]

Georgii Petrovich Vins. De Kerk leeft nog! De Situatie van de Hervormde Baptisten in Rusland. Ed. von Henk Wolzak. J. H. Kok: Kampen, 1981

Georgii Petrovich Vins. Konshaubi: A True Story of Persecuted Christians in the Soviet Union. Baker Book House: Grand Rapids (MI), 1988

Georgii Petrovich Vins. Wie Schafe unter Wölfen: Erfahrungen eines Christen in sowjetischen Straflagern. Verlag Friedensstimme: Gummersbach, 1989^2 [Engl.:]

Georgii Petrovich Vins. Georgii Petrovich Vins. Let the Wars Roar: Evanglists in the Gulag. Baker Book House: Grand Rapids (MI), 1989

Georgi Vins [= Georgii Petrovich Vins]. Auf dem Pfad der Treue. Missionswerk Friedensbote: Gummersbach, 1999

Daniel Voelter. Der Ursprung des Donatismus, nach den Quellen untersucht und dargestellt. Mohr: Freiburg/Tübingen, 1883

J. Vogt. "Christenverfolgung I (in history)". Col. 1159-1208 in: Reallexikon für Antike und Christentum. Vol. 2. Hirsemann: Stuttgart, 1954

Eugen Voss, Otto v. Luchterhandt, Rudolf Bohren (Ed.). Die Religionsfreiheit in Osteuropa. G2W-Verlag: Zollikon (CH), 1984

John Wagner. The Big Book of Martyrs. Paradox Press: New York, 1997 (Juvenile literature on Catholic martyrs)

Hendrik B. Weijland. Augustinus en de kerkelijke tucht. J. H. Kok: Kampen, 1965

Eugen Weiner, Anita Weiner. The Martyr's Conviction: A Sociological Analysis. Scholars Press: Atlanta (GA), 1990 (Psychology, Judaism)

William Carl Weinreich. Spirit and Martyrdom. University Press of America: Washington D.C., 1981 [Diss. Basel, 1977]

K. Wessel. "Christenverfolgungen in den ersten Jahrhunderten". Col. 1730-1732 in: Kurt Galling (Ed.). Die Religion in Geschichte und Gegenwart. Vol. 1. J. C. B. Mohr: Tübingen, 1986^3 (Repr from 1957^3)

Abram J. Wiebe. "Special Problems with Islamic Governments": pp. 95-102 in: Edwin L. Frizen, Wade T. Coggins (Ed.). Christ and Caesar in Christian Missions. William Carey Library: Pasadena (CA), 1979

Ludwig Wiedemann. "Länderberichte: Indien". Katholische Missionen 115 (1996) 4 (Jul/Aug): 133-136

James Michael Weiss. "Luther and His Colleagues on the Lives of the Saints". The Harvard Library Bulletin 33 (1983): 174-195

Helen C. White. Tudor Books of Saints and Martyrs. University of Wisconsin Press: Madison (WI), 1963

Thomas Wilson. A Sermon on Martyrdom. Davis: Oxford, 1682

Johannes Wirsching. "Bekenntnisschriften". pp. 487-511 in: Gerhard Krause, Gerhard Müller (Ed.). Theologische Realenzyklopädie. Vol. 5. Walter de Gruyter: Berlin, 1980

Selected Bibliography on Persecution of Christians 173

Diana Wood (Ed.). Martyrs and Martyrologies. Papers Read at the 1992 Summer Meeting and the 1993 Winter Meeting ... Ecclesiastical History Society. B. Blackwell: Oxford, 1993

Herbert B. Workman. Persecution in the Early Church. Charles H. Kelly: London, 1906; Epworth Press: London, 1960; Oxford University Press: Oxford, 1980

World Evangelical Fellowship. The Geneva Report 2001. Religious Liberty Commission: Kokkola (Finland) & Geneva, 2001. 24 S. (auch unter www.advocatesinternational.org/geneva_report.htm)

Jürgen Wüst. Menschenrechtsarbeit im Zwielicht: Zwischen Staatssicherheit und Antifaschismus. Schriftenreihe Extremismus und Demokratie 13. Bouvier: Bonn, 1999

(Richard Wurmbrand) United States. Congress. Senate. Committee on the Judiciary. Subcommittee to Investigate the Administration of the Internal Security Act and Other Internal Secutity Laws. Communist exploitation of religion. Hearing, Eighty-ninth Congress, second session, May 6, 1966: testimony of Rev. Richard Wurmbrand. , U.S. Govt. Print. Off.: Washington, 1966

Richard Wurmbrand. Het getuigenis van Richard Wurmbrand. Internationale Raad van Christelijke Kerken: Amsterdam, 1966. 40 pp.

Richard Wurmbrand. Gefoltert für Christus. R. Brockhaus: Wuppertal, 1968[1]; 1975[13]; Stephanus Edition: Seewis, 1987[17]; Stephanus Edition: Uhldingen, 1993[18] [Engl. Hodder & Stoughton: London, 1967; Living Sacrifice Book Bartlesville (OK), 1993; 1998]

Richard Wurmbrand. Christ in Communist Prisons. Coward-McCann: New York, 1968[USA]

Richard Wurmbrand. Stärker als Kerkermauern: Predigten. Aussaat: Wuppertal, 1969 [Engl.: Sermons in Solitary Confinement. Hodder & Stoughton: London, 1969; Stronger than Prison Walls. Revell: Old Tappan (NJ), 1969[USA]]

Richard Wurmbrand. Blut und Tränen. Evangelisationsverlag: Berghausen, 1969

Richard Wurmbrand. In Gottes Untergrund. Evangelisationsverlag: Berghausen, 1969 [Engl. In God's Underground. Hodder & Stoughton: London, 1969]

Richard Wurmbrand. The Church in Chains. Hodder & Stoughton: London, 1974

Richard Wurmbrand. Wo Christus noch leidet. Stephanus Edition: Uhldingen, 1983

Richard Wurmbrand. Wenn Gefängnismauern sprechen können. Stephanus Edition: Uhldingen, 1995

Richard Wurmbrand. Jesus, Freund der Terroristen. Stephanus Edition: Uhldingen, 1995 [Engl.: Jesus: Friends of Terrorists. Voice of the Martyrs: Bartlesville (OK), 1995]

"The Yakunin Hearing July 22-26, 1983 Vancouver ..." (Christian Solidarity International). Programmheft

Gabriele Yonan. Ein vergessener Holocaust: Die Vernichtung der christlichen Assyrer in der Türkei. Pogrom Taschenbücher 1018. Gesellschaft für bedrohte Völker: Göttingen, 1989

Ravi Zacharias. "Christians are Compelled to Help". pp. 91-93 in: Nina Shea. In The Lion's Den: A Shocking Account of Persecution and Martyrdom of Christians Today and How We Should Respond. Zum Tode verurteilt. Offene Grenzen: Prilly (CH), 1993 (on Oswaldo Magdangal, Phillipines)

Broadman & Holman: Nashville (TN), 1997

Web-adresses

Important German Web Sides

www.ead.de/akref [Gebetsanliegen und Nachrichten des AKREF]
https://gebet.ead.de/ [verschiedene Gebetsinitiativen, z. B. '30 Tage Gebet für die islamische Welt', 'Gebetstag für verfolgte Christen']
www.opendoors.de [evangelikal, dort auch 'Verfolgungsindex' anklicken]
www.verfolgte-christen.org [evangelikal]
www.hoffnungszeichen.de [evangelikal]
http://csi-de.de/ / http://csi-schweiz.ch/
www.bucer.de/institute/iirf.html [evangelikal]
www.kirche-in-not.de [katholisch]
www.daskirchenjahr.de/tag.php?name=heiligenkalender [ev. Namenskalender]
Menschenrechtsorganisationen:
www.igfm.de
www.amnesty.de
www.amnesty.at
www.gfbv.de

Important English Web Sides

www.iirf.eu/about-us/wea-rlc/ [RLC of WEA]
www.worldevangelicals.org/rlc/prayer-idop.htm [IDOP]
www.idop.org [IDOP]
www.iirf.eu [International Institut for Religious Freedom]
www.persecutedchurch.org [IDOP USA]
www.advocatesinternational.org [lawyers working for RLC]
www.advocatesinternational.org, than 'Current Issues' [important texts and links]
www.opendoors.org [Open Doors]
www.persecution.com [Voice of the Martyrs]
www.persecution.org [Int. Christian Concern]
https://csi-usa.org/ [Christian Solidarity International]
www.worldwatchmonitor.org [WorldWatch Monitor]
www.barnabasfund.org [Islam]
www.domini.org/openbook/ [Islam]
Reports on Religious Freedom:
www.uscirf.gov [Commission of the US-Government for Religious Freedom]
www.freedomhouse.org
Human Rights Organisations:
www.hrw.org
www.hrwf.net
www.ihf-hr.org
www.ohchr.org

Regular email news

subskribiere-gebetsanliegen@akref.de [German, AKREF, a selection under http://www.ead.de/gebet/gebet-fuer-verfolgte/aktuelle-anliegen.html]

http://worldea.org/whoweare/newsletter-signup [English; Religious Liberty Prayer News (monthly), RLC of WEA]

https://www.opendoors.de/nachrichten/kostenlos-informiert-bleiben/bestellformular-meldungen-e-mail [German]

https://www.worldwatchmonitor.org/subscribe/ [English]

About the Author

Prof. Dr. theol. Dr. phil. Thomas Schirrmacher, PhD, DD, (born 1960) is President of the International Council of the International Society for Human Rights, and Associate Secretary General for Theological Concerns (Theology, Theological Education, Intrafaith and Interfaith Relations, Religious Freedom, Research), which networks churches with appr. 600 million conservative Protestant Christians, chair of its theological commission, and director of the International Institute for Religious Freedom (Bonn, Cape Town, Colombo, Brasilia), the largest research network for religious freedom and against persecution of Christians and other religions and world views.

Schirrmacher is extraordinary professor of the sociology of religion at the state University of the West in Timisoara (Romania) and Distinguished Professor of Global Ethics and International Development at William Carey University in Shillong (Meghalaya, India). He is also president of 'Martin Bucer European Theological Seminary and Research Institutes' with campuses in Berlin, Bielefeld, Bonn, Chemnitz, Hamburg, Innsbruck, Istanbul, Izmir, Linz, Munich, Pforzheim, Prague, Sao Paulo, Tirana, Zurich, where he teaches social ethics and comparative religions.

Bishop Schirrmacher has given guest lectures at more than 100 universities in more than 50 countries and travels to appr. 15 countries each year.

He studied theology from 1978 to 1982 at STH Basel (Switzerland) and since 1983 Cultural Anthropology and Comparative Religions at Bonn State University. He earned a Drs. theol. in Missiology and Ecumenics at Theological University (Kampen/Netherlands) in 1984, and a Dr. theol. in Missiology and Ecumenics at Johannes Calvin Foundation (Kampen/Netherlands) in 1985, a Ph.D. in Cultural Anthropology at Pacific Western University [today: California Miramar University] in Los Angeles (CA) in 1989, a Th.D. in Ethics at Whitefield Theological Seminary in Lakeland (FL) in 1996, and a Dr. phil. in Comparative Religions / Sociology of Religion at State University of Bonn in 2007. In 1997 he received a honorary doctorates (D.D.) from Cranmer Theological House, in 2006 one from Acts University in Bangalore.

He has authored and edited 102 books, which have been translated into 17 languages. His newest books include 'Corruption' (2016), 'Human Rights' (2015), 'Human trafficking' (2014), 'Fundamentalism: When Religion turns violent' (2013), 'Racism' (2012), 'The Persecution of Christian

Concerns us All: A Systematic Theology' (2011) and in German: 'Suppressed Women' (2013) and 'Internet-Pornography' (2008). For a full list of his books please have a look on https://www.thomasschirrmacher.net/bio/books-published/.

Schirrmacher regularly testifies in Parliament, in High Courts and at the United Nations and OSCE, e.g. in the German parlament (Deutscher Bundestag), the House of Lords, the EU Pparliament, the US Houses of Representatives or the Supreme Court of Brazil.

Bishop Schirrmacher has visited and worked with most of the heads of Christian churches, as well as leaders from all world religions. He met the old as well as the new Pope, the Ecumenical Patriarch as well as many other patriarchs on behalf of religious freedom. The German major newspaper 'Die Welt' calls him one of the three leading experts on religious freedom globally and "Pope Francis' most loved Protestant". He is known for his role in the five years process leading towards the first ever joint statement by the Vatican (PCID), the World Council of Churches and World Evangelical Alliance on world mission and human rights, published mid 2011.

He is listed in Marquis' Who's Who in the World, Dictionary of International Biography, International Who is Who of Professionals, Kürschners Gelehrten-Kalender, EU-Who is Who, Who is Who in der Bundesrepublik Deutschland, 2000 Outstanding People of the 21st Century, 2000 Outstanding Intellectuals of the 21st Century, International Who's Who in Distance Learning, and other biographical yearbooks.

Beside his honorary doctorates he received several other honours. In 2002 he was named 'Man of Achievement' by the International Biographical Center Oxford for his achievements in the area of the ethics of international development. 2007 he received the Franz-Delitzsch-Award for his dissertation on Hitler and in 2008 the International ProFide Award (Finland) for advocating human rights and religious freedom worldwide, especially for refugees from Iraq. 2016 he received the Order of Merit of the Royal House of Ghassan (Jordan/Lebanon) and 2017 the Stephanus-Price for Religious Freedom by the Stephanus-Foundation (Frankfurt).

World Evangelical Alliance

World Evangelical Alliance is a global ministry working with local churches around the world to join in common concern to live and proclaim the Good News of Jesus in their communities. WEA is a network of churches in 129 nations that have each formed an evangelical alliance and over 100 international organizations joining together to give a worldwide identity, voice and platform to more than 600 million evangelical Christians. Seeking holiness, justice and renewal at every level of society – individual, family, community and culture, God is glorified and the nations of the earth are forever transformed.

Christians from ten countries met in London in 1846 for the purpose of launching, in their own words, "a new thing in church history, a definite organization for the expression of unity amongst Christian individuals belonging to different churches." This was the beginning of a vision that was fulfilled in 1951 when believers from 21 countries officially formed the World Evangelical Fellowship. Today, 150 years after the London gathering, WEA is a dynamic global structure for unity and action that embraces 600 million evangelicals in 129 countries. It is a unity based on the historic Christian faith expressed in the evangelical tradition. And it looks to the future with vision to accomplish God's purposes in discipling the nations for Jesus Christ.

Commissions:

- Theology
- Missions
- Religious Liberty
- Women's Concerns
- Youth
- Information Technology

Initiatives and Activities

- Ambassador for Human Rights
- Ambassador for Refugees
- Creation Care Task Force
- Global Generosity Network
- International Institute for Religious Freedom
- International Institute for Islamic Studies
- Leadership Institute
- Micah Challenge
- Global Human Trafficking Task Force
- Peace and Reconciliation Initiative
- UN-Team

Church Street Station
P.O. Box 3402
New York, NY 10008-3402
Phone +[1] 212 233 3046
Fax +[1] 646-957-9218
www.worldea.org

International Institute for Religious Freedom

Purpose and Aim

The "International Institute for Religious Freedom" (IIRF) is a network of professors, researchers, academics, specialists and university institutions from all continents with the aim of working towards:

- The establishment of reliable facts on the restriction of religious freedom worldwide.
- The making available of results of such research to other researchers, politicians, advocates, as well as the media.
- The introduction of the subject of religious freedom into academic research and curricula.
- The backing up of advocacy for victims of violations of religious freedom in the religious, legal and political world.
- Serving discriminated and persecuted believers and academics wherever they are located. Publications and other research will be made available as economically and as readily available as possible to be affordable in the Global South.

Tools

The IIRF encourages all activities that contribute to the understanding of religious freedom. These include:

- Dissemination of existing literature, information about archives, compilation of bibliographies etc.
- Production and dissemination of new papers, journals and books.
- Gathering and analysis of statistics and evidence.
- Supplying of ideas and materials to universities and institutions of theological education to encourage the inclusion of religious freedom issues into curricula.
- Guiding postgraduate students in research projects either personally or in cooperation with the universities and educational institutions.
- Representation at key events where opportunity is given to strengthen connections with the wider religious liberty community and with politicians, diplomats and media.

Online / Contact:

- www.iirf.eu / info@iirf.eu

International Institute for Religious Freedom
Internationales Institut für Religionsfreiheit
Institut international pour la liber té religieuse
of the World Evangelical Alliance
Bonn – Cape Town – Colombo

Friedrichstr. 38	PO Box 535	32, Ebenezer Place
2nd Floor	Edgemead 7407	Dehiwela
53111 Bonn	Cape Town	(Colombo)
Germany	South Africa	Sri Lanka

Board of Supervisors
- *Chairman:* **Godfrey Yogarajah** (Sri Lanka)
- *Chairman emeritus:* Dr. Paul C. Murdoch
- Esme Bowers (South Africa)
- Julia Doxat-Purser (European Evangelical Alliance)
- John Langlois (World Evangelical Alliance)

Executives
- *Director:* **Prof. Dr. Dr. Thomas Schirrmacher** (Germany)
- *Co-Director:* **Prof. Dr. Christof Sauer** (South Africa)
- *Director Colombo Office:* **Roshini Wickremesinhe**, LLB (Sri Lanka)
- *CFO:* Manfred Feldmann (Germany)
- *Legal Counsel:* Martin Schweiger (Singapore)
- *Representative to UN, OSCE, EU:* Arie de Pater (Netherlands)
- *Senior research writer:* Fernando Perez (India)
- *Research Coordinator:* Joseph Yakubu (Nigeria)
- *Public relations:* Ron Kubsch (Germany)

Academic Board
with areas of research
- *Honorary Chairman:*
  Prof. Dr. Dr. John Warwick Montgomery (France)
- Tehmina Arora, LLB (India):
  Anti-conversion laws
- Prof. Dr. Janet Epp Buckingham (Canada):
  Human rights law
- Dr. Rosalee Velosso Ewell (Brazil):
  Consultations
- Prof. Dr. Lovell Fernandez (South Africa):
  Transitional justice
- Prof. Dr. Ken Gnanakan (India):
  Universities, Social justice
- Dr. Benyamin Intan (Indonesia):
  Peacebuilding
- Prof. Dr. Thomas Johnson (Czech Republic):
  Natural law ethics
- Max Klingberg (Germany):
  Human rights organizations
- Drs. Behnan Konutgan (Turkey):
  Orthodox Churches
- Dr. Paul Marshall (USA):
  Religious liberty research, Islam
- Patson Netha (Zimbabwe): Africa
- Ihsan Yinal Özbek (Turkey): Turkish Islam
- Prof. Glenn Penner † (Canada)
- Prof. Dr. Bernhard J. G. Reitsma (Netherlands): Islam and Christianity
- Prof. Dr. Christine Schirrmacher (Germany):
  Islamic Sharia
- Prof. Dr. Donald L. Stults (USA): Training
- Anneta Vyssotskaia (Russia):
  Central and Eastern Europe

The institute operates under the oversight of the World Evangelical Alliance and is registered as a company in Guernsey with its registered office at PO Box 265, Suite 6, Borough House, Rue du Pré, Saint Peter Port, Guernsey, Channel Islands, GY1 3QU.

The Colombo Bureau is registered with the Asia Evangelical Alliance, Sri Lanka.
The Cape Town Bureau is registered as 'IIRF Cape Town Bureau' in South Africa.
The Bonn Bureau is registered under ProMundis e. V. (Bonn, 20 AR 197/95)

Institute of Islamic Studies

The protestant "Institute of Islamic Studies" is a network of scholars in Islamic studies and is carried out by the Evangelical Alliance in Germany, Austria and Switzerland.

Churches, the political arena, and society at large are provided foundational information relating to the topic of 'Islam' through research and the presentation thereof via publications, adult education seminars, and democratic political discourse.

Research Focus

As far as our work is concerned, the focus is primarily on Islam in Europe, the global development of Islamic theology and of Islamic fundamentalism, as well as a respectful and issue-related meeting of Christians and Muslims. In the process, misunderstandings about Islam and Muslims can be cleared up, and problematic developments in Islamic fundamentalism and political Islam are explained. Through our work we want to contribute to engaging Muslims in an informed and fair manner.

What we do

Lectures, seminars, and conferences for public authorities, churches, political audiences, and society at large

- Participation in special conferences on the topic of Islam
- The publication of books in German, English, and Spanish
- The preparation of scholarly studies for the general public
- Special publications on current topics
- Production of a German-English journal entitled "Islam and Christianity"
- Regular press releases with commentaries on current events from a scholarly Islamic studies perspective
- Academic surveys and experts' reports for advisory boards of government
- Regular news provided as summaries of Turkish and Arab language internet publications
- Fatwa archive
- Website with a collection of articles

Islam and Christianity

Journal of the Institute of Islamic Studies and the International Institute of Islamic Studies

- German/English. All articles in both languages
- Topics of current issues: Women in Islam, Human Rights in Islam, Sharia law, Shii Islam.
- Editor: Prof. Dr. Christine Schirrmacher
  Executive Editor: Carsten Polanz
- ISSN 1616-8917
- 48 pp. twice annually
- 9,20 € per year including postage (airmail on request)
- **Sample copies and subscription**:
  Ifl · Pf 7427 · D-53074 Bonn · Germany
  info@islaminstitut.de
- **Download** under www.islaminstitut.de/zeitschrift.20.0.html

Institute for Islamic Studies (IfI)
of the Evangelical Alliance in Germany, Austria, Switzerland

International Institute of Islamic Studies (IIIS)
of the World Evangelical Alliance

Ifl · Pf 7427 · D-53074 Bonn · Germany · info@islaminstitut.de

www.islaminstitute.net

International Institute
of Islamic Studies

Giving Hands

GIVING HANDS GERMANY (GH) was established in 1995 and is officially recognized as a nonprofit foreign aid organization. It is an international operating charity that – up to now – has been supporting projects in about 40 countries on four continents. In particular we care for orphans and street children. Our major focus is on Africa and Central America. GIVING HANDS always mainly provides assistance for self-help and furthers human rights thinking.

The charity itself is not bound to any church, but on the spot we are co-operating with churches of all denominations. Naturally we also cooperate with other charities as well as governmental organizations to provide assistance as effective as possible under the given circumstances.

The work of GIVING HANDS GERMANY is controlled by a supervisory board. Members of this board are Manfred Feldmann, Colonel V. Doner and Kathleen McCall. Dr. Christine Schirrmacher is registered as legal manager of GIVING HANDS at the local district court. The local office and work of the charity are coordinated by Rev. Horst J. Kreie as executive manager. Dr. theol. Thomas Schirrmacher serves as a special consultant for all projects.

Thanks to our international contacts companies and organizations from many countries time and again provide containers with gifts in kind which we send to the different destinations where these goods help to satisfy elementary needs. This statutory purpose is put into practice by granting nutrition, clothing, education, construction and maintenance of training centers at home and abroad, construction of wells and operation of water treatment systems, guidance for self-help and transportation of goods and gifts to areas and countries where needy people live.

GIVING HANDS has a publishing arm under the leadership of Titus Vogt, that publishes human rights and other books in English, Spanish, Swahili and other languages.

These aims are aspired to the glory of the Lord according to the basic Christian principles put down in the Holy Bible.

Baumschulallee 3a • D-53115 Bonn • Germany
Phone: +49 / 228 / 695531 • Fax +49 / 228 / 695532
www.gebende-haende.de • info@gebende-haende.de

Martin Bucer Seminary

Faithful to biblical truth
Cooperating with the Evangelical Alliance
Reformed

Solid training for the Kingdom of God
- Alternative theological education
- Study while serving a church or working another job
- Enables students to remain in their own churches
- Encourages independent thinking
- Learning from the growth of the universal church.

Academic
- For the Bachelor's degree: 180 Bologna-Credits
- For the Master's degree: 120 additional Credits
- Both old and new teaching methods: All day seminars, independent study, term papers, etc.

Our Orientation:
- Complete trust in the reliability of the Bible
- Building on reformation theology
- Based on the confession of the German Evangelical Alliance
- Open for innovations in the Kingdom of God

Our Emphasis:
- The Bible
- Ethics and Basic Theology
- Missions
- The Church

Our Style:
- Innovative
- Relevant to society
- International
- Research oriented
- Interdisciplinary

Structure
- 15 study centers in 7 countries with local partners
- 5 research institutes
- President: Prof. Dr. Thomas Schirrmacher
  Vice President: Prof. Dr. Thomas K. Johnson
- Deans: Thomas Kinker, Th.D.;
  Titus Vogt, lic. theol., Carsten Friedrich, M.Th.

Missions through research
- Institute for Religious Freedom
- Institute for Islamic Studies
- Institute for Life and Family Studies
- Institute for Crisis, Dying, and Grief Counseling
- Institute for Pastoral Care

www.bucer.eu • info@bucer.eu
Berlin I Bielefeld I Bonn I Chemnitz I Hamburg I Munich I Pforzheim
Innsbruck I Istanbul I Izmir I Linz I Prague I São Paulo I Tirana I Zurich

www.ingramcontent.com/pod-product-compliance
Lightning Source LLC
Chambersburg PA
CBHW071456150426
43191CB00008B/1361